HIKING OREGON'S FIRE LOOKOUTS

HIKING OREGON'S FIRE LOOKOUTS

CHERYL HILL

MOUNTAINEERS BOOKS

To my sister and best friend, Deb.
Thank you for being my confidant, my cheerleader,
and my greatest inspiration.

....

MOUNTAINEERS BOOKS is dedicated to the exploration, preservation, and enjoyment of outdoor and wilderness areas.

1001 SW Klickitat Way, Suite 201, Seattle, WA 98134
800-553-4453, www.mountaineersbooks.org

Printed in China

First edition, 2026

Design: Jen Grable
Additional design and layout: Kim Thwaits Moehring
Cartographer: Erin Greb
All photographs by the author unless credited otherwise
Cover photographs, from top left: *Odell Butte Lookout (Hike 18), blooming beargrass on Coffin Mountain (Hike 9), an Osborne Firefinder, and a view of Mount Jefferson from Gold Butte (Hike 7);* back, *Bolan Mountain (Hike 28) is a great place to watch the sunset.*
Frontispiece: *Replica of a fire lookout at the Tillamook Forest Center, northeast of Tillamook*
Part openers: page 45, *Sunrise at Gold Butte (Hike 7);* page 125, *Mount Scott Lookout (Hike 25) is the highest elevation fire lookout in Oregon;* page 181, *Hat Point Lookout (Hike 45) has a sweeping view of the Wallowa Mountains.*
Last page: *View from Little Grayback Trail (Hike 29)*

Leave No Trace Seven Principles © Leave No Trace, www.LNT.org

Library of Congress Cataloging-in-Publication Data is on file for this title.

Mountaineers Books titles may be purchased for corporate, educational, or other promotional sales, and our authors are available for a wide range of events. For information on special discounts or booking an author, contact our customer service at 800-553-4453 or mbooks@mountaineersbooks.org.

Printed on FSC-certified materials®

MIX
Paper | Supporting responsible forestry
FSC® C188448

ISBN (paperback): 978-1-68051-708-8
ISBN (ebook): 978-1-68051-709-5

An independent nonprofit publisher since 1960

CONTENTS

NORTHWEST

SOUTHWEST

CENTRAL AND EAST

LOOKOUTS AT A GLANCE

LOOKOUT	ROUNDTRIP DISTANCE	ELEVATION GAIN	LOOKOUT ELEVATION
NORTHWEST			
1. Saddle Mountain	5.2 miles	1600 feet	3290 feet
2. Marys Peak	2.6 miles	620 feet	4100 feet
3. Devils Peak	7.5 miles	3200 feet	5050 feet
4. Fivemile Butte	7.4 miles	1300 feet	4630 feet
5. Flag Point	8.8 miles	1740 feet	5650 feet
6. Pechuck	5.6 miles	1670 feet	4340 feet
7. Gold Butte	3 miles	790 feet	4620 feet
8. Hawk Mountain	4 miles	760 feet	5280 feet
9. Coffin Mountain	3 miles	1000 feet	5770 feet
10. Iron Mountain	6.5 miles	1800 feet	5450 feet
11. Sand Mountain	3.6 miles	760 feet	5460 feet
12. Black Butte	4.2 miles	1500 feet	6440 feet
13. Carpenter Mountain	2 miles	770 feet	5350 feet
14. Little Cowhorn Mountain	2.2 miles	900 feet	4240 feet
15. Waldo Mountain	6.2 miles	1930 feet	6360 feet
16. Round Mountain	2.8 miles	700 feet	5900 feet
17. Lava Butte	3.3 miles	540 feet	5020 feet
18. Odell Butte	1.6 miles	490 feet	7030 feet
SOUTHWEST			
19. Illahee Rock	1.4 miles	560 feet	5390 feet
20. Pig Iron	6.8 miles	1850 feet	4880 feet
21. Garwood Butte	3 miles	1000 feet	7020 feet
22. Hershberger Mountain	7.9 miles	1400 feet	6200 feet
23. Acker Rock	3 miles	950 feet	4110 feet

LOOKOUT	ROUNDTRIP DISTANCE	ELEVATION GAIN	LOOKOUT ELEVATION
24. The Watchman	1.8 miles	390 feet	8010 feet
25. Mount Scott	4.4 miles	1250 feet	8930 feet
26. Snow Camp Mountain	6.4 miles	1420 feet	4220 feet
27. Pearsoll Peak	5.4 miles	1400 feet	5100 feet
28. Bolan Mountain	3.2 miles	780 feet	6270 feet
29. Acorn Woman Peak	11.2 miles	1940 feet	4980 feet
30. Dutchman Peak	1 mile	160 feet	7420 feet
31. Soda Mountain	4.3 miles	840 feet	6090 feet
CENTRAL AND EAST			
32. Green Mountain	0.3 mile	50 feet	5190 feet
33. Hager Mountain	5 miles	1490 feet	7190 feet
34. Lookout Rock	0.6 mile	220 feet	6500 feet
35. Morgan Butte	6.7 miles	1050 feet	7230 feet
36. Madison Butte	8.2 miles	2200 feet	5710 feet
37. Tower Mountain	11.4 miles	1800 feet	6850 feet
38. Indian Rock	8.2 miles	1500 feet	7350 feet
39. Mount Ireland	7 miles	2330 feet	8320 feet
40. Strawberry Mountain	7.4 miles	1200 feet	9040 feet
41. Table Rock	5 miles	1900 feet	7820 feet
42. Mule Peak	10.6 miles	3780 feet	8550 feet
43. Summit Point	1.8 miles	580 feet	7010 feet
44. Russel Mountain	4.2 miles	950 feet	7510 feet
45. Hat Point	0.5 mile	50 feet	6980 feet

INTRODUCTION

The allure of fire lookouts is easy to understand. Even though fewer are staffed now than ever before, these cabins and towers perched on high points, usually with spectacular views, have captivated the public's imagination. If you have read a travel magazine or skimmed social media in the past few years, you'll know. Instagram is filled with photos of lookouts. Hikers love trekking to them and sometimes even staying in them—their recent popularity has made reservations difficult to obtain. Charming and photogenic, they serve as an added bonus for hikers reaching a summit. Pitching a tent on an exposed summit can be a recipe for a sleepless night in bad weather, but when you're warm and cozy inside a lookout, the only time you care about the wind howling outside is when you have to run to the outhouse.

My interest in fire lookouts began when I embarked on the Oregon Forest Fire Lookout Challenge, which requires geocachers to find or hide geocaches at fifty fire lookout sites. It was fun to seek out these high places by road and by trail. I quickly grew interested in lookout history and decided to create a personal challenge: visit every publicly accessible standing lookout in Oregon and document it on my website. I also wrote a book about the history of Oregon lookouts, published by Arcadia. My interest in visiting lookouts expanded to wanting to rent one. There were more than fifteen lookouts available to rent in Oregon at that time, and I picked Gold Butte, managing to grab a September reservation. Despite the cold, rainy weather, I was totally hooked. I've now rented more than a dozen lookouts in three states; to learn how to rent one yourself, see How to Rent a Fire Lookout later in this guide.

For several years I had toyed with the idea of writing a hiking guidebook for Oregon's lookouts. A little over a decade after the Lookout Challenge, I felt ready to combine my love of hiking, photography, writing, and lookouts to create a guidebook, so I made a list of hikeable lookouts in Oregon. Some of the hikes I had done before, but most I had not. I thought I would do some more research and then submit a proposal to Mountaineers Books, which had recently published Amber Casali's *Hiking Washington's Fire Lookouts*. That December, Mountaineers Books asked me if I would be interested in writing a guidebook to Oregon's lookouts. The timing was uncanny, and I agreed. I made many weekend trips to lookouts the following two summers, plotting and planning around rain, fresh snowfall and lingering snowpack, heat, smoke, and closures from wildfires both past and present—all to make this guide as comprehensive a resource as possible.

This guidebook describes forty-five hikes across the state of Oregon, ranging from the lush green Coast Range, to the snowcapped Cascades (which harbor the state's five tallest peaks), to the biodiverse Klamath Mountains, to the drier Blue Mountains and rugged peaks of the Wallowa Mountains. Forty of these hikes are to lookouts that are still standing, and five are to sites of former lookouts. Whether you want a leisurely family outing, wildflowers, fall colors, solitude, or easy road access, there's something for everyone in this book.

In the early days of lookouts, most of them could only be reached by trail. Nowadays the vast majority in Oregon are accessible via roads. In some cases, the construction of those roads obliterated the trail network around lookouts, but in other cases, some of the trails remain. These hikes are a mix of trail-only, trail and road, and road-only. There is nothing wrong with driving up to a lookout, of course, but this book is aimed at people who like to hike in order to appreciate fire lookouts and the incredible vistas they offer.

I love to talk about hiking and lookouts. Message me anytime via my website (cherylhill.net) with your questions or reports, and please let me know about any changes or updates so that I can post them on my website. I hope you have as much fun hiking to the lookouts in this book as I had researching them all!

Note: As this book was being finalized, the Bureau of Land Management, the US Forest Service, and the National Park Service all faced significant reductions in their budgets and staffing. These cuts will likely have substantial and lasting impacts on the maintenance and accessibility of roads and trails. For the most current information, please consult the respective agency websites.

A BRIEF HISTORY OF FIRE LOOKOUTS

Long before Europeans arrived on this continent, many Indigenous peoples used fire on the landscape. It was seen as medicine and served different purposes in different places. Fire was used to increase the density of huckleberry fields, create better hunting conditions, promote the growth of plants used to make medicine and basket-making material, and increase biodiversity. However, those practices were put to a halt as white settlers spread across the country. They saw fire as destructive and bad, whereas fire suppression was important and necessary, especially in the West with its vast reserves of profitable timber.

One of the suppression methods was early detection through the use of fire lookouts. (The word *lookout* refers to both the structure and the person staffing it.) Early fire lookouts were simple camps placed on high spots with a good view of the landscape. Sometimes a platform called a crow's nest would be constructed high up in a tree to provide a better vantage point. Tools included a compass and/or an alidade (a device used to determine directions or measure angles), and communication occurred via heliograph (a signaling device that relied on the sun's reflection).

After three million acres of forest in Washington, Idaho, and Montana burned in the Big Burn of 1910, the five-year-old US Forest Service became diligent about fire suppression. An extensive network of lookouts began to grow so that fires could be spotted as soon as possible. When a fire was reported, firefighters were dispatched from ranger stations or guard stations and used the large trail network to reach their destination. Traveling from their base to the location of the fire could take a while, so early detection was extremely important. Sometimes the lookouts themselves hiked to the fire and started work on putting it out.

In 1911, the forester William Bushnell Osborne Jr. invented a device that he called a firefinder. A map circle with the location of the lookout at its center was affixed to a round brass plate. A rotating sight mechanism allowed the lookout to determine the location of the fire by obtaining an azimuth, the horizontal bearing of a point measured clockwise from true or astronomic north. If another lookout also had eyes on the fire, a more accurate location could be determined by using triangulation.

FIRE LOOKOUTS OVERVIEW

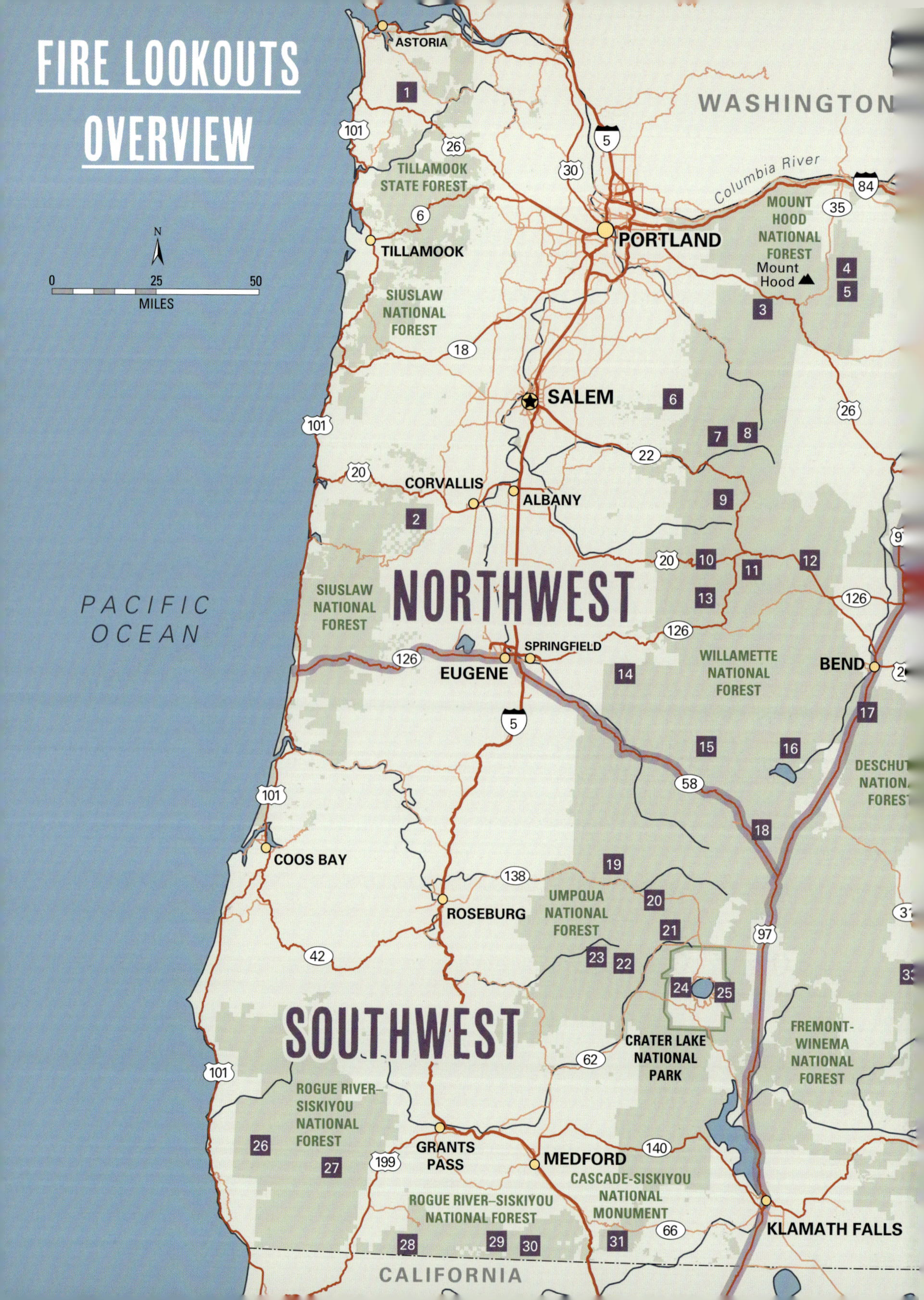

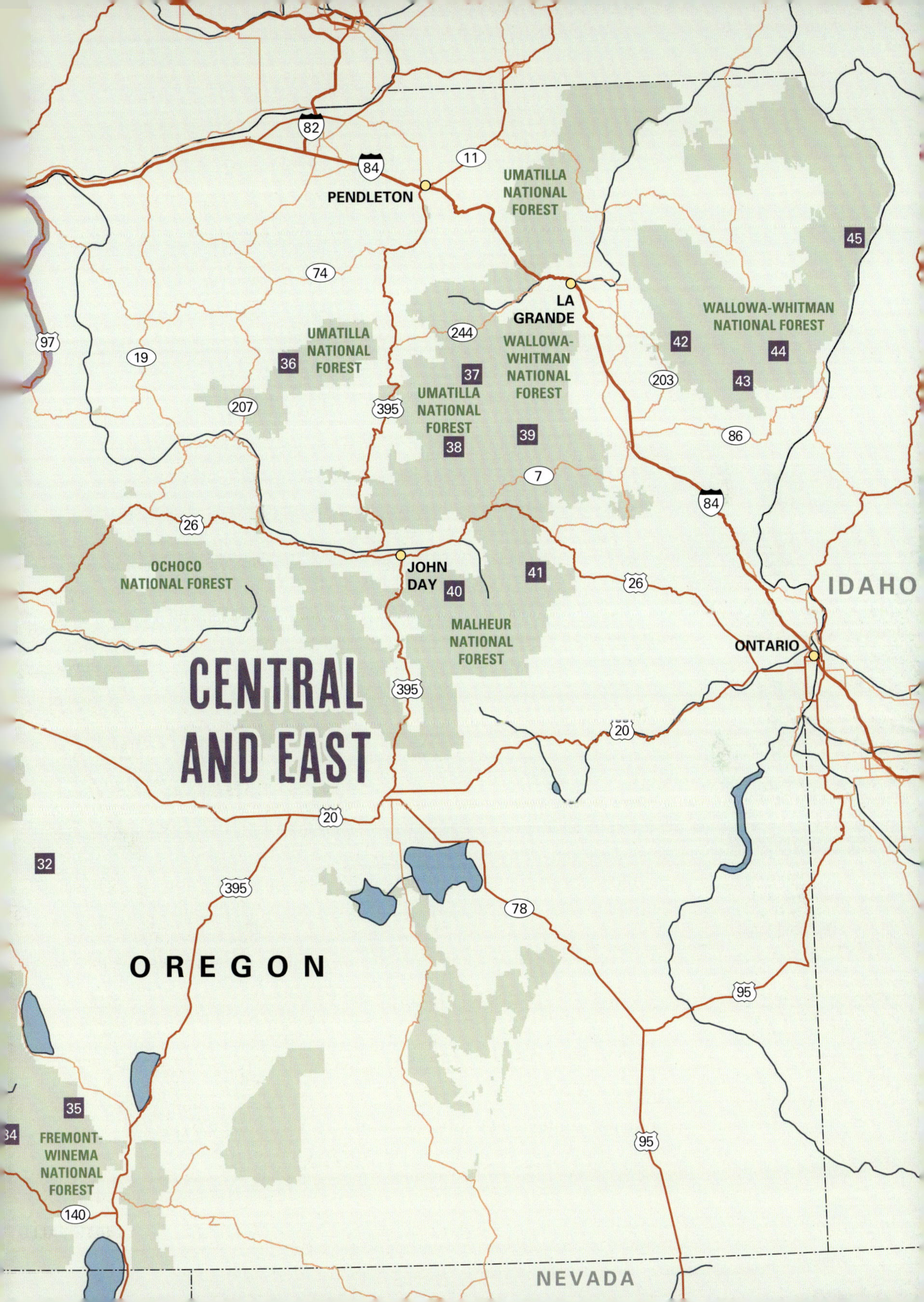

CENTRAL AND EAST
OREGON
IDAHO
NEVADA
PENDLETON
LA GRANDE
JOHN DAY
ONTARIO
UMATILLA NATIONAL FOREST
UMATILLA NATIONAL FOREST
UMATILLA NATIONAL FOREST
WALLOWA-WHITMAN NATIONAL FOREST
WALLOWA-WHITMAN NATIONAL FOREST
OCHOCO NATIONAL FOREST
MALHEUR NATIONAL FOREST
FREMONT-WINEMA NATIONAL FOREST
32
34
35
36
37
38
39
40
41
42
43
44
45

The cupola lookout on Illahee Rock (Hike 19) was built in 1925.

The Osborne Firefinder was tested in several locations in Oregon and Washington, where it was hauled up steep mountain trails by horse or mule. Proving to be a useful tool, it was then deployed to all lookouts. The device underwent a few modifications over the years, but the basic design remains the same and is still used in lookouts today.

In the early years, lookouts had a challenging task of communicating with the ranger station. Heliographs were sometimes used, but they required the sun to be out. Carrier pigeons were tried for a while. These unreliable methods were soon replaced with a telephone system. Thousands of miles of phone lines were strung along roads and trails through the forest—attached to poles and trees via ceramic insulators—so that lookouts could report fires and weather quickly and efficiently. While it was an improvement, the system was far from perfect. Falling branches and trees could break the connection and require someone (frequently the lookout) to locate the problem and repair it.

Early radios were heavy, cumbersome, and often unreliable. In the 1920s and 1930s, the Forest Service tested the use of radios, but due to their limitations, radio technology was not widely adopted until the 1940s. As radio technology improved and equipment became lighter and more reliable, the phone lines were phased out. Even though the telephone lines are now long gone, you can still sometimes spot old brown or white ceramic insulators up on tree trunks along roads and trails.

President Franklin Roosevelt established the Civilian Conservation Corps (CCC) in 1933. The goal of the program was to improve the forests, parks, and public lands and put men to work during a time of high unemployment. Three million men found work with the CCC before the program ended in 1942. In the Pacific Northwest, CCC crews built campgrounds, planted trees, and fought fires, including the 1933 Tillamook Burn that engulfed 350,000 acres. They strung fifty-eight thousand miles of telephone line and built or improved eighty-five thousand miles of roads and forty-two thousand miles of trails. They also built more than six hundred fire lookouts. The road network was expanding, but many lookouts could still only be reached by trail. Sometimes thousands of pounds of material had to be hauled by pack trains to the lookout site before construction could begin.

Around the 1930s, all fire lookouts started being equipped with lightning protection, involving copper wire that extends from the roof down the four corners of the cabin and to the ground. If a lookout is hit by lightning and the protection system hasn't been properly maintained, the current can damage radios and other equipment and can even burn down the lookout. Many lookouts also had lightning stools or chairs, which were simply regular stools or chairs with glass insulators on the ends of the legs to protect the occupant from getting shocked.

In 1933, the Forest Service undertook a project to photograph the forest from lookouts and other high points, using a special camera that could rotate 360 degrees and record a series of three panoramic photos. The camera was invented by William Osborne Jr., the inventor of the firefinder. For the next five years, two-man crews lugged the heavy equipment to high points throughout the region, taking fourteen thousand photographs. Copies of the photos were located at both the lookout and the ranger station as another tool to make sure fire locations were accurately reported.

In 1935, the Forest Service adopted the 10 a.m. policy: When a fire was spotted (no matter how big or small), it had to be under control by 10 a.m. the following morning. Since fire was still seen as wholly bad, this was the policy for decades. It wasn't until 1978 that the Forest Service abandoned the 10 a.m. policy, when it started focusing on fire management instead of fire suppression.

Some women served as lookouts in the first decades of the twentieth century, but the job was mostly given to men. The first female Forest Service lookout was Hallie M. Daggett. In 1913, she was hired to work at Eddy Gulch lookout in California's Klamath National Forest, where she ended up working for fourteen seasons. The number of women lookouts increased during World War II—with so many men involved in the war effort, women took on the role.

The Aircraft Warning Service (AWS) was established in 1941 with the goal of spotting and reporting enemy aircraft entering US airspace. Although supervised by the military, the jobs were filled by civilians. More than five hundred observation posts were in service in Oregon during the peak of the AWS, and many of these were at lookout sites. Spotters relied on charts, flash cards, and three-dimensional models to learn the size and shape of different types of aircraft. They reported their airplane observations to a control center, and those were then compared to known flights. If a plane could not be identified, then fighter planes would intercept it.

Job requirements for the AWS were similar to those of a fire lookout, and indeed prior experience as a lookout was desirable. Sometimes two men were stationed together and other times it was a husband and wife. Because observations occurred year-round, observers often had to endure cold, snowy winters at high elevations. The AWS was disbanded in 1944.

After World War II, timber harvesting increased in the national forests, which resulted in a rapidly expanding road network. By the 1950s and 1960s, fire lookouts were less utilized than they once were. Many remote corners of the forests were now reachable due to thousands of miles of new roads. Aerial detection, better communication, and easier access meant fewer and fewer lookouts were staffed. Many of the aging structures attracted vandalism or were deemed a liability and were therefore removed (sometimes by burning them down!). Others were simply abandoned. However, after decades of fire suppression and fuel buildup, fires are becoming a bigger problem, compounded by summers that are longer, hotter, and drier than a century ago. Increased human recreation has led to an increase in the number of fires

LEFT *A rusted teakettle on Mule Peak (Hike 42)* **RIGHT** *Lookout ruins on Hawk Mountain (Hike 8)*

started by humans. In this era of increasing wildfires, fire lookouts are still needed and still staffed across Oregon.

In the 1990s, the Forest Service started converting no-longer-needed lookouts into rentals that could be reserved by the public. Some lookouts that were staffed in summer were included in the rental program for winter reservations. The program has become hugely popular, and demand now far outstrips supply.

Whether a lookout is staffed, rented, or no longer in use, preserving these weather-beaten buildings is a monumental task. Volunteers have taken on a bigger role in recent decades to repair and maintain lookouts. One of these volunteer groups is the Sand Mountain Society, an Oregon-based nonprofit dedicated to the preservation and restoration of historic lookouts. The Forest Fire Lookout Association is a nationwide nonprofit that was established in 1990. Among other things, they help organize lookout restorations and provide grants for restoration projects.

There are approximately 150 standing lookouts left in Oregon. Not all of them are on public land and less than half of them are staffed. Planes and helicopters have aided in the detection of fires for decades, and recently drones have been added to that mix, but in certain conditions none of these can fly. Some lookouts are being replaced by a different technology: remotely monitored cameras. These cameras scan the landscape, and someone sitting at a desk in another location watches the video feed for smoke. Experiments are underway to test the ability of artificial intelligence to detect fires from these cameras. Google has invested millions in a project to deploy more than fifty low-orbit satellites that can detect fires as small as 16 by 16 feet. The first prototype launched in 2025.

It remains to be seen what long-term impact this technology will have on fire detection, but it's important to remember that none of these technologies can perform the "other duties as assigned" that lookouts perform, such as serving as a communications relay. In addition, a staffed lookout is far less likely to become the target of vandalism than an unstaffed lookout. (In August 2022, vandals broke into the unstaffed lookout at White Point in Oregon's southern Cascades and stole batteries, solar panels, and other equipment used for the remote camera that had been installed there.)

TYPES OF LOOKOUTS

There have been numerous lookout types over the past century, but some styles were more commonly used in Oregon than others.

The D-6 cupola was the first standardized lookout used by the Forest Service. (D-6 referred to District 6, the Pacific Northwest region of the US Forest Service; it is now known as Region 6.) It was designed by Lige Coalman, who built the first one on the summit of Mount Hood in 1915. This design consisted of a 12-by-12-foot cabin and a small second-story cupola observatory accessible by an interior ladder. This style of lookout was widely used through the 1920s.

The L-4 was by far the most popular and widely used style. The 14-by-14-foot wood frame cabin could sit on the ground or up on a tower. It has either a gable roof or a hip roof and shutters that are propped open above the windows. Intended to be both home and office, L-4 kits were specifically packaged for transport, often by pack animals, and designed to be easily assembled at their destination. The Aladdin Company in Portland manufactured many of these kits. Many L-4 lookouts still stand in Oregon.

The R-6 style came along in the 1950s. The 15-by-15-foot cabin has a flat roof that extends beyond the walls. Like the L-4, it could sit on the ground or on a tower, and it was designed to be lived in and worked in. Unlike the L-4, however, the shutters are not propped open but removed entirely during fire season and stored underneath the lookout or in a garage or shed on the summit. R-6 refers to US Forest Service Region 6 where it was designed.

The Aermotor towers were made of galvanized steel. They came in a dozen different styles, but they usually had a 7-by-7-foot room (referred to as a cab) at the top that was designed only for observation. A separate cabin on the ground served as living quarters. Although these towers were built in Oregon, they were far more common on the East Coast. The tallest tower ever built is the 175-foot Woodworth Fire Tower in Louisiana's Alexander State Forest.

STAFFING A LOOKOUT

Many people think that staffing a lookout involves a summer of admiring the scenery and reading a pile of books, or maybe penning an entire memoir or writing some music. While lookouts certainly have some downtime to pursue such hobbies, they also have a job to do that requires more work than you might realize.

In the early days, staffing a lookout was a very rustic experience. Remote and isolated, a lookout may not see another human for weeks and it could be a lonely life. This was not a job for extroverted social butterflies, although men would often bring their wives with them. (These women performed unpaid duties at the lookout.) Food and supplies were occasionally delivered by pack animals. The nearest water source might be a spring, lake, or creek that required miles of hiking to reach, and the return trek uphill was made all the more difficult by carrying the heavy water. (Needless to say, lookouts were very judicious in their water usage!) A lookout may also have to serve as the first responder to a nearby wildfire, hiking some distance to the fire to put it out. If a tree or branch fell across the phone line, a lookout would have to hike out to find the break and repair it.

The impressive vista from Acorn Woman Peak (Hike 29) on a clear day

In Oregon, most staffed lookouts are far less remote than they once were, thanks to the extensive road network that now exists. Many more lookouts today have road access than fifty years ago, but accessing some still requires a hike. Today lookouts are often equipped with many modern amenities, such as solar panels and refrigerators, and rather than relying on a woodstove for heating and cooking, many have a propane range and sometimes a propane heater. If a lookout shares the summit with communications equipment with an underground electrical line, it may have full electricity and even air-conditioning! Cell phones and mobile hotspots allow you to stay connected to friends and family during your stay. Regardless of the amenities a lookout has, it can still be a rustic experience with bad weather, insects, and the inconvenience of being far from civilization.

Despite the help of modern conveniences, the duties of a lookout remain largely the same: conduct regular scans to check for smoke, report smoke to dispatch, record lightning strikes during storms and keep an eye on those spots afterward, keep the lookout and grounds tidy, keep windows clean inside and out, maintain an accurate daily log, and learn every peak, ridge, hill, road, trail, lake, creek, and building in your

Bald Knob Lookout in Rogue River–Siskiyou National Forest is available for rent.

field of view. Modern lookouts also serve as a relay when firefighters may be down in a canyon or valley that blocks radio and cell signals to dispatch. They may alert fire crews about weather pattern shifts and fire behavior. Some lookouts encounter a lot of visitors in the summer and may serve as ambassadors of sorts, sharing their knowledge of the area, answering questions, and talking about the duties of a lookout.

Lookout life can vary widely from one season to the next. Some years are bad for wildfires, with multiple fires burning many thousands of acres of forest. Depending on the location and the wind, lookouts can be shrouded in smoke for days at a time. Other years are quieter, with less lightning and fewer fires.

An excellent way to learn about lookouts and the job they do is to visit the Tillamook Forest Center, located twenty miles northeast of Tillamook on Oregon Route 6. This museum, opened in 2006, contains exhibits related to the history of the Tillamook State Forest, forestry practices, and the Tillamook Burn. In front of the museum is a forty-foot replica fire lookout with a mini museum inside showcasing the history of lookouts. Admission is free (with a small suggested donation). The museum is closed during the winter, generally from December through February.

HIKING TIPS

While I have made every effort to provide the most accurate information possible about these trails and lookouts, the dynamic nature of our wild landscapes means that on-the-ground conditions may differ substantially from what is described. Winter storms, wind, fire, landslides, and other natural events can alter roads and trails. Always check for recent reports before heading out, and call the land agency for any updates on closures. See the Resources section at the end of the book for contact information.

While checking for conditions ahead of time is important, also remember that conditions can change rapidly. A hiker may have reported online that a trail was in great shape last week, but that rainstorm over the weekend has since created a rockslide across the trail. Always check for fire-related closures, even if there are no active fires in the area. Post wildfire closures of roads and trails can last for years, long after the fire has been extinguished.

While doing your prehike research, check which permits or passes are required. Each hike in this book includes pass and permit information, but those requirements can change. If you do a lot of hiking, it's worth buying an annual Northwest Forest Pass, which is sold at many ranger stations and outdoor retailers. This pass is displayed on your car's dashboard at the trailhead. You can also purchase a one-day pass at recreation.gov/pass. Do this ahead of time, since there is often no cell signal at the trailhead. Your license plate number is used to confirm compliance when employees check for passes at trailheads.

Some specific sites have their own permitting rules. Entrance into Crater Lake varies depending on the season and type of vehicle, and the park does not accept cash. The annual interagency America the Beautiful pass is a good deal if you regularly visit both national forests and national parks. As of this writing, it costs eighty dollars. You can buy this pass online, at national park entrance booths, and at many national forest ranger stations. Other iterations of this pass are available, including ones for seniors and veterans. Visit recreation.gov/pass for more information.

If you're new to hiking, you may want to start off with some of the shorter hikes in this book. Lookouts, by their very nature, sit on high points that require an uphill trek. Sometimes the hike is a steady climb on a well-graded trail; other times it's much steeper. If you plan to do a lot of hikes in this book, consider investing in a pair of trekking poles, which can help you maintain both your balance in either direction and your footing when descending a steep rocky trail.

You don't have to spend a lot of money on gear to go hiking. Whether it's the aforementioned trekking poles, a pack, or a rain jacket, you can acquire what you need without breaking the bank. Check for sales at outdoor gear stores, especially during the holidays. Look for gently used items for sale on eBay, Facebook Marketplace, Craigslist, and so on. Also check your local Buy Nothing group and ask your network of friends and family. It may take some time and patience, but decent gear can be obtained for an affordable price (or even for free). See the Ten Essentials list below for what you should bring when hiking.

If you're going to splurge on one item, it should be footwear. Plenty of people hike in sneakers and have no problems, but rough terrain can be hard on sneakers, and they may not provide the support you need. Some hikers prefer boots and other hikers prefer trail running shoes. Boots cover more of your feet and ankles and can be good in wet or snowy conditions. Trail runners (which usually have more durable soles than running shoes) weigh less than boots and are becoming increasingly popular. Everyone's feet are different, so the footwear that works for your friend may not make your feet happy. Go to an outdoor store such as REI and get properly fitted. I cannot emphasize enough the importance of taking care of your feet.

The trail to Hager Mountain (Hike 33) winds through wildflowers in season.

Every time you head out for a hike, make sure you tell someone where you're going. Provide them with the name of the trail and your destination; your car's make, model, and plate number; and your expected return time. If you become injured, have car trouble, or encounter another type of emergency and don't have a signal to make a call, the person you designated can contact authorities to let them know you're overdue. Hikers should always do this, but it's especially important when traveling solo. (For extra peace of mind, you can carry an emergency SOS device; see Safety Considerations, below.)

Whenever you hike through a burn area, always keep an eye out for falling snags, especially on windy days. It is never a good idea to camp in a burn area because the risk of a snag falling on your tent or hammock is much higher than in an unburned forest. Also keep in mind that road signs and trail signs may have burned and not been replaced.

When hiking in designated wilderness areas, remember that special rules apply, including limits on group size and restrictions on drones, dogs, and bicycles.

Hiking in different seasons brings different pros and cons. The benefits of hiking early in the season are seeing wildflowers and having a much lower chance of wildfires and smoke. On the other hand, later in the season there is a higher chance that trails and roads have been cleared of winter blowdown and other obstacles; by this time, winter snow has melted and mosquitoes are gone. (However, in recent years widespread wildfire smoke has become a significant problem in August and September.) In the fall, trails are often less crowded and you can enjoy the fall colors.

Trekking to lookouts in the winter is not impossible, but it can be a challenge. Even if you're up for the trek over snowy trails, forest roads can be buried in snow, preventing you from even reaching the trailhead. There are several hikes in this book that are safe bets in the winter because they can be accessed from a low-elevation trailhead or Sno-Park. The Oregon Department of Transportation keeps Sno-Parks accessible through the winter by plowing snow, making them an ideal jumping-off point for recreationists who want to ski or snowshoe. Keep in mind that you always need to display a Sno-Park Pass on your vehicle's dashboard when parked at a Sno-Park from November 1 through April 30.

Finally, remember that all public land was once occupied by Indigenous peoples, and many of the sites where lookouts have been built are sacred to them. Treat the land with the respect it deserves and leave it better than you found it.

THE TEN ESSENTIALS

Whenever you go for a hike in the backcountry, it's a good idea to carry any supplies you need to prevent and survive an emergency situation, as well as safely spend a

The outstanding views from Black Butte (Hike 12) stretch from the Three Sisters (South and Middle shown here) all the way to Mount Hood.

night, or more, outside. The Ten Essentials, a list originated by The Mountaineers, should always be in your pack:

1. **NAVIGATION:** Carrying a paper map is best (no batteries!) along with a compass you know how to use. Many hikers supplement paper maps with the use of a handheld GPS device, or smartphone GPS apps such as Gaia or OnX. Other tools, depending on altitude and weather, include an altimeter and a personal locator beacon.
2. **SUN PROTECTION:** Broad-spectrum sunscreen rated at least SPF 30 will protect you from getting burned. Sunglasses and a sun hat, as well as other sun-protective clothing, are lifesavers during long summer days when the sun is high in the sky. Shade is often lacking on exposed summits and in burn areas.
3. **EXTRA CLOTHES:** Dress in layers so you can add and subtract clothing according to the conditions. Wear clothes that will wick sweat away from your body, and avoid wearing cotton. A jacket, hat, and gloves come in handy if the weather shifts or you find yourself stranded overnight. When choosing layers, consider the worst conditions you could realistically encounter during your trip.
4. **ILLUMINATION:** Don't rely solely on your phone's flashlight. Carry a headlamp or flashlight and check the batteries regularly, and bring extra with you.
5. **FIRST AID:** Assemble your own first aid kit from supplies you have at home, or purchase one of the many preassembled lightweight kits designed for hiking. Good items to include are dressings for wounds and other injuries; blister prevention and treatment; nonprescription painkillers, antidiarrheals, and antihistamines; and any personal prescriptions you use regularly.
6. **FIRE:** Waterproof matches and/or a butane lighter plus firestarters can help you build a signal fire that also keeps you warm.

7. **KNIFE OR MULTITOOL:** A sharp blade can be used for first aid, gear repair, or starting a fire. Carrying other items such as gear repair tape, duct tape, and safety pins is also recommended.
8. **FOOD:** Bring more food and snacks than you think you need, in case of an emergency; for shorter trips, consider what you would need for one additional day. Nutritious snacks that don't need cooking are best, including nuts and energy bars.
9. **WATER:** Always carry more water than you think you need, and be sure to stay hydrated during your hike, especially if it's a hot, sunny day. Not every trail has a water source, but carrying water treatment supplies, such as water purification tablets, and knowing how to use them helps ensure you'll drink clean water when you come across it.
10. **SHELTER:** A chilled person who is wet from rain or sweat can suffer from hypothermia even at temperatures above 40 degrees. An emergency space blanket takes up very little room, weighs only a few ounces, and can mean the difference between life and death in an emergency situation. Additional items include a rain shell, single-use bivy sack, tube tent, or even a jumbo plastic trash bag.

LEAVE NO TRACE SEVEN PRINCIPLES

When people hear "leave no trace," they often think of one thing: Pack out your trash. This is definitely an important practice to follow, but there are actually seven Leave No Trace Principles developed by the Center for Outdoor Ethics.

1. **PLAN AHEAD AND PREPARE.** Before you leave home, do some research so you know the regulations and special concerns for the trail you want to hike. Check the weather forecast and prepare accordingly. Visit in small groups when possible, and avoid high-use periods (remember that some of these lookouts take up nearly the entire summit with little room to spare!).
2. **TRAVEL AND CAMP ON DURABLE SURFACES.** Durable surfaces include maintained trails and designated campsites, rock, gravel, sand, dry grasses, and snow. Camp at least two hundred feet from lakes and streams. Use an existing campsite where possible instead of creating a new one, keeping your site as small as possible. When hiking, stick to the middle of the trail.
3. **DISPOSE OF WASTE PROPERLY.** Pack it in, pack it out! That includes toilet paper and *all* of your food (even apple cores and pistachio shells). Deposit solid human waste in catholes dug six to eight inches deep, at least two hundred feet from water, camping areas, and trails. Bag up your dog's poop and take it with you (never leave it sitting beside the trail for any length of time).

4. **LEAVE WHAT YOU FIND.** Take as many photos as you like, but do not take any items you find inside or outside a lookout. Leave rocks, plants, and other natural objects as you find them.
5. **MINIMIZE CAMPFIRE IMPACTS.** Use established fire rings and keep your fires small. Only use down and dead wood from the ground. Burn all wood to ash, extinguish your campfire completely before leaving (you should be able to touch it and feel no heat), and scatter the cooled ashes. Never build a campfire during high fire danger or during a fire ban.
6. **RESPECT WILDLIFE.** Let wildlife be wild; don't approach them, but rather observe from a distance. Never feed birds or other wildlife, no matter how cute they are. Feeding wildlife damages their health, changes their natural behaviors, and exposes them to predators and other dangers. Protect wildlife—and your food—by storing food and trash securely. Control your pets at all times or leave them at home. (Note that dogs are not allowed on trails in national parks.) Avoid wildlife at sensitive times, such as mating or nesting seasons.
7. **BE CONSIDERATE OF OTHER VISITORS.** Respect other visitors and protect the quality of their experience. Let nature's sounds prevail. Avoid loud voices and noises. If you like to listen to music, use earbuds instead of speakers. Be courteous. Yield to other users on the trail. The general rule is that uphill hikers have the right-of-way; cyclists yield to hikers; both hikers and cyclists yield to horses and other pack stock. When you encounter pack stock, greet riders and ask which side of the trail they prefer to use, stay visible, and speak calmly.

SAFETY CONSIDERATIONS

Hiking is fun and rewarding, but safety should always come first. In this section you'll find some tips to help you stay safe in the face of weather, critters, lack of communication, and fire danger in order to make the most of your time outdoors.

WEATHER

The weather conditions at the trailhead may be vastly different from conditions at the summit. It may be pleasantly warm when you start your hike, but temperatures are cooler the higher you go, so make sure you pack a long-sleeved shirt and even a jacket. Early in the season, you may also encounter lingering winter snow on the upper stretches of the trail, especially on north-facing slopes and in shaded areas.

Always remember that conditions can change quickly in the mountains. Check the forecast before you head out and plan accordingly. If you find yourself in a thunderstorm, seek shelter immediately. Open areas such as meadows and exposed high points are not safe places during a thunderstorm. Check for red flag warnings, which

The expansive vista from Summit Point (Hike 43)

are raised when high temperatures, strong winds, and low humidity combine to create an elevated fire risk. Being in the backcountry during a red flag warning requires extra vigilance because existing fires can grow rapidly and a smoldering stump from a recent lightning strike can quickly turn into a wildfire.

Summers are getting hotter in Oregon. Everyone's heat tolerance is different, but if you are engaging in outdoor activities during extreme heat and you feel faint or weak, the Oregon Health Authority advises stopping all activity and getting to a cool environment. They also advise limiting or avoiding activity in the afternoon when the sun is hottest, wearing loose lightweight clothing, wearing sunscreen, and drinking more water than usual. If you're hiking with a dog, make sure you bring plenty of water for them too.

WILDLIFE

Negative human-wildlife encounters are quite rare in Oregon. Keeping dogs on a leash, being alert, and practicing situational awareness will help you be prepared if you do encounter wildlife. Grizzlies no longer exist in Oregon, but the state is home to approximately twenty-five thousand black bears. Their fur is usually black, but it can also be cinnamon colored. Bears usually steer clear of humans, but it's important to secure food and garbage against bears so that they do not become habituated to

LEFT *Western pasqueflower in bloom* **RIGHT** *False hellebore on Madison Butte (Hike 36)*

people. The Oregon Department of Fish & Wildlife (ODFW) recommends that if you encounter a bear while hiking, do not approach it. Give it plenty of space, make sure it has an escape route, and leave the area if you see cubs.

The cougar population in Oregon is more than six thousand. Cougars (also known as mountain lions) usually stay away from people and are rarely sighted. If you do see one, make sure it has a path of retreat. If a cougar does not retreat, it is very important that you do not run away, which would trigger a chase response. ODFW recommends that you stand your ground, maintain eye contact, and back away slowly. Raise your voice, yell, and clap your hands. Pick up small children without bending down or turning your back on the cougar. Raise your arms to make yourself appear larger. If the cat does attack, fight back. Use your trekking poles, rocks, and sticks—any tool you have at your disposal. Call the ODFW if you have a face-to-face encounter with a bear or cougar.

The last wolf in Oregon was killed in 1947. Wolves from Canada were relocated and reintroduced into Yellowstone National Park and Idaho in 1995, and some of these wolves have since migrated into Oregon. As of 2022, there were at least 170 gray wolves in Oregon. Wolves are not considered a threat to humans, and there have been no wolf attacks on humans since they reappeared in Oregon.

There are about twenty species of tick in Oregon, but only four are a nuisance to humans: the Rocky Mountain wood tick, American dog tick, Pacific Coast tick, and western black-legged tick (the only one of the four known to carry Lyme disease). Ticks are found in areas with tall grass and brush. You can protect yourself by wearing long pants and tucking your pant legs into your socks, wearing long-sleeved shirts, and wearing light-colored clothing that will enable you to more easily spot a tick and remove it. Inexpensive tick removal tools can be purchased online and should be part of your first aid kit in case you are bitten by a tick.

The only venomous snake in Oregon is the rattlesnake, which lives in the dry, rocky areas of the state. There are several ways to tell them apart from other snakes, but the two most obvious ones are the rattles at the end of their tail and their diamond-shaped heads. Rattlesnakes are not aggressive unless threatened, and they use those rattles to warn you if you're getting too close. When you're hiking in rattlesnake country, watch your step, especially when stepping over a log or rock, since a snake might be resting underneath or on the other side. When sitting down to rest, always check the area for rattlesnakes first.

Cows may be domestic animals, but you should treat them as if they are wild. Ten of Oregon's thirty-six counties don't allow cows to wander freely. The others have areas of open range, where cows are allowed to roam on public land. You are most likely to encounter free-range cows in eastern Oregon. Watch your speed when driving on forest roads; it can be hard to spot dark cows in shadows or at night. If you encounter cows on a trail, give them space and don't approach or try to touch them. They usually run away when hikers come into their view.

SATELLITE MESSENGERS

Some hikers choose to carry a satellite messenger such as a Garmin inReach, Spot, or Zoleo. These devices allow you to summon help if you find yourself in an emergency without a cell phone signal (or your cell phone has died). Some of them also allow you to send texts to loved ones back home and to fellow hikers carrying the same kind of device. Prices, subscription plans, and features vary, so if you are interested in carrying a satellite messenger, do your research before making a purchase to choose the best device and subscription plan for your needs.

Newer iPhone and Android phones now have SOS capabilities that allow you to get help in an emergency when there is no regular signal. Before you head out for a hike, make sure you research how this works on your specific phone. The last thing you want to be doing in an emergency is trying to figure out how the SOS feature works!

Remember, do not use this technology as a crutch. Satellite messengers are no substitute for common sense. That said, accidents can happen to anyone, anytime, anywhere, and many hikers like knowing they have a way to summon help.

FIRE SAFETY

Summers are hotter than ever, and fire season is longer than it used to be. Wildfires burn bigger and longer. The Oregon Department of Forestry reported that from 2000

From The Watchman (Hike 24) in Crater Lake National Park, you can enjoy views of Hillman Peak up close and Mount Thielsen off in the distance.

to 2022, 73 percent of wildfires were started by humans. Of those, the top cause is equipment use, which includes vehicles, tractors, lawn mowers, chain saws, and so on. The next category is debris burning. The third category is recreation, which includes things like campfires and fireworks.

It's extremely important to practice fire safety when recreating on public land. While fire lookouts are there to spot and report fires, the fewer preventable wildfires caused by abandoned campfires and dragging trailer chains, the better. Every user of public land is responsible for practicing fire safety. Be careful where you park and drive. If your vehicle's hot exhaust system comes into contact with dry grass, it could spark a fire. If you're towing a trailer, make sure you secure the tow chain. Dragging chains can send sparks into roadside grass and start a fire. Never toss a cigarette onto the ground. Not only is such behavior littering, but it could start a fire.

Be responsible with campfires. Check with the land agency ahead of time for any fire restrictions; fire bans are common in late summer. Keep your fires at a manageable size, especially during windy weather. Always extinguish your campfire completely before leaving the area, even if you plan to return later. Properly extinguishing a campfire means drowning it with a lot of water. Nothing should be smoldering, and the spot where the fire was burning should be cool to the touch. If it's too hot to touch, it's too hot to leave. Even if there is no fire ban, consider campfire alternatives such as a propane fire pit or gas lantern. If staying warm isn't a concern, some campers create a pile or coil of battery-powered twinkle lights instead of a fire.

Setting off fireworks on public land is illegal year-round. If you see fireworks or an illegal campfire, or if you spot the start of a wildfire, report it to the authorities immediately.

APPS AND TECHNOLOGY

There are hundreds of hiking-related apps available for your smartphone. I cannot possibly mention them all, but here are a few to be aware of.

AllTrails is a directory of trails (albeit an incomplete one). It is great for hike discovery, but not great at providing details. The data is provided by users; land agencies have nothing to do with the information you find here. If you find a hike on AllTrails, conduct further research to find out more about it. Another big downside is that it relies on an external app such as Google Maps to provide driving directions to the trailhead. Google Maps is notoriously unreliable on public land, showing roads that don't exist or have been closed, while not showing roads that do exist. Some features of AllTrails are free, but a yearly subscription is required to access all features.

I've lost track of the number of times I've helped fellow hikers identify peaks visible from a lookout. Two apps on my phone help make this possible. PeakFinder and PeakVisor use your phone's GPS to determine where you are. When you hold your phone up horizontally, the app will show you the profile of the mountains and their names. This is a much easier method for identifying peaks than looking at a two-dimensional map, plus it includes peaks that are off the edge of your map. PeakFinder is a one-time purchase, whereas PeakVisor is free to download but limits you to one location a day. For multiple locations per day, it requires a yearly subscription.

Many hikers carry a handheld GPS device or use an app on their phone such as Gaia or OnX. It's important to remember that while these apps work without a signal, you do need to download offline maps while you have a signal. Traditional mapping apps like Google Maps and Apple Maps should never be used to navigate roads or trails on public land. (See How to Use This Guide for more information.)

Wildfires and weather events can cause road and trail closures that sometimes last for several years. In addition to checking the managing agency's website for news and updates (listed for each hike; you can also check the agency's Facebook page), a couple of helpful apps are worth a look. Watch Duty tracks current wildfires big and small and is always worth checking before heading out for a hike, and AirNow provides air quality measurements as well as a smoke map.

ETIQUETTE FOR VISITING LOOKOUTS

The fire lookouts in this book are on public land, and the public is allowed to visit them. However, that doesn't mean that anything goes. Always practice Leave No Trace (see Hiking Tips). Pack out all your trash, don't leave graffiti, and leave the place better than you found it.

Lookouts fall into one of three categories: not staffed or abandoned, staffed, and rentable.

NOT STAFFED OR ABANDONED

Some lookouts have ceased to be staffed for the purposes of fire detection. With a few exceptions, these lookouts are locked and not open to the public. When visiting these lookouts, obey any warning signs about not climbing the stairs or entering the cabin due to the structural integrity of the lookouts. Don't tamper with locks or cut holes to break into a locked lookout.

Two of the lookouts in this book are first-come, first-served: Pechuck (Hike 6) and Little Cowhorn Mountain (Hike 14). Devils Peak (Hike 3) is often used by overnight hikers, but the structure is considered unsafe. Accepted etiquette dictates that if someone is staying in the cabin, then anyone who shows up later should not expect to also stay inside unless the weather is terrible. Therefore, many overnighters come prepared with a tent or hammock so they can camp nearby if necessary. Some people think that if they were the first to arrive at the lookout, then no one else should camp anywhere nearby on the summit. Others feel that it is unrealistic and misguided to expect solitude and to have the entire summit to themselves when staying at a non-reservable lookout. Neither the Forest Service nor the Bureau of Land Management provides guidance on the proper etiquette for these situations. Ultimately this is public land open for all to use, so exercise your best judgment and above all, remember to be respectful.

OPPOSITE *Table Rock Lookout (Hike 41)*

STAFFED AND RENTABLE

I have grouped staffed and rentable lookouts together because there is a lot of overlap in the etiquette for these two.

- **STAFFED:** A staffed lookout is occupied by a paid employee (or sometimes a volunteer) during part or all of the fire season.
- **RENTABLE:** Some lookouts have been completely converted into rental cabins and are never staffed. Others are rentable part of the time and staffed part of the time, depending on the needs of the Forest Service.

When you approach a staffed or rented lookout on foot, it's easy to go unnoticed, especially if it's a tower, so be sure to announce your presence by calling out "hello," although be aware that if the occupants are busy, they may not acknowledge you. You can then proceed to quietly explore the summit. Keep dogs leashed at all times.

Never enter a staffed or rented lookout without permission from the occupants. Be a good visitor and respect their privacy. Whenever you visit a staffed or rented lookout, you should never expect to be able to climb the tower or go inside. (If that does happen, consider it a bonus.) Don't throw rocks or any other objects at the windows to get the attention of someone inside. Feel free to look around outside and walk around the summit. Keep in mind that this is easier at some locations than at others where the summit area is small and may be totally occupied by the lookout.

If you're invited in, be respectful of the occupants' space and ask before touching anything. Don't pick up their stuff or sit on the bed, unless invited to do so. Be polite and courteous, and don't overstay your welcome.

Visiting a staffed or rented lookout very early or very late in the day is considered disruptive and disrespectful. Some staffed lookouts actually have posted hours. Regardless of the time of day you visit, watch your noise level while you're hanging around the lookout. Don't be the rowdy group blasting music on your Bluetooth speaker and letting your barking dogs run around off-leash.

When visiting a staffed lookout, remember that you are visiting someone's home and office. While many lookouts are happy to interact with visitors and even show them around, they may be too busy. They are, after all, up there to do a job: Lookout staff may be monitoring a fire or multiple fires, in which case they won't have time to be your tour guide or answer questions.

Think of a rented lookout as a campsite in a campground or as a hotel room. (This only applies to the structure, not the surrounding land.) Renters have paid for the privilege of staying in the lookout and may not want visitors. It's okay to ask, because some renters may have no problem with a visitor coming onto the catwalk, but never assume they will be okay with visitors climbing the stairs or coming inside.

Hat Point (Hike 45) offers an interesting perspective on Hells Canyon.

You should be carrying enough water, food, and supplies for your hike. Don't expect a lookout or a renter to have extra food and water for you.

Never assume it's okay to fly your drone around the lookout. Be sure to ask first, and be accepting if the answer is no. Drones are never allowed to take off or land in designated wilderness areas.

It is never okay to camp next to a staffed lookout. It is frowned upon to camp next to a rented lookout that someone has paid to stay in, and some lookouts have No Camping signs.

Keep in mind that lookout staffing can change from one year to the next. You may encounter a friendly lookout who invites visitors up, but a few years later someone else may be working there who doesn't wish to have visitors.

HOW TO RENT A FIRE LOOKOUT

With the rebuilding of the Bolan Mountain lookout (Hike 28), there are eighteen Forest Service lookouts for rent in Oregon at the time of publication. (Other states have lookout rentals too, including Washington, Idaho, Montana, and California.) Lookouts can be reserved on recreation.gov. The reservation window opens six months in advance at 7 a.m. Pacific Time, meaning that if you want to book a lookout for July 10, for example, you will be able to make your reservation starting on January 10. However, the rental program is enormously popular, and there may be dozens of other people ready on their phones and computers at 7 a.m. when the window opens, attempting to book the same lookout for the same date you are. There is no secret trick to getting a reservation when so many other people are trying too. Because demand is so high, you will most likely need to try numerous times before you're successful, so it's good to have different dates in mind. Be patient and keep trying.

Before you make a reservation, do research about the lookout you're trying to book. Some lookouts are ground cabins and some are towers with steep stairs. If you have a fear of heights or have mobility issues, consider staying in a ground cabin, not a tower. Most Oregon rentals have road access, but a few require a hike. Lookouts that are available for rent in winter usually require a trek by snowshoes or skis, and you have to haul your gear in an overnight pack or pull it behind you on a sled.

Also research road conditions, which vary widely from one location to another. The district's ranger station can give you information about this. In my experience, lookout access roads are usually quite rough. Some require a high-clearance vehicle, or even four-wheel drive.

Once you've successfully obtained a reservation and know how to get there, here are some things to keep in mind as you prepare for your stay.

Most lookouts have a combination lock on a gate and/or the cabin door, and you'll need to get the combo beforehand. Your confirmation email will tell you whether you need to call the ranger station to get this number or if you'll receive it via

OPPOSITE *Bald Butte Lookout in Fremont-Winema National Forest can be rented for overnight visits.*

Hager Mountain Lookout (Hike 33)

email from recreation.gov. Keep in mind that ranger stations are not open on weekends.

Staying in a lookout is a rustic experience! If you're used to camping, you'll probably do fine, but if you're used to staying in hotels, you'll need to adjust your expectations. Amenities vary from one lookout to another. Some have a single bed, some have a double bed, and some even have multiple beds. A small table and at least one chair will usually be available. Some have a small refrigerator. Some have a gas stove for cooking. Many of them have a woodstove, although sometimes you have to bring your own firewood. Those that do not have a woodstove sometimes have an electric or propane heater, but some have no heat source at all. This is usually not a problem in the summer, but it can get chilly in the fall.

Lookouts do not have plumbing. You will need to bring as much water as you need for cooking, cleaning, and drinking, or plan to melt and filter snow in the winter. An outhouse or vault toilet will be nearby. It's a good idea to bring some toilet paper with you, as the supply may be out.

Supplies available on-site vary. You may find a variety of pots, pans, and dishes in various states of cleanliness. Sometimes none of these things are available. Because the availability of supplies varies so much from one lookout to the next, it's a good idea to bring everything you think you'll need, including pots, pans, silverware, and whatever you need to prepare and eat your meals.

Consider where you will get firewood. Some lookouts have firewood on-site, but sometimes you have to bring your own. Do not chop firewood inside the lookout. It damages the floor and makes a mess. If firewood is provided on-site, it's a nice gesture to bring some in from the woodshed before you leave so that it's all ready for the next renter. If an outside fire ring is provided, make sure your fire is completely out before you leave the area. This means dumping water on it and being able to touch the coals without feeling any heat. If there is a fire ban in effect (often the case in late summer), don't build an outside fire at all.

Rodents, bees, flies, and other pests can occasionally be a problem, especially if past renters have not properly cleaned up after themselves. Most lookouts do not have screened windows or a screen door, so if it's hot and you need ventilation, you might have some insect visitors. It's very important to clean up after yourself so that you don't attract pests.

Don't feed birds or other wildlife that comes calling while you're at the lookout. They are wild animals, not pets, and their reliance on humans for food may turn them into annoying pests for future renters.

Not all lookouts allow dogs, so check before you make your reservation. If you do bring your dog, please make sure to clean up after it, both inside the lookout (clean up that dog hair) and out (get rid of the poop). Ground cabins are no problem for dog access, but if you stay in a tower, the stairs may be too steep for your dog to handle.

Cell phone signals can be spotty. Sometimes you'll have a full signal only to find it's gone ten minutes later. Do not count on having service while staying at a lookout. It's nicer if you put your phone into airplane mode and just enjoy your surroundings.

Don't count on having the summit to yourself. Remember that you are on public land and that you may have visitors on the summit, especially on weekends. However, the lookout itself is not fair game, and you are never obligated to let visitors into the lookout or on the catwalk. (See Etiquette for Visiting Lookouts for how to be a respectful visitor when you're not the renter.)

Pack out *all* of your trash. Do not burn your trash in the woodstove or in the outside fire pit. And definitely don't throw it in the toilet!

Always leave the lookout in better shape than you found it. Clean up after yourself, haul out your garbage, and sweep the floor. Close all the windows before you leave and shut the door firmly behind you. It is okay to leave nonperishable canned food for future visitors, but don't leave anything that can be easily raided by rodents. Don't leave flowers, pinecones, balloons, streamers, and so on; just because you enjoyed having these things around during your stay doesn't mean the next person will, and you are just adding to the amount of trash the next renter has to haul out.

The following table features only lookouts available for rent on public land. It does not include sites that have non-lookout cabins, such as Fremont Point in the Fremont-Winema National Forest, which has a rentable cabin but no lookout. It also does not include lookouts that have been built on private land (you'll find those listed on sites like Airbnb). Ten of these lookouts do not have trails and therefore are not included in this book. Corresponding hike numbers are provided for the others. This information could change at any time. Check with the Forest Service for the latest information.

OREGON LOOKOUTS FOR RENT

LOOKOUT	TYPE	ACCESS	SEASON
MOUNT HOOD NATIONAL FOREST			
Clear Lake Butte	Tower	Hike	Winter
Fivemile Butte (Hike 4)	Tower	Hike (winter), drive-up (summer)	Year-round
Flag Point (Hike 5)	Tower	Hike	Winter
WILLAMETTE NATIONAL FOREST			
Gold Butte (Hike 7)	Ground cabin	Hike	Summer
Indian Ridge*	Tower	Drive-up	Summer
Warner Mountain*	Tower	Hike	Winter
DESCHUTES NATIONAL FOREST			
Green Ridge*	Tower	Drive-up	Summer
UMPQUA NATIONAL FOREST			
Acker Rock (Hike 23)	Ground cabin	Hike	August 1 through November 15
Pickett Butte	Tower	Drive-up	Mid-October through early June
ROGUE RIVER-SISKIYOU NATIONAL FOREST			
Acorn Woman Peak* (Hike 29)	Ground cabin	Drive-up	Summer
Bald Knob*	Tower	Drive-up	Summer
Bolan Mountain (Hike 28)	Ground cabin	Drive-up	Summer
Lake of the Woods	Tower	Drive-up	Summer
Snow Camp Mountain (Hike 26)	Ground cabin	Drive-up	Summer
FREMONT-WINEMA NATIONAL FOREST			
Bald Butte	Ground cabin	Drive-up	Summer
Drake Peak	Ground cabin	Drive-up	Summer
Hager Mountain (Hike 33)	Ground cabin	Hike	Winter
MALHEUR NATIONAL FOREST			
Fall Mountain	Tower	Drive-up	Summer

* *Pets are prohibited inside the lookout.*

HOW TO USE THIS GUIDE

The hikes in this book are grouped by geographical location. Northwest Oregon includes the area north of the portion of Oregon Route 126 between the coast and Eugene and the area north of Oregon Route 58. Southwest Oregon includes the area south of OR 126 and OR 58. The central and east region includes the area east of US Highway 97.

The best time to hike to fire lookouts is during the summer after the snow has melted. Fall is also a good time; the days are often cooler, and there can be less wildfire smoke in the air. If you like snowshoeing or cross-country skiing, some lookouts near plowed roads and Sno-Parks can be visited in the winter without too much effort. When you are hiking in the backcountry in the winter, it's important to be aware of avalanche danger. Avalanche forecast information can be obtained online from the Northwest Avalanche Center (nwac.us).

Never trust apps like Google Maps or Apple Maps as your sole source for navigating to a trailhead. These apps work great in the city, but they are terrible on public land. They frequently lead drivers astray, routing along unmaintained roads or those closed by snow, particularly in winter and spring. Don't rely on AllTrails either; it doesn't provide directions, instead diverting users to an external mapping app such as Google Maps. Best practice is to use turn-by-turn directions from guidebooks like this one in conjunction with a paper map. You can print out road maps and trail maps from websites like Caltopo.com.

Each hike begins by listing some key information.

Year constructed is the year that the current lookout was built. For the hikes to former lookout sites, this category will say "removed."

Lookout access provides information about whether it is closed to the public or is open for day use and/or overnight use.

Location is the jurisdiction of the trail. Most of the hikes in this book are in national forests, and the respective ranger district is listed for those. A few are located in Oregon's only national park—Crater Lake—or on Bureau of Land Management land.

Western larches in Malheur National Forest turn golden in fall.

Roundtrip distance is the length in miles to complete the entire out-and-back (or loop) hike as described. A few of the hikes have options for different approaches or add-ons, which will have different mileage. These distances were measured by my Gaia GPS app but are not guaranteed to be exact.

Elevation gain is the amount of vertical feet you'll gain during the entire course of the hike.

Lookout elevation ranges from 3290 feet to 9040 feet in this book. The higher the elevation, the longer it will take snow to melt in early summer. All elevations are taken directly from the US Geological Survey topographic maps.

Maps recommends which map you should bring on your hike, to supplement the simple topographic map shown in each hike. All the recommended maps are United States Geological Survey (USGS) 7.5-minute maps with a 1:24,000 scale and can be downloaded for free at store.usgs.gov.

GPS coordinates provides the Global Positioning System location for the trailhead. The format is in decimal degrees using the WGS 84 datum, with north and west values.

Permits and fees lists any required parking passes for the trailhead, or wilderness permits you may need to acquire. (See Hiking Tips for more about passes.)

Getting to the Trailhead features driving directions from the nearest town, community, or major landmark.

MAP LEGEND

5 Interstate highway	Bridge
26 US highway	Campsite
22 State route	Direction of travel
1230 Forest road	Fire lookout
Main trail	Gate
Other trail	Mountain or peak
Powerline	Parking
Paved road	Point of interest
Gravel road	Trailhead
Body of water	Alternate trailhead
River or stream	Viewpoint
Meadow or marsh	Restroom
Park, forest, or wilderness area	Picnic area

On the Trail references road and trail signage where I saw it during my research; however, do not expect signage to be intact on public land. Signs frequently fall victim to target shooting, graffiti, and other vandalism, as well as falling trees and winter weather, and are often not replaced, or at least not immediately. Always carry a good map.

A NOTE ABOUT SAFETY

Safety is an important concern in all outdoor activities. No guidebook can alert you to every hazard or anticipate the limitations of every reader. Therefore, the descriptions of roads, trails, routes, and natural features in this book are not representations that a particular place or excursion will be safe for your party. When you follow any of the routes described in this book, you assume responsibility for your own safety. Under normal conditions, such excursions require the usual attention to traffic, road and trail conditions, weather, terrain, the capabilities of your party, and other factors. Keeping informed on current conditions and exercising common sense are the keys to a safe, enjoyable outing.

—*Mountaineers Books*

NORTHWEST

1 SADDLE MOUNTAIN

YEAR CONSTRUCTED	LOOKOUT ACCESS	LOCATION
1953	Removed	Saddle Mountain State Natural Area

Roundtrip distance: 5.2 miles
Elevation gain: 1600 feet
Lookout elevation: 3290 feet
Map: USGS Saddle Mountain
GPS coordinates: 45.96284°, –123.69009°
Permits and fees: None

The northern Coast Range of Oregon once boasted dozens of lookouts. Today not a single one remains, but on Saddle Mountain the views that make it a good spot to watch for fires still abound. It is a stiff climb, but come in June for the wildflower displays and you will feel like you are in paradise. If you bring your dog, consider booties because the wire mesh near the top of the trail can be abrasive on dogs' foot pads.

Coast Range peaks are visible above the clouds from the slopes of Saddle Mountain. (Photo by Greg Lief)

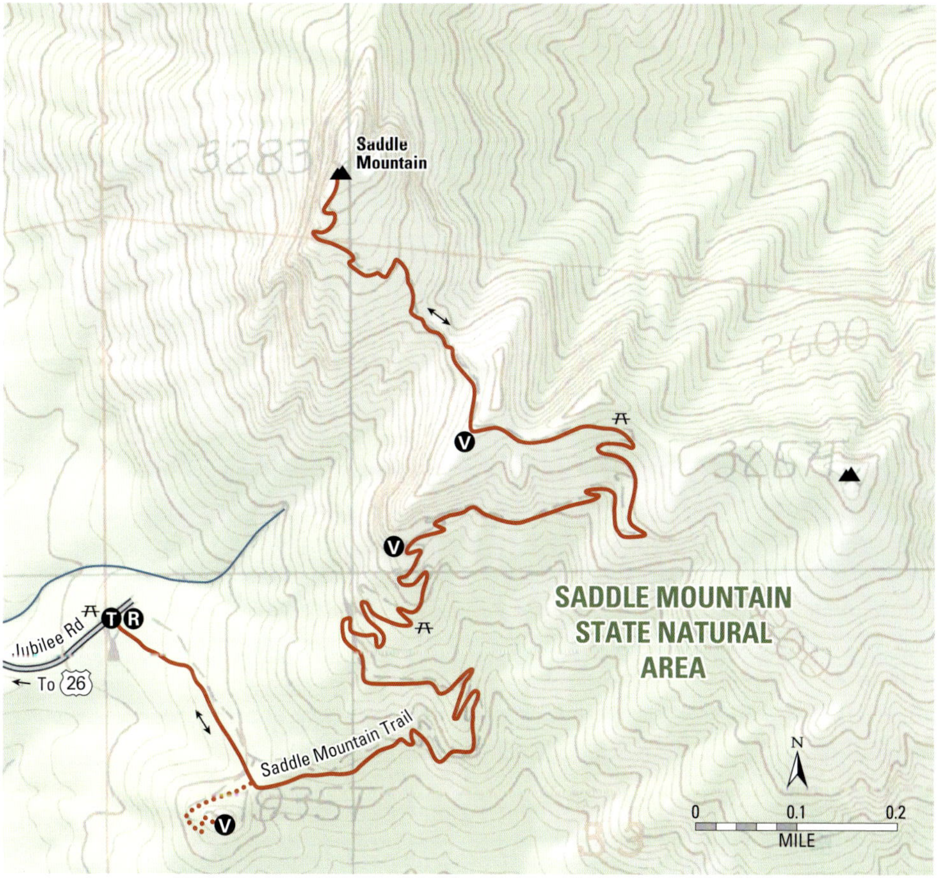

GETTING TO THE TRAILHEAD

From North Plains, drive west on US Highway 26 for 47 miles. If you are coming from Seaside, drive south on US Highway 101 for 3.5 miles, then drive east on US 26 for 10 miles.

From US 26, turn north onto Jubilee Road (also called Saddle Mountain Road), signed for Saddle Mountain Natural Area. Follow this paved road for 7.1 miles to the Saddle Mountain trailhead at the road's end. There is a picnic area and a toilet; however, the area is day use only with overnight camping prohibited.

ON THE TRAIL

From the east side of the parking lot by the signboards, the Saddle Mountain Trail starts out paved but then soon turns to dirt. Alder trees tower above you, and moss covers everything in this wet forest, which receives many inches of rain each year.

LEFT *Rosy plectritis blooms in abundance on Saddle Mountain in June.* **RIGHT** *New vegetation sprouts on a large old stump on Saddle Mountain.*

Notice the enormous stumps; the huge old-growth forest that once stood here was logged long ago, but the stumps left behind are fostering the next generation of trees. Sorrel, ferns, salmonberry, and vine maple fill the understory. In June, the trail is lined with bleeding heart, fringecup, and candy flower.

After 0.2 mile, reach the junction with a 0.1-mile side trail to a viewpoint of Humbug Mountain. You can see it even better later in the hike, so feel free to skip this detour.

The trail continues climbing through a forest of Sitka spruce and Douglas-fir, switchbacking up the mountain. Stay on the trail and do not cut the switchbacks, a practice that causes erosion and eventually landslides, resulting in extra work for trail crews and sometimes even trail closures.

At the 1-mile mark, pass a thoroughly vandalized picnic table at a switchback. There is not really anything to see here, but it is a good place to take a breather. The trail now starts to cross open slopes carpeted with monkeyflower, chickweed, plectritis, and paintbrush, providing a colorful distraction as you climb ever upward. In many spots, the trail is held in place by wire mesh. At 1.2 miles, there is a good viewpoint on the left where the trail switchbacks uphill to the right and a rock formation sticks up out of the mountainside—another good spot for a break.

After traversing slopes awash with wildflowers (if you hike it in late spring through early summer), the trail reenters the forest at 1.5 miles. Pass a picnic table on your right, and just beyond that, the trail emerges from the forest into another open rocky area dotted with yet more wildflowers. The trail reaches another stop-and-catch-your-breath viewpoint on the left and turns right at this spot, heading briefly into the forest. Emerge from the trees and spot your destination ahead, as well as the final stretch of trail you have to climb to get there. Do not be discouraged; it looks more daunting than it is. Descend to a saddle, then begin your final ascent to the summit. Switchback up the rocky slope on more wire mesh to the end of the trail at the summit of Saddle Mountain, which is surrounded by a wire cable.

Up here on Clatsop County's highest point, vistas stretch in all directions. To the north you can see the town of Astoria and the mighty Columbia River. If you have really good vision or powerful binoculars, you can spot the 125-foot-tall Astoria Column on the hill above town. On a clear day, you may even see the prominent Cascade volcanoes to the east: Mount Rainier, Mount St. Helens, Mount Adams, and Mount Hood. If it is especially clear, you might also be able to spot Mount Jefferson. To the southeast is the other hump of Saddle Mountain. To the south is Humbug Mountain and just to the right of it, but more distant, are Angora Peak, Onion Peak, and Sugarloaf Mountain. To the west is the Pacific Ocean.

The Clatsop Indians call this peak Swallalahoost. Legend tells of a great chief who was killed by enemies and assumed the form of an eagle, becoming the creator of thunder and lightning atop this mountain. Visible from the town of Astoria, this mountain was noted by Meriwether Lewis and William Clark in their journals while they wintered at Fort Clatsop west of there. Lieutenant Charles Wilkes of the US Navy named the peak Saddle Mountain in 1841 due to the saddlelike shape formed by its two summit peaks. A geologist with the Wilkes party, James D. Dana, led the first recorded ascent that year.

The first lookout on Saddle Mountain was a log cabin built in 1913. Ten miles of telephone line had to be erected between Jewell and the summit so that fires could be reported in a timely manner. The federal government set aside 1400 acres for a park here in 1916, later donating it to the state. In 1920, a frame cabin was built with an observation platform on top of it. A Civilian Conservation Corps (CCC) camp was built near the highway in 1935. In addition to many other projects, CCC crews built the entrance road between the highway and the base of the mountain.

A 14-by-14-foot lookout cabin was proposed for construction in 1953. Hauling more than twenty thousand pounds of material up the narrow trail by pack animal was deemed too time-intensive and costly, so helicopter pilot Dean Johnson and his copilot Fred Hill volunteered to fly the material up. Using wood from the old lookout, workers built a small helicopter pad at the summit. Johnson and Hill made eighty-five flights over the course of a week, transporting lumber, concrete blocks, tools,

Mount St. Helens and Mount Rainier are visible on the horizon from the wildflower-covered slopes of Saddle Mountain. (Photo by Greg Lief)

sacks of cement, and other building materials. Fog and constantly changing conditions made for challenging flights. One time a gust of wind nearly blew the parked helicopter off the summit, but Johnson jumped in the cockpit and took off at the last second—disaster averted. The lookout was removed just a decade later. No evidence of it remains.

Several lookout sites are visible from Saddle Mountain, including Green Mountain to the north and Wickiup Mountain and Nicolai Mountain to the northeast. These and every other lookout structure in the Coast Range down to Reedsport are now gone. Of the remaining lookouts to the south, only one west of Interstate 5 is still staffed—Dutchman Peak near Ashland (Hike 30). The rest are either abandoned, are rented out to the public, or have been converted into remote camera sites.

Return the way you came.

2 MARYS PEAK

YEAR CONSTRUCTED	LOOKOUT ACCESS	LOCATION
1963	Removed	Siuslaw National Forest, Central Coast Ranger District

Roundtrip distance: 2.6 miles
Elevation gain: 620 feet
Lookout elevation: 4100 feet
Map: USGS Marys Peak
GPS coordinates: 44.51001°, –123.56097°
Permits and fees: Northwest Forest Pass

Marys Peak is the highest point in Oregon's Coast Range. Its distinctive humpback shape can be seen from numerous spots in the Willamette Valley, Coast Range, and Cascades. This short hike to the summit has a little bit of everything: a beautiful forest, wildflower meadows, and sweeping views.

GETTING TO THE TRAILHEAD

From Philomath, head west on US Highway 20; then, 0.1 mile after the eastbound and westbound lanes reunite, at the edge of town, turn left onto Oregon Route 34, signed for Marys Peak and Alsea Falls. Drive for 8.8 paved, curvy miles. Turn right onto paved Forest Road 30 (Marys Peak Road), signed for Marys Peak Recreation Area. Drive for 5.3 miles to a junction where FR 30 goes left. Stay straight on FR 3010 and drive 3.4 miles, then turn right into the Marys Peak Campground. Make an immediate left turn into the parking area where there are about a dozen parking spots.

ON THE TRAIL

Walk down the road into the campground and turn left at the signboard, following the road to the far end of the turnaround loop, where the trail starts between two signboards.

The trail heads into a forest of hemlock and noble fir. The forest floor is carpeted with sorrel. After 0.1 mile, reach a junction where your loop on Meadowedge Trail #1325 begins. There is a signboard here with a helpful trail map. Turn right and begin a gradual descent. This area receives around a hundred inches of precipitation annually, creating a lush environment with abundant moss. All around you, decaying stumps and logs host a new generation of trees and plants.

Cross Parker Creek on a wooden footbridge, then begin ascending. The trail switchbacks up the mountain through the trees. Now the forest floor is carpeted with thousands of star-flowered lily-of-the-valley. At 0.8 mile, the trail emerges from the forest into an expansive meadow. The summit communication towers are visible above you, and views start appearing to your right. The trail switchbacks, then reenters the forest.

At the 1-mile mark, reach another junction. Your return loop will be the left fork. For now, you will take the uphill right fork. After 0.1 mile, reach another junction. Again, your return route will be the left fork. Turn right onto Summit Loop Trail #1388. The trail heads back out into the meadow, climbing steeply. Columbia lily and lupine bloom here in late June and early July. Reach an unsigned junction and turn right (to the left is an unofficial closed path), then reach the summit where the trail ends.

A tent camp was established on Marys Peak in 1915. In 1941, the Civilian Conservation Corps built a three-story combination lookout and observation tower.

The Meadowedge Trail winds through the forest.

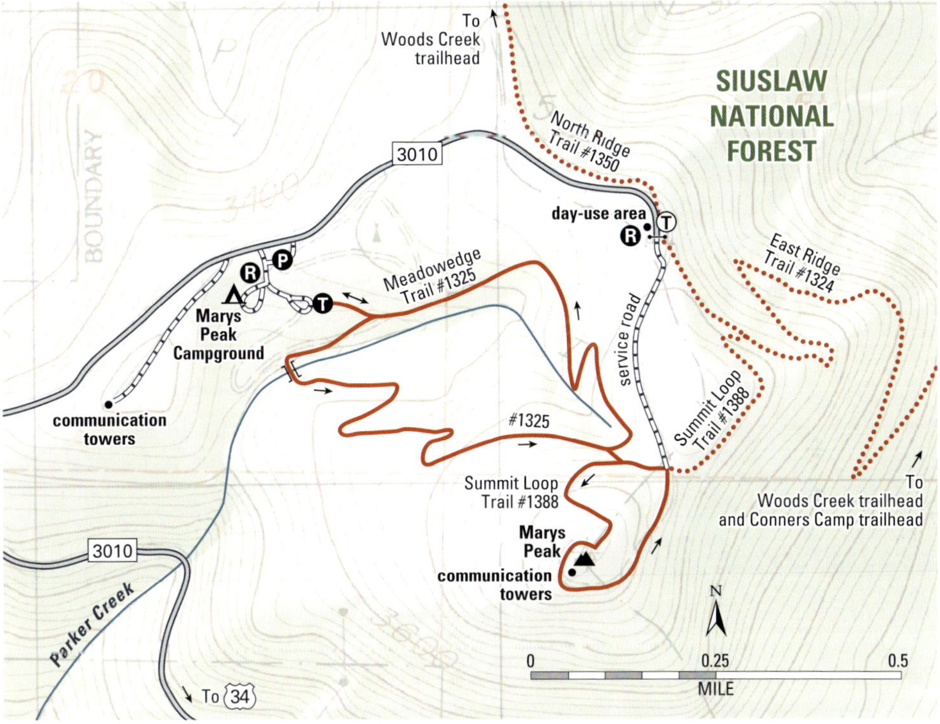

The first level was a large log base to provide extra height, the second level was a public observation area with glass windows and a deck, and the third level was the 14-by-14-foot lookout cabin. The Forest Service removed the entire structure by burning it down in 1959, replacing it with a 41-foot R-6 tower. Just three years later, the tower was destroyed in the 1962 Columbus Day storm (peak gusts reached 127 miles per hour in nearby Corvallis). A new tower was built a year later with a lower viewing deck for visitors and an R-6 lookout cabin above. It ceased being staffed in the 1970s and was removed.

The area on the summit where the lookout once stood is now occupied by a cluster of communication towers, all surrounded by a fence. It's unsightly, but the landscape beyond them is spectacular. To the east, the Cascade Mountains are on display, and on an especially clear day, you can see all the way from Mount Rainier to the northeast to Diamond Peak to the southwest, with an abundance of major and minor peaks in between. Due east is Mount Jefferson and the Three Sisters.

The Siuslaw National Forest established the 924-acre Marys Peak Scenic Botanical Special Interest Area in 1989 in recognition of its botanical, scenic, and recreational value, including the 130 acres of summit meadows. The noble fir forest on the summit

Phlox blooms on the summit of Marys Peak in June.

is the largest stand of such trees in the entire Coast Range and contains trees that are 150 to 200 years old. However, the area covered by the summit meadows has decreased by 34 percent over the past fifty years as the noble firs have spread into the meadow. Restoration efforts in recent years have included the removal of these encroaching trees.

Marys Peak is an important spiritual site for Indigenous peoples, including the Kalapuya, Alsea, and Yaquina. The Marys Peak Alliance worked with the Confederated Tribes of the Grand Ronde and the Confederated Tribes of Siletz Indians to rename ten creeks on Marys Peak to reflect Indigenous history and culture. These names were approved by the Oregon Geographic Names Board in 2019. The Kalapuya call this place Chateemanwi, meaning Spirit Mountain. The modern name comes from the Marys River, which may have been named for the daughter of John Lloyd, a settler from Missouri who lived in Benton County. (And no, the lack of an apostrophe is not a typo. The US Board on Geographic Names discourages apostrophes in official place names, so "Marys Peak" is correct.)

Turn right onto the gravel service road and follow it as it curls down around the west and south sides of the summit. From early June to mid-July, a rainbow of different flowers bloom in the rock gardens alongside this road, including larkspur, phlox, paintbrush, groundsel, and penstemon. Be sure to stay on the roadbed and do not go off-trail through the fragile meadows.

Continue descending the service road to its junction with the Summit Loop Trail. The road continues to the summit parking area, and the continuation of the Summit Loop Trail to the right meets up with East Ridge Trail #1324, but you will turn left onto a trail that immediately heads into the trees. You will soon reach a familiar junction where you were earlier. Take the right fork downhill. At the next junction, turn right.

The trail descends through the forest, then traverses a meadow at the edge of the forest before turning and dropping back into the woods. After a pleasant descent through the trees, reach that first junction with the signboard and bear right to return to the trailhead.

EXTEND YOUR HIKE

Numerous trails in the area invite further exploration. You can start your hike farther down the mountain at Woods Creek trailhead where the North Ridge Trail begins, or at Conners Camp trailhead where the East Ridge Trail begins. You can also drive to the day-use area near the gate just below the summit and start a hike on the North Ridge or East Ridge Trails, or hike past the gate on the service road to reach the summit.

3 DEVILS PEAK

YEAR CONSTRUCTED	LOOKOUT ACCESS	LOCATION
1933	Unlocked but unsafe for public access	Mount Hood National Forest, Zigzag Ranger District

Roundtrip distance: 7.5 miles
Elevation gain: 3200 feet
Lookout elevation: 5050 feet
Maps: USGS Government Camp and USGS Rhododendron
GPS coordinates: 45.29745°, −121.88455°
Permits and fees: None

The only remaining lookout in the Mount Hood National Forest without a road leading to it, Devils Peak is the highest point in the Salmon-Huckleberry Wilderness.

GETTING TO THE TRAILHEAD

From the Zigzag Ranger Station, drive east on US Highway 26 for 1.3 miles and turn right onto paved Still Creek Road (Forest Road 2612). In 0.3 mile, keep right at the fork. Drive another 2.5 miles of pavement and 0.5 mile of good gravel—that is drivable in any vehicle—until you reach the trailhead sign on your right. There is parking for about a dozen vehicles along the shoulder here.

ON THE TRAIL

Devils Peak has the unique distinction of having four different access routes. This hike describes the most commonly used route up Cool Creek Trail #794. Do not let the name fool you, as this trail never comes within sight of Cool Creek.

The current lookout tower on Devils Peak was built in 1933.

The trail starts on the south side of the road and immediately enters the Salmon-Huckleberry Wilderness. You have more than 3000 feet to gain, so the trail wastes no time in climbing. As you head steeply through the forest, you will gain 1000 feet of elevation in the first mile. For much of this hike, you will pass wild rhododendrons, which bloom in June. You may also see beargrass, sorrel, columbine, bunchberry, paintbrush, and Oregon grape. At 1.2 miles, enjoy a flat stretch with Mount Hood to your left and sounds of traffic on US 26 far below. This is a good spot to pause and drink some water before continuing on.

The trail continues to climb steadily with occasional flat sections that never seem to last long enough. There may not be any sweeping expanses to distract you, but take the time to appreciate the big old Douglas-firs and hemlocks that make up this beautiful forest. In late summer and early fall, huckleberries make a tasty snack, as well as a good excuse to stop and catch your breath.

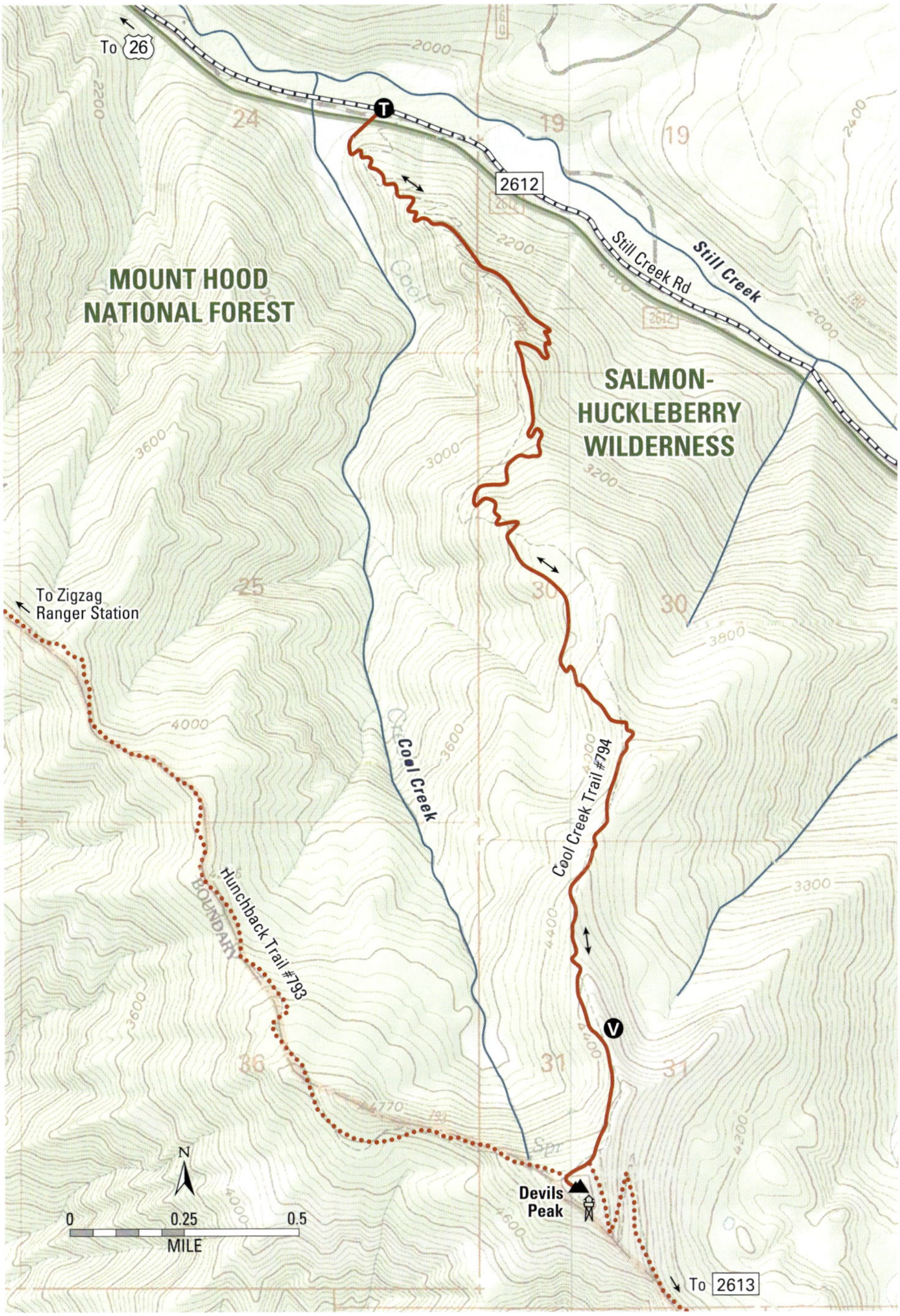
To 26
2000
24
19
19
2400
2612
2200
Still Creek Rd
Still Creek
MOUNT HOOD
NATIONAL FOREST
Cool
2612
2000
SALMON-
HUCKLEBERRY
WILDERNESS
3600
3000
3200
To Zigzag
Ranger Station
25
30
30
3800
4000
Cool Creek
3600
Cool Creek Trail #794
Hunchback Trail #793
BOUNDARY
4400
3300
3600
36
31
31
4770
793
Spr
4200
N
Devils
Peak
0
0.25
0.5
MILE
4000
4600
To 2613

At 3.1 miles, watch for a user path to the left that climbs 100 feet up a gentle rocky slope. At the top of this slope is the best view of the hike. Mount Hood is front and center, flanked by Zigzag Mountain on the left and Tom Dick and Harry Mountain on the right. Still Creek (where you started this hike) is out of sight down in the canyon far below you. Much of the clear-cut-free forest you can see from here is in the Salmon-Huckleberry Wilderness or the Mount Hood Wilderness.

Back on the trail, at 3.5 miles reach the junction with Hunchback Trail #793, where you turn right. (The trailhead on FR 2613 is 1.2 miles to your left.) In short order, reach another junction. The Hunchback Trail continues straight, but you will turn left onto the short spur trail to the summit of Devils Peak, the highest point on the long ridge known as Hunchback Mountain.

The rocky summit provides plenty of places to sit and take a break. Because the 8-foot-tall L-4 lookout tower has not been staffed for many decades, the trees have been allowed to grow tall and now obstruct most of the scenery around you. If you climb the stairs and stand in the doorway of the cabin, you will be able to see Mount Hood through a gap in the trees to the northeast. From the ground and from the catwalk, you can also see partial views to the southeast looking out over the Salmon-Huckleberry Wilderness and beyond.

While the Forest Service has officially closed this lookout due to structural issues, the closure is not posted on the structure, so the lookout, left unlocked and open, is frequently used by both day hikers and overnighters. As the structure is no longer maintained, if you decide to go up the stairs and into the cabin, proceed at your own risk. Conditions inside are quite rustic: The cabin still contains a table, a couple of rickety folding chairs, two metal bed frames with mattresses of questionable cleanliness and comfort, and a woodstove; there is no water access or provision of firewood. Be sure to leave the cabin better than you found it and do not leave any food behind that will attract critters.

The first lookout on Devils Peak was a 12-by-12-foot log building with a 6-by-6-foot cupola, built in 1924. In 1933, that building was replaced with the tower that still stands today, along with a garage at the end of FR 2613 (to the southeast, which has long since collapsed), making it the oldest lookout in the Mount Hood National Forest.

When the Salmon-Huckleberry Wilderness was created in 1984, the lookout ended up just outside the wilderness boundary. The entirety of Devils Peak, including the lookout—as well as the Cool Creek Trail you hiked up—became part of the wilderness when the boundary was expanded in 2009. Now covering more than 62,000

OPPOSITE *Striking view of Mount Hood through the door at Devils Peak* acres, the Salmon-Huckleberry Wilderness protects numerous pockets of old-growth trees. The name comes from two prominent peaks: Salmon Butte is a former lookout site, and the Salmon River flows along its northeast base. Huckleberry Mountain is west of there. The Salmon River originates from the Palmer Glacier on Mount Hood and was designated a Wild and Scenic River in 1988.

Return the way you came.

ALTERNATIVE ROUTES

The shortest and easiest hike to Devils Peak starts above Kinzel Lake at the end of FR 2613 (Sherar Burn Road). This easy route is 2.4 miles roundtrip with 600 feet of elevation gain. However, the road is so rough and rocky that it took me an hour to drive just 9 miles. Do not attempt this road in your minivan!

The longest route starts at the Zigzag Ranger Station and follows the Hunchback Trail 9 miles to the lookout, gaining about 3000 feet.

You can also start across the road from Green Canyon Campground on FR 2618 (Salmon River Road), where it is 5.3 miles one way to take the route up Green Canyon Way #793A and the Hunchback Trail, gaining about 3500 feet.

4 FIVEMILE BUTTE

YEAR CONSTRUCTED	LOOKOUT ACCESS	LOCATION
1957	Closed to the public for day use; open for year-round overnight rental by reservation	Mount Hood National Forest, Barlow Ranger District

Roundtrip distance: 7.4 miles
Elevation gain: 1300 feet
Lookout elevation: 4630 feet
Map: USGS Fivemile Butte
GPS coordinates: 45.40622°, –121.45451°
Permits and fees: Northwest Forest Pass; Sno-Park Permit in winter

Hike through the forest on the dry side of the Cascades to reach a lookout atop a broad flat butte. Mountain bikers are more common on this route than hikers, so keep your eyes and ears open for them.

Fivemile Butte Lookout is set in a meadow dotted with ponderosa pines, grand fir, and manzanita.

GETTING TO THE TRAILHEAD

From exit 64 on Interstate 84 in Hood River, drive south on US Highway 30 for 0.3 mile. Continue straight onto Oregon Route 35 at the four-way stop. Drive for 25 miles, then turn left at Forest Road 44, signed for Lookout Mountain, Camp Baldwin, and Dufur. (If you are coming from Government Camp, drive east on US Highway 26 for 3 miles, then take the exit for OR 35. Drive north on OR 35 for 13 miles. Just past Little John Sno-Park, turn right onto FR 44.) Drive east for 5.2 miles, then make a sharp right turn to stay on FR 44. Drive for an additional 4.7 miles to Billy Bob Sno-Park.

If you are coming from Dufur, drive south on Heimrich Street for 0.4 mile. Turn right onto Dufur Valley Road, which becomes FR 44, and drive for 16.7 miles to Billy Bob Sno-Park.

From Billy Bob Sno-Park, turn north onto FR 4430. Drive 0.3 mile and turn right into Eightmile Campground. Follow the one-way counterclockwise loop road into the campground, then turn left into the day-use parking area; there you will find the trailhead, a toilet, and room for about a dozen cars. A Northwest Forest Pass is required here.

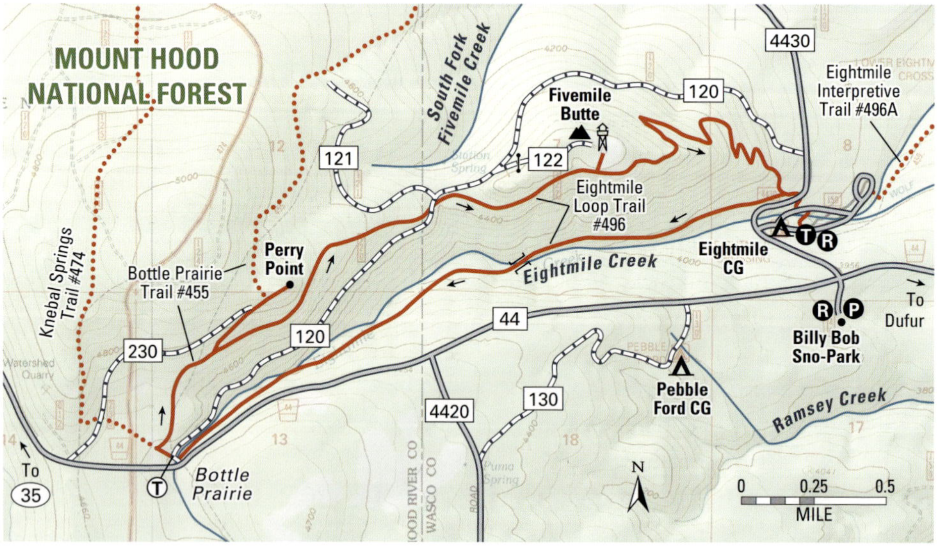

Alternatively, you could park at the Bottle Prairie trailhead (45.3951°, –121.5002°), which requires no pass, but also has no toilet and limited parking. It is 2.4 miles west of Billy Bob Sno-Park, just off FR 44. There is no sign from the road.

Winter access: If you have rented Fivemile Butte during winter, you will not be able to approach Billy Bob Sno-Park via OR 35 from the west because FR 44 is not plowed west of the Sno-Park. Instead, from the town of Dufur, drive south on Heimrich Street for 0.4 mile. Turn right onto Dufur Valley Road, which becomes FR 44 and is usually plowed in winter. Drive for 16.7 miles to Billy Bob Sno-Park, where a Sno-Park Permit is required between November 1 and April 30.

Walk back out to FR 44, cross over it, and follow FR 4430 for 0.8 mile. Turn left onto FR 120 and follow it uphill for 1.4 miles. Turn left onto Forest Road 122 and follow it for 0.5 mile to the lookout. Skis or snowshoes are required to navigate this snow-covered route in winter. The cabin contains a bed, propane cookstove, and a woodstove, and you'll find firewood in the woodshed stocked by the Forest Service.

ON THE TRAIL

The trail starts on the north side of the parking area and heads into a forest of hemlock, Douglas-fir, and grand fir. Immediately cross Eightmile Creek on a footbridge. Cross the other half of the campground loop road. The trail heads west, then north, then crosses over FR 4430. At 0.3 mile, reach a T junction where you meet up with Eightmile Loop Trail #496 and your loop begins. (Your return route is on the right.)

Stay straight at the junction. As you head west through the forest, Eightmile Creek can be heard to the left, but not seen. At the 1.3-mile mark, you finally get to see the creek you have been hearing as you cross it on a footbridge, an extremely pleasant spot if you need a break.

The trail continues upstream along the south bank of the creek through a forest of hemlock, pines, and larches. At the 2.8-mile mark, the trail reaches FR 120 and the Bottle Prairie trailhead (an alternate spot from which to start the hike). Turn right onto the road and pick up the trail again on the north side of the small trailhead parking area, at the spot where FR 120 makes a sharp right turn.

Quickly reach a junction where the Knebal Springs Trail #474 goes straight. You will turn right onto Bottle Prairie Trail #455. Cross a meadow where larkspur bloom in early summer, and continue on, hiking through a forest of grand fir and lodgepole pine. Cross another meadow, this one dotted with clumps of buckwheat.

At the 3.3-mile mark, reach another trail junction, where you can begin a worthwhile 0.6-mile detour. Bear left to stay on the Bottle Prairie Trail. After 0.2 mile, the Bottle Prairie Trail makes a sharp left turn at a sign for Perry Point. You will take the trail on the right that heads out to the point. Cross an open area where larkspur, balsamroot, and groundsel bloom in June. Follow the trail 0.1 mile past the sign to its end at a jumble of rocks. Just beyond the rocks, a huge old Douglas-fir was once home to a crow's nest lookout, a treetop platform used in the 1930s and reachable via a wooden ladder. Very little of it remains, but you can stand here and imagine what it was like to be stationed up there, swaying in the wind and watching for fires. A few weathered boards lie scattered on the ground, and a couple of boards still cling to the tree up high. Also look for the black ceramic phone line insulator embedded in the bark about 10 feet up the trunk.

As you retrace your steps to return to the main hike, you can clearly see Lookout Mountain to the south. Back at the junction with Eightmile Loop Trail, turn left. Continue east through a pleasant shady forest until you reach FR 120, at the 5.4-mile mark.

The trail continues on the other side of the road and now traverses the south side of Fivemile Butte, passing in and out of meadows where balsamroot and lupine bloom in June and ponderosa pines tower overhead. The distant sound of Eightmile Creek far below drifts up the hillside. You can spot landmarks to the south, such as Jordan Butte, Flag Point, and Lookout Mountain.

Reach an unsigned junction in an open rocky area 0.6 mile from FR 120. Turn left for the short side trail to the fire lookout. You will not see anything from the ground here, but if you walk past the tower and follow a path north past the toilet, you will reach a viewpoint where you can see Mount Rainier and Mount Adams to the north. Be sure not to disturb the renters.

The summit of Fivemile Butte is a broad flat area of meadows, ponderosa pines, grand fir, and manzanita, and its history as a lookout site goes back more than a century. In the 1920s, a 30-foot tower was built here. In 1932, it was replaced by a new 30-foot tower with an L-4 cabin, which collapsed in winter snow in 1942. The tower was rebuilt, then replaced in 1957 with the 30-foot R-6 tower that still stands today. It was converted into a rental in the 1990s and is the only year-round lookout rental in Oregon.

Fivemile Butte is named after Fivemile Creek, which starts from a spring on the butte's west side and is so named because the pioneer road from The Dalles into central Oregon crossed it about five miles from town.

Return to the main trail and turn left. This quarter mile of trail is lovely in June as it passes through a series of wildflower-dotted meadows. It then begins switchbacking down the hill, passing through a forest where an abundance of western larches grow; they turn bright orange in late October. Because this forest was thinned in 2003, you can get glimpses through the trees of Mount Rainier and Mount Adams to the north. Cross an old logging spur and then leave the thinned forest, entering a forest that is much denser and shadier. At 1.6 miles from the lookout, reach the T junction from the beginning of your hike. Turn left, cross FR 4430, and follow the trail back to your car.

Starry winter sky at Fivemile Butte

5 FLAG POINT

YEAR CONSTRUCTED	LOOKOUT ACCESS	LOCATION
1963	Accessible by invitation only during fire season; open for overnight rental in winter by reservation	Mount Hood National Forest, Barlow Ranger District

Roundtrip distance: 8.8 miles
Elevation gain: 1740 feet
Lookout elevation: 5650 feet
Map: USGS Flag Point
GPS coordinates: 45.34964°, –121.47227°
Permits and fees: None in summer; Sno-Park Permit in winter

Hike through the Badger Creek Wilderness to reach this lookout in summer, or ski or snowshoe 10 miles one way on snow-covered roads in winter. The Divide Trail has a lot of ups and downs, so be prepared to hike uphill in both directions.

GETTING TO THE TRAILHEAD

From exit 64 on Interstate 84 in Hood River, drive south on US Highway 30 for 0.3 mile. Continue straight onto Oregon Route 35 at the four-way stop. Drive for 25 miles, then turn left onto Forest Road 44, signed for Lookout Mountain, Camp Baldwin, and Dufur. (If you are coming from Government Camp, drive east on US Highway 26 for 3 miles, then take the exit for OR 35. Drive north on OR 35 for 13 miles. Just past Little John Sno-Park, turn right onto FR 44.) Drive east for 5.2 miles, then make a sharp right turn to stay on FR 44. Drive for an additional 3.7 miles to the junction with FR 4420 (Cold Springs Road), signed for Flag Point Lookout and Fifteenmile Campground.

If you are coming from Dufur, drive south on Heimrich Street for 0.4 mile. Turn right onto Dufur Valley Road, which becomes FR 44, and drive for 18.2 miles to the junction with FR 4420 (Cold Springs Road), signed for Flag Point and Fifteenmile Campground.

From FR 44, turn south onto paved FR 4420. Drive 2.1 miles to a junction where FR 4420 makes a sharp right. You will drive straight, following paved FR 2730; from that junction, drive 2.2 miles until you reach the Fret Creek trailhead. Parking is available next to a signboard on the wide left shoulder, with room for five to six cars.

Flag Point Lookout on a clear day

The trail begins on the right side of the road. There is no toilet here, but there is one at Fifteenmile Campground, which you passed on the left 0.2 mile before the trailhead.

Winter access: If you rent this lookout during the winter, you will have to snowshoe, ski, or ride a snowmobile over 10 miles of snowy, unplowed roads. Traveling over snow is much slower than on bare ground, so know your abilities and allow yourself plenty of time. Follow the winter driving directions to Billy Bob Sno-Park provided in Hike 4; a Sno-Park Permit is required in winter. From the Sno-Park, ski or snowshoe west on FR 44. After 1.5 miles, turn left onto FR 4420. Follow this road for 2.1 miles to the junction with FR 2730. Travel 3.3 miles on FR 2730, then turn right onto Flag Point Lookout Road (FR 200). Follow this road 3.2 miles to its end at the lookout. The cabin contains a bed, propane cookstove, and woodstove. Firewood is provided.

ON THE TRAIL

Cross the road and head south on Fret Creek Trail #456A, immediately entering the Badger Creek Wilderness. Climb steadily through a forest of grand fir and hemlock. The understory contains many huckleberry bushes, which makes for delicious snacking in late summer. Fret Creek tumbles down the mountain to your left.

At 0.4 mile, cross Fret Creek on a wooden footbridge, where you will continue south along the east bank of the creek. This section is a pleasant, level forest ramble with the sound of the gurgling creek to your right.

At 0.8 mile, cross back over Fret Creek on another wooden footbridge. At 1 mile, cross a little unnamed creeklet with no bridge. At 1.2 miles, cross back over the creeklet on a wooden footbridge.

Notice how some of the old trees have blazes on them: a longer rectangle topped by a smaller one, like the letter *i*. Carving this shape into the bark of trees was once a common practice to mark the route of a trail. While marking trails with blazes is no longer done, in areas like this that have not burned since the blazes were made, they can still be seen.

At 1.6 miles, cross Fret Creek yet again, but this time without the benefit of a bridge. A jumble of logs here may aid in your crossing. You'll now start climbing away from the creek, first gradually, then steeply, as if the trail builders had never heard of switchbacks. Pass Oval Lake on your left, which is really more of a pond. The ground here isn't flat, but hikers have eked out a few campsites anyway—mosquitoes lie in wait for backpacker blood in July.

Continue past the lake. At the 2.2-mile mark, reach the junction with Divide Trail #458. Should you turn right, in 1.6 miles you would reach Lookout Mountain, a former fire lookout site. However, today you will turn left.

From the junction, you'll head east through the forest, climbing up the north side of the ridge. The trail makes several switchbacks, climbs to the top of the ridge, then at the 2.5-mile mark arrives at an area of rocky pinnacles where stonecrop grows in any crack or crevice it can find. Have fun scrambling around in and exploring this area, but use caution, especially if you have pets or kids, as there are steep drop-offs. From here, you get sweeping views to the south, including the Three Sisters and Mount Jefferson, and you'll be able to see the lookout on Flag Point sticking up above the trees to the east. To the west is Lookout Mountain.

Continuing east through the rock pinnacle area, the trail then descends into a forest of subalpine fir, hemlock, and western larch. Larches turn a vivid shade of orange during the second half of October, when on a beautiful fall day, they practically glow. A member of the pine family, this is the only native larch in Oregon, and while it is common on the east side of the state, it is harder to find in the Cascades. The

Badger Creek Wilderness is a reliable place to see their brilliant display in autumn. As the season transitions into winter, the golden needles drop to the ground and the trees are bare until spring, when their pale-green, new growth makes them stand out from their neighbors' darker needles. Mature larches can withstand fires of moderate intensity and can live to be more than five hundred years old.

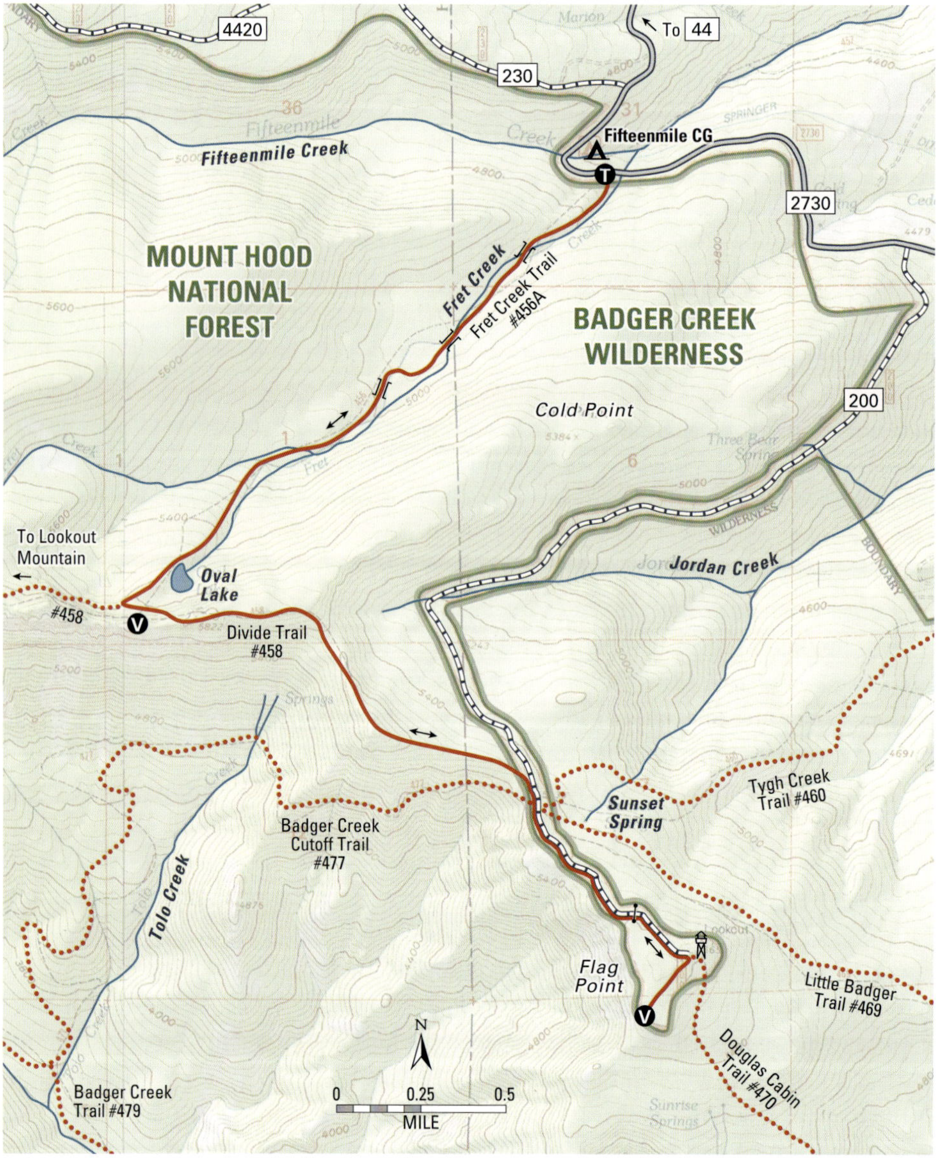

Western larches turn yellow in October along the Divide Trail.

Now make a short ascent before leveling off. Pass another rocky viewpoint on the right, then descend again. After a level stretch, the trail again descends, heading down a rocky open slope where balsamroot and larkspur bloom in late June.

The trail levels out, crosses a meadow, then reenters the trees and climbs again. It tops out on a viewless rise, descends again, and levels out. Pass two empty signposts as you cross the wilderness boundary, emerge from the trees, and cross a meadow. At the 3.6-mile mark, the Divide Trail ends at FR 200, the narrow, rough, rocky dirt road that is used to service the lookout.

Other trails fan out from this spot: Badger Creek Cutoff Trail #477 heads downhill to the west to Badger Creek, 2000 feet below. On the other side of the road, Little Badger Trail #469 heads southeast toward Felt Tip and Ball Point. Tygh Creek Trail #460 heads east toward Jordan Butte. However, you will turn right onto FR 200 and follow the road through the forest, once again ascending. Arrive at a locked gate, hike around it, and continue up the road. After 0.8 mile on the road, reach the lookout.

Flag Point first became a lookout site in 1924 with the construction of a 40-foot tower. It was replaced by a 30-foot tower in 1932, which itself was replaced in 1963 by a 41-foot tower with a 14-by-14-foot R-6 cabin, the tower that still stands today and is staffed during fire season. It was a winter rental until 2016 when the Forest Service removed it from the rental program due to damage caused by renters and vandals. The Forest Service added it back to the rental program in 2023.

The tower is surrounded by a forest of larches, ponderosa pines, and hemlock. From the rock pile on the tower's south side, you can spot the Three Sisters to the south and Mount Jefferson. If you turn around, you can also see Mount Adams and

On a clear day, Flag Point offers a picture-perfect view of Mount Hood.

Mount Rainier. To the west lie the vast forests of the Cascades, and to the east the flat brown farmland and grassland of central Oregon.

If you want even better views, or if the lookout is inaccessible during your visit, find the start of an unsigned trail to the south of the toilet and follow it southwest for 0.2 mile to a rocky sagebrush-covered viewpoint where you can see Broken Top, the Three Sisters, Mount Jefferson, Olallie Butte, and Mount Hood. You can also see the rock pinnacles from earlier in the hike, as well as Lookout Mountain. There is plenty of room here to sit down, take a break, and soak in the scenery.

Flag Point is surrounded by the twenty-nine-thousand-acre Badger Creek Wilderness, which was designated in 1984. When the wilderness boundaries were established, the roads to Flag Point and Badger Lake were excluded, maintaining vehicle access to both sites, although both roads are presently in rough shape. The Douglas Cabin Trail #470 heads south from Flag Point, toward Gordon Butte. This little-used and seldom-maintained trail is marked by a broken, weathered sign.

Return the way you came.

6 PECHUCK

YEAR CONSTRUCTED	LOOKOUT ACCESS	LOCATION
1932	Open to the public for day use; overnight use is first-come, first-served	Bureau of Land Management, Northwest Oregon District

Roundtrip distance: 5.6 miles
Elevation gain: 1670 feet
Lookout elevation: 4340 feet
Map: USGS Rooster Rock
GPS coordinates: 44.94154°, –122.32398°
Permits and fees: None

Hike through the Table Rock Wilderness to Oregon's last remaining lookout built of stone, Pechuck, a Chinook word for "green." (The origin of the name is not documented.) Stay the night if you like; the lookout is open for overnight visits on a first-come, first-served basis.

GETTING TO THE TRAILHEAD

From downtown Molalla at the intersection of N. Molalla Avenue and Oregon Route 211 (W. Main Street), drive east on OR 211 for 0.6 mile, then turn right onto Mathias Road. After 0.2 mile, turn left onto S. Feyrer Park Road. After 1.6 miles, reach a

Sign on the way to Pechuck Lookout

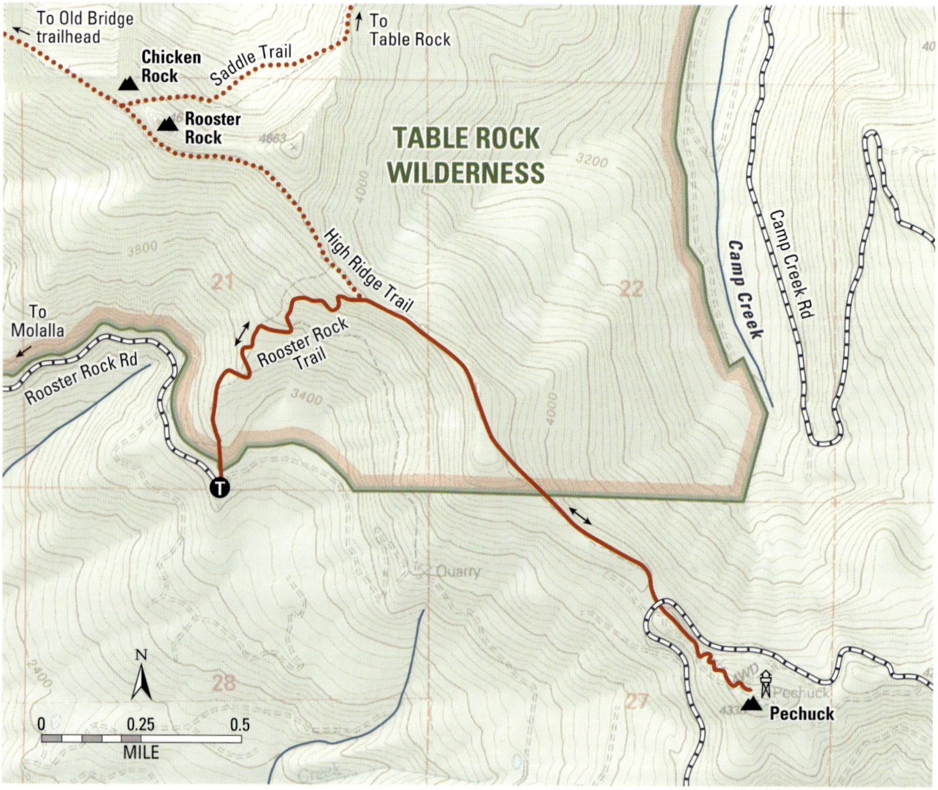

T intersection and turn right onto S. Dickey Prairie Road. Stay on Dickey Prairie for 3.6 miles, then turn right onto S. Molalla Forest Road and cross the Molalla River; continue for 0.2 mile, then turn left to stay on S. Molalla Forest Road.

Continue for 12.8 paved miles, then turn right onto gravel Copper Creek Road. Continue for 0.5 mile and take the left fork uphill onto Rooster Rock Road. Continue for 2.8 gravel miles and keep left at the junction to stay on Rooster Rock Road, then drive the final 3.5 miles to the Rooster Rock trailhead at the road's end.

ON THE TRAIL

Head to the far end of the parking area and look for the Rooster Rock Trail heading uphill to the north. (Do not follow the now-closed continuation of the road.) Climb steeply through a shady forest with an understory of rhododendron that blooms pink in June and vine maple that turns yellow in October.

After 1.1 miles and 900 feet of elevation gain, you will reach the ridge crest at an unsigned junction with the High Ridge Trail. Take a look around at this easy-to-miss junction so you do not pass it on the way back. Rooster Rock is to the left (see Extend Your Hike at the end of this entry). Turn right and follow the trail southeast along the ridge as it travels up and down. Beargrass and other summer wildflowers bloom here.

At the 1.9-mile mark, enter an area of forest burned in the lightning-caused Beachie Creek Fire, which destroyed more than 190,000 acres in 2020. Here at the edge of the burn, many trees survived. The trail leaves the wilderness and descends to a road crossing marked by a blank crumbling signboard. (Unfortunately, you cannot start the hike here as a shorter alternative, as the road is gated.)

The trail continues on the other side of the road. The last 0.4 mile from the road crossing climbs steeply up to the summit. As you pass above a scree slope, look back for a view of prominent Table Rock behind you. From this angle it doesn't so much resemble a table as a pyramid. Continue climbing through the forest. If you are planning to stay the night, note the composting toilet on your right about a tenth of a mile before the lookout.

Pechuck Lookout is the only stone lookout in Oregon.

View of Table Mountain from Pechuck Lookout

Despite trees burning west, south, and east of the summit in 2020, amazingly the lookout escaped the fire unharmed. Live trees and burned snags alike block much of the scenery, but to the north you can see Table Rock. Through gaps in the trees, you can also see some of the other surrounding peaks.

The 12-by-12-foot lookout is a D-6 cupola design built of native stone and wood, left unlocked and available for visitors. The accommodations are very rustic, consisting primarily of two wooden platforms that can be used as either tables or beds. A ladder provides access to the 7.5-by-7.5-foot cupola, where the views are a little bit better than below. If you visit in winter and take the shutters off, be sure to put them back on before leaving.

The first lookout here consisted of a range finder on a stand accompanied by a small wood-plank cabin that served as living quarters and was first staffed around 1918 or 1919. The current structure was built in 1932 by John Oblack from Molalla. Construction materials, including rocks from a local source, were packed in by mule. By the time this lookout was built, however, the L-4 style was in favor, so Pechuck may be one of the last D-6 cupolas to be constructed in the state.

Pechuck was last staffed in 1964, and in the following decades it started deteriorating. The chimney collapsed, windows were broken out, and mortar between the stones began crumbling. Many other abandoned lookouts around Oregon were being removed during this time, but Pechuck may have escaped that fate due to the effort involved in dismantling a building made of stone instead of wood. In the early 1990s, a group of volunteers worked to restore the lookout, including replacing windows and the roof and adding a deck in front of the door.

The lookout sits just outside the boundary of the Table Rock Wilderness; designated by Congress in 1984, its 5,700 acres contain approximately 17 miles of hiking trails, including a popular trail that leads to the summit of the wilderness's 4881-foot namesake, Table Rock.

Return the way you came.

EXTEND YOUR HIKE

Views from the lookout are limited by trees, so if you do not want to head back without getting some better vistas, you can add on the detour to Rooster Rock. Retrace your steps back to the junction with the Rooster Rock Trail, then continue straight 1 mile on the High Ridge Trail to another trail junction. (Here, the High Ridge Trail continues straight; Table Rock is 1.9 miles to the right.)

Rooster Rock itself is a technical climb, but a spur trail heads up to a rocky viewpoint northwest of Rooster Rock that is often referred to as Chicken Rock. Turn right onto the Saddle Trail, walk 300 feet, then watch for an obvious path on the left heading across a meadow and up Chicken Rock. From there you can see many peaks on a clear day, including the Three Sisters, Mount Jefferson, and Mount Hood.

7 GOLD BUTTE

YEAR CONSTRUCTED	LOOKOUT ACCESS	LOCATION
1934	Closed to the public for day use; open for seasonal overnight rental by reservation	Willamette National Forest, Detroit Ranger District

Roundtrip distance: 3 miles
Elevation gain: 790 feet
Lookout elevation: 4620 feet
Map: USGS Mother Lode
GPS coordinates: 44.81881°, –122.08688°
Permits and fees: None

Gold Butte Lookout all lit up at night

This historic lookout was once in a state of disrepair, but it has been lovingly restored by volunteers, who continue to maintain it. The cabin is a hike-in rental in the summer.

GETTING TO THE TRAILHEAD

From Oregon Route 22 in the town of Detroit, turn east onto Forest Road 46. Drive for 4.4 miles, then turn left onto FR 4696. Continue for 0.7 mile, then turn left onto FR 4697. Drive this potholed road for 4.5 miles, and then turn right onto FR 451. High clearance and reliable tires are strongly recommended because the final mile is very rough and rocky. After a few hundred feet, you'll reach the junction where the gated FR 453 heads uphill to the right. There is room for two to three cars to park on the shoulder, but do not block the gate, as renters are given access. If you are renting, you will have received a code to open it.

ON THE TRAIL

From the gate, start hiking up FR 453. The road passes through a pretty forest full of Douglas-fir, hemlock, huckleberries, bracken fern, beargrass, rhododendron, and vine maple, golden in the fall. After half a mile, reach the second locked gate. (Renters must park here and carry their gear the rest of the way, including all the water they will need for their stay, as there is no water source at the cabin.)

Hike around the second gate and continue for another 0.5 mile until you reach the end of the road. Gold Butte Trail #3350 begins on your right, heading up the mountain. Climb steadily among a sea of rhododendrons. (The first time I rented this lookout, I was inexperienced; I tried to transport my gear up this trail by wheelbarrow, but I only made it part of the way up before leaving it alongside the trail to retrieve on my way out because it was too heavy and difficult to steer. As you huff and puff up this trail, be thankful you are not pushing a wheelbarrow!)

The trail makes a switchback, and then another. Just after the second switchback, you get a good view of Mount Jefferson through the trees. An even better viewpoint is just ahead on the left, which is also an excellent spot to return to for a break if renters ask for privacy on the summit. Purple bunches of penstemon bloom periodically along the trail.

After one final switchback, the trail makes a right turn, then reaches the summit where the woodshed and lookout sit. Vegetation up here is dominated by vine maple, thimbleberry, and boxwood. A toilet is located just down the hill on the west slope. It may be one of the nicest and cleanest backcountry toilets you will ever encounter!

The Civilian Conservation Corps built the Gold Butte lookout in 1934, but after it stopped being staffed in the 1970s, it fell into serious disrepair. By the time volunteers from the Sand Mountain Society began restoring the cabin in 1999, the building was in bad shape and full of carpenter ants. Although it would have been quicker to rebuild using new lumber, volunteers salvaged and reused every original board that could be saved—such as the original tongue-and-groove flooring, siding, wallboards, and ceiling boards—eventually restoring the interior to look exactly how it would have looked in the 1930s, with a woodstove, cabinet, single bed, and firefinder. Volunteers also constructed a new outhouse. The restored lookout was dedicated in 2006, and volunteers from the Sand Mountain Society continue to maintain the cabin.

The lookout has been repeatedly threatened by wildfires, including the 2017 Scorpion Fire, the 2020 Lionshead Fire, and the 2021 Bull Complex Fire. Each time,

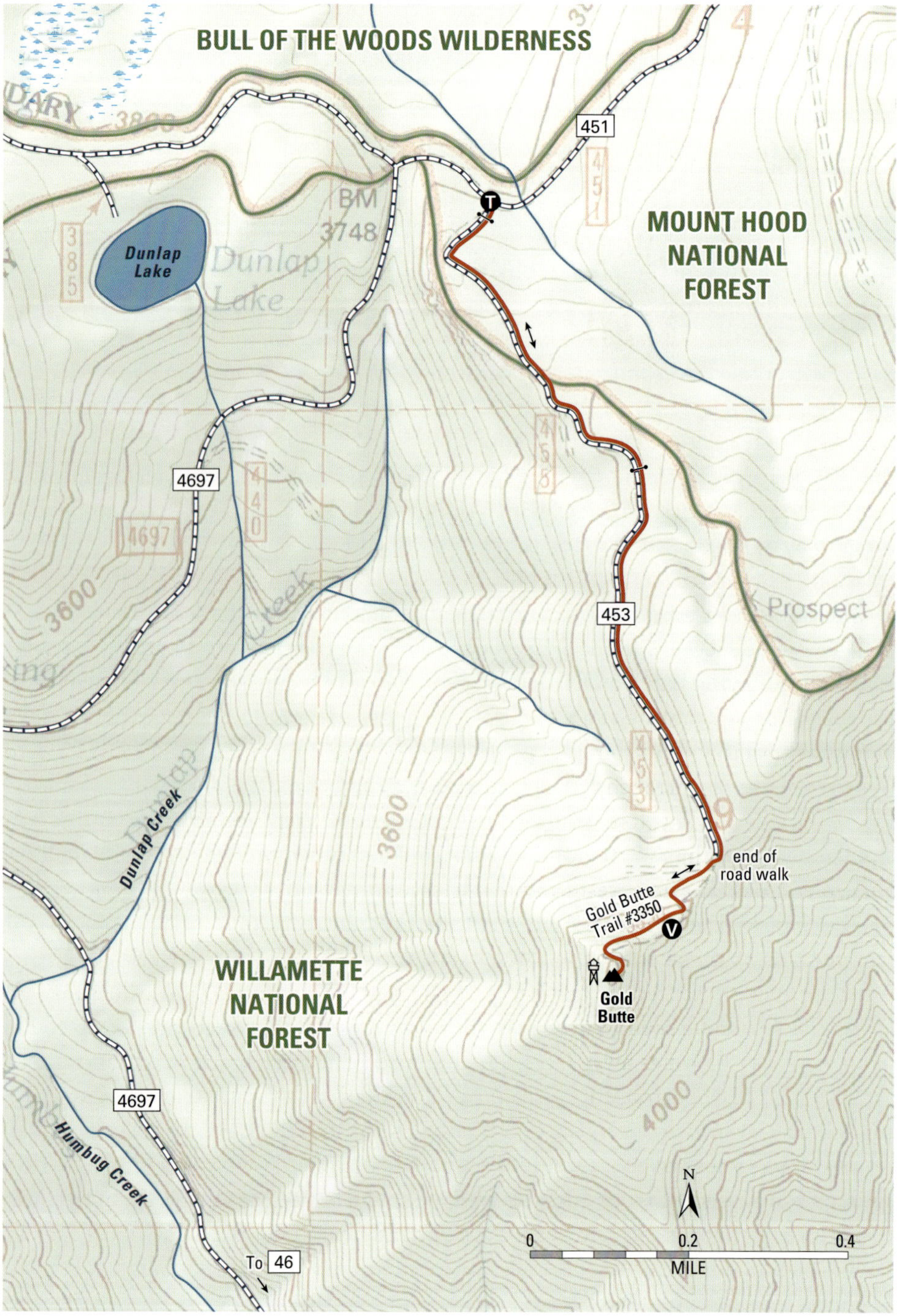
BULL OF THE WOODS WILDERNESS
MOUNT HOOD NATIONAL FOREST
WILLAMETTE NATIONAL FOREST
Dunlap Lake
Dunlap Creek
Humbug Creek
451
453
4697
To 46
BM 3748
3600
4000
end of road walk
Gold Butte Trail #3350
Gold Butte
Prospect
N
0
0.2
0.4
MILE

LEFT *View of Mount Jefferson from Gold Butte at sunset* **RIGHT** *Wild rhododendron on the hike up Gold Butte*

it was wrapped in protective material and managed to survive. The Lionshead Fire, along with the Beachie Creek and P-515 Fires, was started by lightning in mid-August 2020. Labor Day Weekend was hot and dry that year and ended with powerful east winds that caused the three fires to blow up and merge, roaring west down the Santiam Canyon. More than four hundred thousand acres burned and 1,500 structures were destroyed, along with much of the towns of Detroit and Gates. Other fires around the state also exploded due to the strong east wind, like the human-caused Riverside Fire just to the north that started on Labor Day. Ultimately more than 1.2 million acres burned in the 2020 fires, resulting in the second-most-destructive Oregon wildfire season on record as of this writing.

Evidence of those fires is visible all around you in the form of burned forest. But if you raise your eyes to the horizon, the mountains along it are still stunning. Mount Hood can be seen to the northwest, but of course the best view is of Mount Jefferson, just 17 miles away. To the right of Mount Jefferson are Three Fingered Jack, Mount Washington, the Three Sisters, and Coffin Mountain's distinctive boxy shape (Hike 9).

You can also see the flat summit of Battle Ax (a former lookout site) to the northwest, and the conical shape of Bull of the Woods can be seen to the north. Its historic 1942 lookout managed to survive the 2020 fires, only to burn the following year in the Bull Complex Fire.

Return the way you came.

8 HAWK MOUNTAIN

YEAR CONSTRUCTED	LOOKOUT ACCESS	LOCATION
1936 (cabin)	Lookout removed; cabin open to the public for day use	Mount Hood National Forest, Clackamas River Ranger District

Roundtrip distance: 4 miles
Elevation gain: 760 feet
Lookout elevation: 5280 feet
Map: USGS Breitenbush Hot Springs
GPS coordinates: 44.84064°, –121.94725°
Permits and fees: None

Visit a historic cabin that sits in a lovely meadow with a spectacular view and is open to visitors. Peek inside and try to imagine living here for a whole summer.

GETTING TO THE TRAILHEAD

From Oregon Route 22 in the town of Detroit, turn east onto Forest Road 46. Drive 17.6 miles, then turn left onto gravel FR 6350.

If you are coming from Estacada, drive south on Oregon Route 224 for 25.5 miles to Ripplebrook and the junction with FR 57. Keep right, as OR 224 becomes FR 46. Continue on FR 46 for another 27 miles, then turn right onto FR 6350.

Drive 4.8 miles on FR 6350 to a four-way intersection, where you turn left onto FR 6355. Continue 0.2 mile to the intersection with FR 150, on the left. The trail is on the right, marked by a small sign. There is parking along the shoulder of both roads here, with room for about six vehicles.

ON THE TRAIL

Rhododendron Ridge Trail #564 starts out in an area burned by the 2020 Lionshead Fire. Life has returned here and vegetation regrowth is well underway: Beargrass has grown back in abundance, and if your timing is right (as it doesn't bloom every year), you will see hundreds of their bulb-shaped white plumes. Huckleberry bushes are also growing back, slowing your pace in late summer when the berries invite numerous snack breaks. Fireweed, lupine, paintbrush, and bleeding heart bloom in these meadows in July, along with an abundance of vivid purple penstemon. Penstemon,

The 1919 cabin on Hawk Mountain has a view of Mount Jefferson.

also known as beardtongue, has nectar-rich flowers that attract pollinators like bees and hummingbirds.

The trail makes a few switchbacks up a slope, where you can spot Olallie Butte and Mount Jefferson to your right now that the trees are gone. Enter a section of forest that has burned twice, first in 2020 and again in the 2021 Bull Complex Fire. Both fires were started by lightning. Unlike the mostly straight snags you hiked past earlier, many of these twice-burned trees are bent and twisted.

The trail begins a gradual descent. Pass through a small cluster of subalpine fir that somehow managed to survive the fires. At 1.1 miles, enter unburned forest with tall shady hemlocks and noble firs. Soon you will hear the sounds of an unnamed creek on your right, then you will cross it.

At 1.7 miles, reach the junction with Hawk Mountain Lookout Trail #564A and turn right. (If you were to continue straight for another 7-plus miles, you would reach Mount Lowe.) The trail climbs up the hill for 0.3 mile, leaving behind the forest and reentering the burn, where arnica and valerian bloom in July.

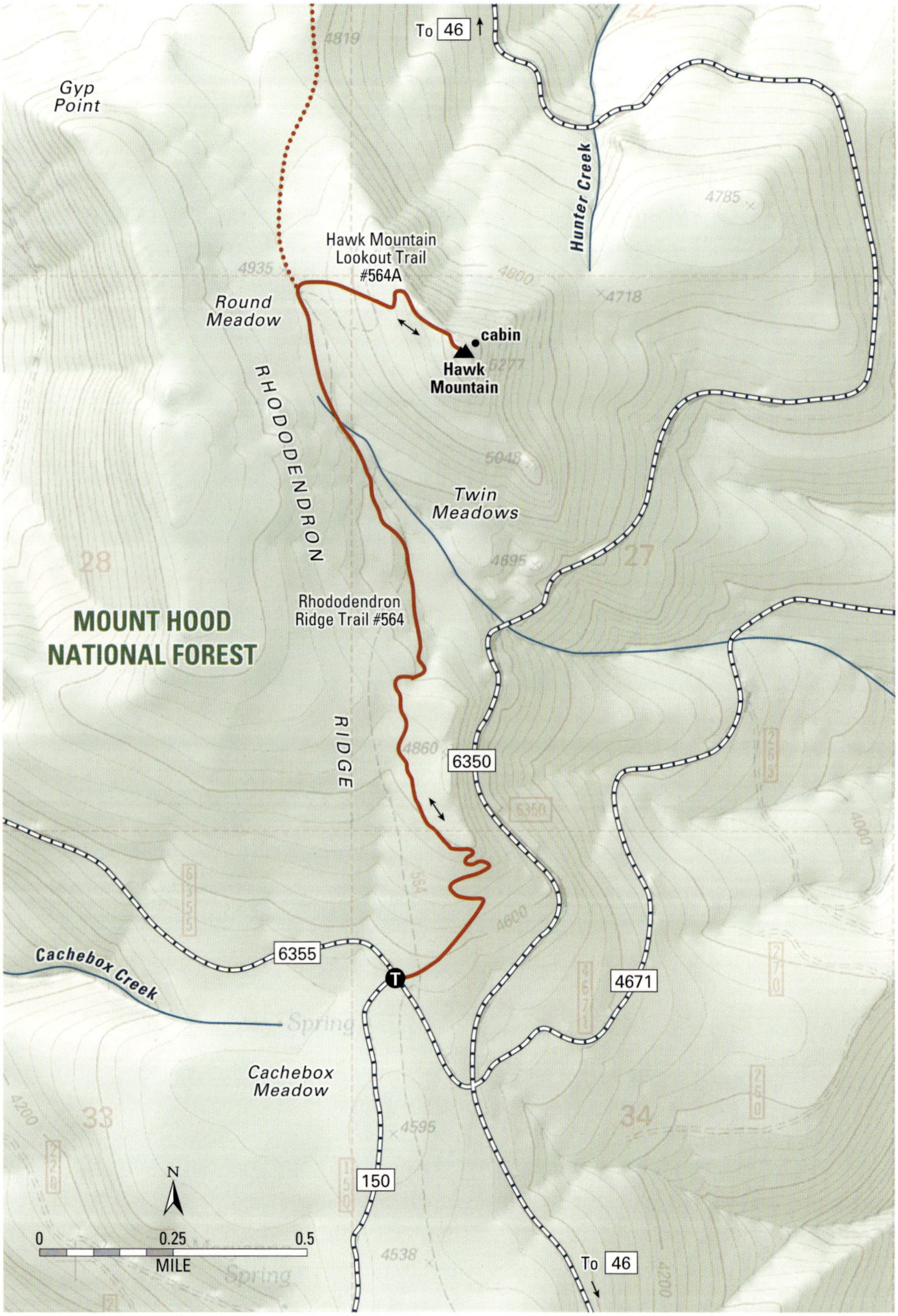
To 46
Gyp Point
4819
Hunter Creek
4785
Hawk Mountain Lookout Trail #564A
4935
4800
4718
Round Meadow
cabin
Hawk Mountain
5277
RHODODENDRON
5048
Twin Meadows
4695
28
27
MOUNT HOOD NATIONAL FOREST
Rhododendron Ridge Trail #564
RIDGE
4860
6350
6350
265
4000
6355
564
4600
6355
Cachebox Creek
4671
4671
270
Spring
Cachebox Meadow
260
4200
33
4595
34
N
150
150
0
0.25
0.5
MILE
4538
Spring
To 46
4200

At 2 miles from the trailhead, you will arrive at the summit. Pass the old lookout footings on your left, then arrive at the cabin. Behind it, a user trail heads out into the meadow with a smashing view of Mount Jefferson. If you come in July, you will notice that the rock gardens at the far end of the meadow bloom with delightful paintbrush, mariposa lily, buckwheat, and Oregon sunshine.

A unique and unusual-looking three-legged, 60-foot tower was built on Hawk Mountain in 1919. Because the tower did not have a cabin on top, only a viewing platform, a log cabin was built on the ground as living quarters. Sometime around 1936, a frame cabin was built, although historical photos show that the old log cabin was left standing for at least another twenty years. The tower was removed in 1967, but the frame cabin was not, and it remains standing to this day.

Hawk Mountain was one of three lookouts on Rhododendron Ridge. Starting in 1915, and 7 miles to the north, Mount Lowe hosted a log cabin lookout with a roof platform. It was replaced by an L-4 ground cabin in 1932 and subsequently removed in the 1960s. Another 3 miles farther north is a peak called Burnt Granite, which had a lookout cabin starting in 1929. The Rhododendron Ridge Trail connected all three to each other and to other trails in this remote corner of the forest before the extensive road system we know today was built.

The Hawk Mountain cabin underwent restoration in 2002. After clearing numerous downed trees across the trail, tools and equipment such as ladders and long boards had to be carried by hand the entire 2 miles from the trailhead. The volunteers weatherproofed the cabin, replaced the roof and missing window panes, repaired shutters, and applied fresh paint inside and out. Efforts were made to match the original paint

Penstemon blooming along the trail up Hawk Mountain

color as closely as possible. The porch was in such disrepair that it had to be entirely removed and rebuilt, using materials that matched what had been used originally.

Many of the trees around the summit burned in the 2020 and 2021 fires, but some survived. The Hawk Mountain cabin was wrapped in fire-resistant material to protect it, and it, too, survived the flames. You can go inside and have a look around. Imagine spending your days on an open-air platform 60 feet above the ground and your nights in this tiny cabin. While it is possible to spend the night in the cabin, it is not recommended, as it is now home to many mice and other critters.

Return the way you came.

9 COFFIN MOUNTAIN

YEAR CONSTRUCTED	LOOKOUT ACCESS	LOCATION
1984	Staffed; accessible to the public when invited in by staff; locked when not staffed	Willamette National Forest, Detroit Ranger District

Roundtrip distance: 3 miles
Elevation gain: 1000 feet
Lookout elevation: 5770 feet
Map: USGS Coffin Mountain
GPS coordinates: 44.60834°, –122.04985°
Permits and fees: None

Hike to a lookout perched on top of a long ridge that resembles a coffin from afar. Come in late June or early July and you will get the bonus of experiencing one of the best wildflower hikes in Oregon.

GETTING TO THE TRAILHEAD

From Detroit, drive east on Oregon Route 22 for 19.1 miles, then turn right onto paved Straight Creek Road (Forest Road 11). After 1.4 miles, make a sharp left to stay on FR 11. After 4 total miles, come to a fork and go uphill to the right onto FR 1168, a good gravel road. Drive for 3.8 miles—following the main gravel road and ignoring

OPPOSITE *Coffin Mountain Lookout*

"CLOSED"

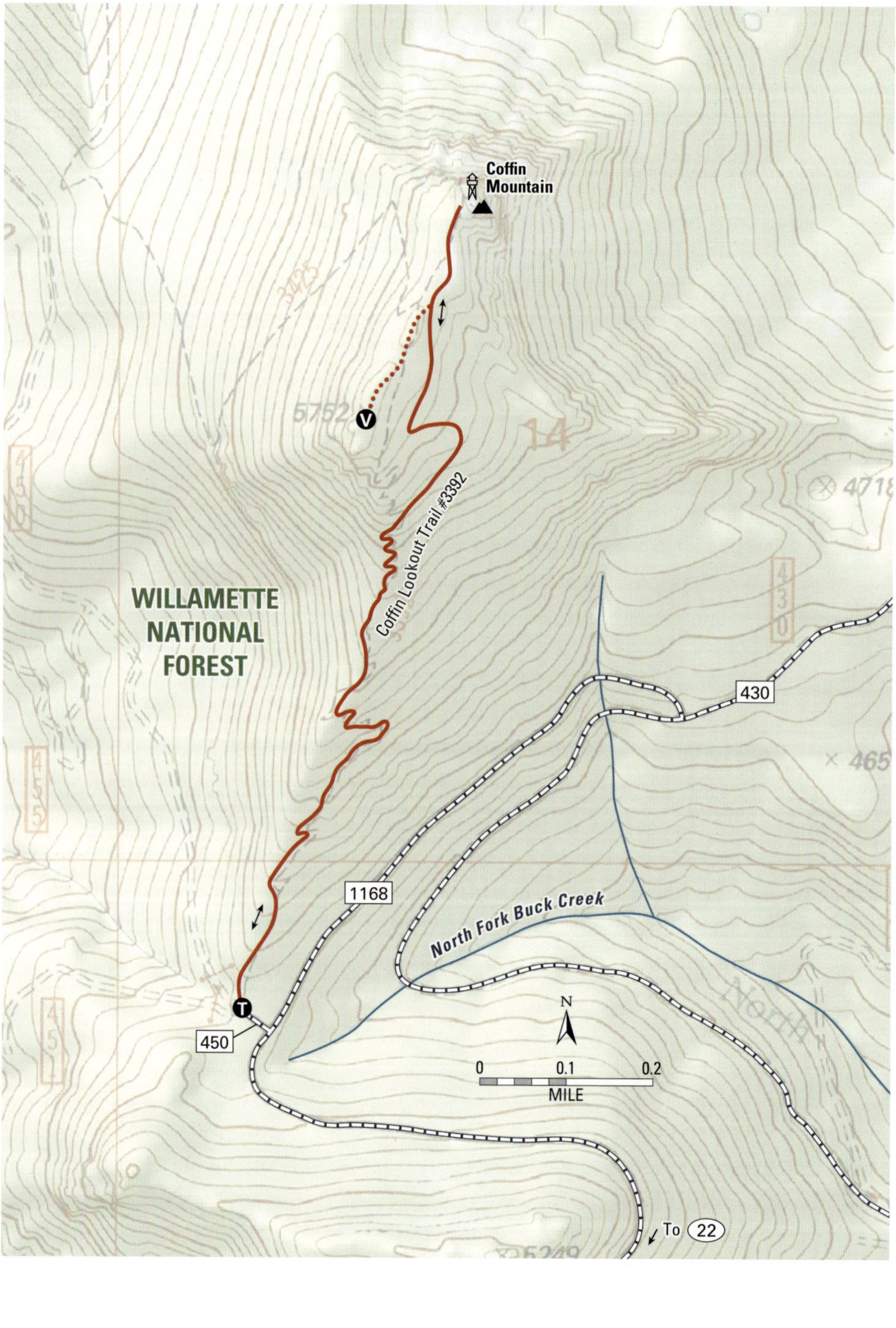
Coffin Mountain
5752
14
Coffin Lookout Trail #3392
WILLAMETTE NATIONAL FOREST
430
1168
North Fork Buck Creek
450
N
0
0.1
0.2
MILE
To 22

View of Bachelor Mountain and Mount Jefferson from Coffin Mountain

logging spurs—then turn left onto Forest Road 450 and park in the trailhead parking area on the right. There is room for about five cars, but there are no toilets or facilities.

ON THE TRAIL

The trail heads northeast from the parking area. You have 1000 feet to gain in just 1.5 miles, so the trail wastes no time in launching uphill, starting out on an old road bed in a forest of hemlock and Douglas-fir. In late June and early July, this first stretch is lined with paintbrush, phlox, and mariposa lilies.

Enter an open area with fewer trees, and after 0.2 mile of steep climbing, you will take the trail angling off to the left where the old roadbed goes straight. Now the south end of Coffin Mountain appears above you. Pass through a glorious rock garden of bluehead gilia, larkspur, and Oregon sunshine. You'll soon get a view of Three Fingered Jack on your right. Much more of that to come!

The trail reenters the forest where beargrass and huckleberries grow, then it emerges from the trees, makes a switchback, and climbs a slope covered with bracken ferns and thimbleberry. Make five more switchbacks and then emerge into another rock garden chock-full of early summer wildflowers. Bachelor Mountain and Mount Jefferson come into view ahead.

Beyond the rock garden, the trail enters the huge south-facing meadow on the upper slopes of the mountain. Beargrass blooms here in profusion every few years or so. This unusual-looking flower resembles a light bulb atop a two-to-five-foot-high stalk. The white "bulbs" are actually a collection of hundreds of tiny tightly packed flowers. These flowers do not bloom every summer, but it is a sight to behold during a good year when the meadow is a sea of white. The common name originates from the Lewis and Clark Expedition, although it is a member of the lily family and not a grass at all. Bears do not eat this plant, but Native Americans use the leaves to make baskets. Elk, deer, mountain goats, and bighorn sheep eat the leaves.

The trail makes several switchbacks on the west side of the meadow before beginning an uphill traverse heading northeast. The trail briefly swings west, then after a switchback heads north.

At the far end of the meadow, at the 1.2-mile mark, the trail heads briefly back into the trees. It then traverses a small meadow, with the lookout ahead. Pass an unofficial user trail on the left, which heads out to the repeater station on the other end of the summit. While you will stay right to head to the lookout, the user trail is a pleasant detour if you are seeking some solitude on a busy summer weekend. There are plenty of spots out that way to stop and take a break, and the viewpoint here is just as good.

The trail follows a ridgeline, then makes one final push to the summit, reaching the lookout at 1.5 miles. The lookout is staffed during the season, so do not go on the deck or enter the cabin without staff permission. There is room to spread out up here and take in the sights. On a clear day you can see Mount Adams and Mount Hood to the north. Due west is Mount Jefferson, partially hiding behind Bachelor Mountain, which once hosted its own fire lookout from 1934 to 1967. To the south you can see Three Fingered Jack, Mount Washington, the Three Sisters, and Diamond Peak. Subalpine fir and mountain hemlock grow on the summit, wider than they are tall due to the short growing season and harsh conditions. Although you wouldn't know looking at it now, an 1893 wildfire burned 5,000 acres on and around Coffin Mountain. In 1967, the Buck Mountain Fire burned 1,400 acres.

Coffin Mountain gets its name from its coffin-shaped appearance from a distance. A succession of lookouts have sat atop this mountain, including a 1906 platform tower and a 1921 D-6 cupola cabin. In 1936, the Civilian Conservation Corps constructed an L-4 ground cabin back when no roads had yet been built to the base of this mountain. Although it was renovated sometime in the late 1970s, it was deemed too weather-beaten to save. In 1984, supplies for a new lookout were transported by helicopter and a new R-6 ground cabin was built, which is the lookout that still stands today.

Return the way you came.

10 IRON MOUNTAIN

YEAR CONSTRUCTED	LOOKOUT ACCESS	LOCATION
1976	Lookout removed and replaced with viewing platform	Willamette National Forest, Sweet Home Ranger District

Roundtrip distance: 6.5 miles
Elevation gain: 1800 feet
Lookout elevation: 5450 feet
Map: USGS Harter Mountain
GPS coordinates: 44.39565°, –122.14121°
Permits and fees: Northwest Forest Pass

Visit the site of the former Iron Mountain lookout for expansive views that stretch from the Coast Range to the Cascades, as well as an amazing wildflower show during summer. If you are just looking for a quick trip to the summit and back, a shorter hike is available from an alternate trailhead.

Iron Mountain's observation platform

GETTING TO THE TRAILHEAD

From Sweet Home, drive 36 miles east on US Highway 20 (or from Santiam Junction drive 11 miles west), until you reach a sign for Tombstone Pass. Park in the paved lot on the south side of the highway. This large lot has room for about twenty cars, but it still fills up on busy summer weekends. A toilet is available.

ON THE TRAIL

Begin by heading east toward the back of the parking area down gravel Forest Road 060 (Santiam Wagon Road Trail #3413). Turn left onto Tombstone Prairie Trail #3420, which descends from the road and into the forest. After 0.4 mile on this trail, reach a junction where the Tombstone Nature Trail #3419 heads off to the right. For a diversion, hike this short loop around the backside of Tombstone Prairie, once known as Indian Prairie. It served as a gathering place for local tribes and later for travelers on the Santiam Wagon Road. The name originates from a grave that was once located here, that of eighteen-year-old James McKnight, who died in 1871 of an

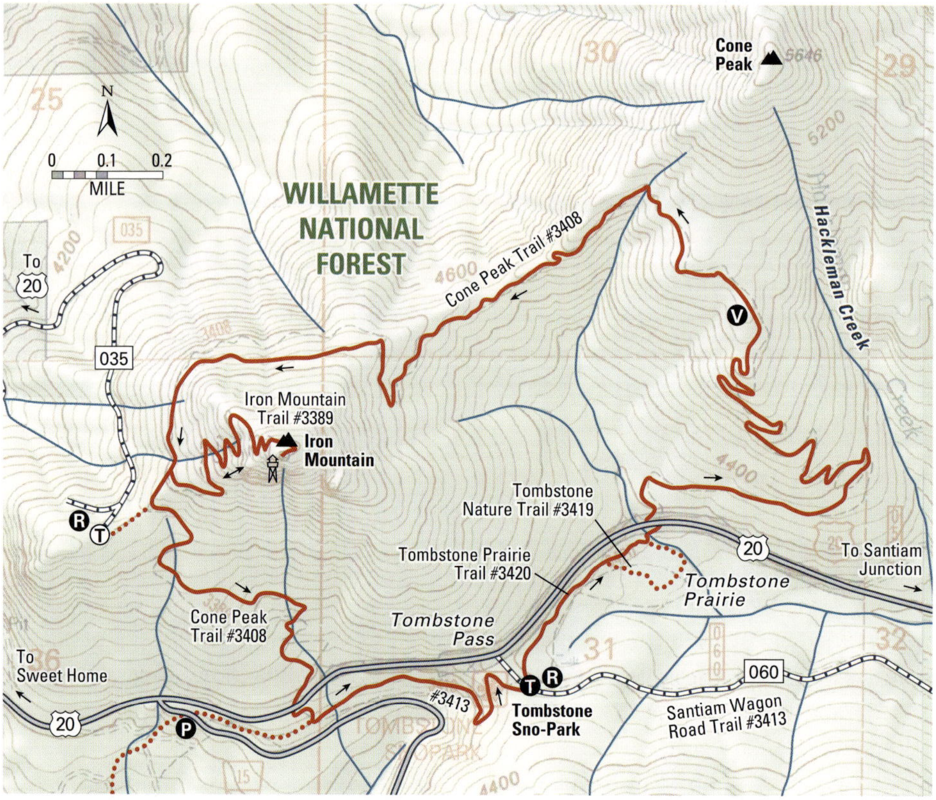

LEFT *View of Iron Mountain from the wildflower-covered slopes of Cone Peak* **RIGHT** *The mountain locator on Iron Mountain helps visitors identify nearby peaks.*

accidental gunshot wound while traveling the Santiam Wagon Road with his family. His remains were later relocated to Sand Ridge Cemetery in Lebanon. A replica gravestone at the edge of the meadow is now gone. The prairie is becoming smaller over time as trees encroach and fill in the edges of the meadow.

If you skip the nature trail, then stay straight at the junction. Soon you will reach another junction, the other end of the Tombstone Nature Trail. Turn left here. Climb uphill to US 20 and use caution here as you cross. The hike continues on the other side where Cone Peak Trail #3408 begins next to a 6 percent downgrade warning sign.

Climb steadily through the forest and enjoy its shade on a hot summer day, as well as forest wildflowers such as bunchberry that bloom here in early summer. The trail switchbacks uphill and passes a series of small lovely rock gardens where larkspur and bluehead gilia bloom. At 2 miles, the trail emerges from the forest into an open area on the lower slope of Cone Peak, which is directly ahead of you. The trail soon makes a left turn, and you will get an excellent view of Iron Mountain to your left. The next 0.3 mile is a delightful wonderland of color in late June and early July: Watch for larkspur, paintbrush, mariposa lily, buckwheat, blue-eyed Mary, and many more, but please do not pick them, and make sure you stay on the trail.

After you have enjoyed the wildflower show, the trail heads back into the trees, briefly traverses an open rocky slope, and reenters the forest. The trail now heads southwest through the trees as it makes its way toward Iron Mountain. You will cross several more open areas with buckwheat, coneflower, and Sitka valerian.

At the 3.7-mile mark, reach a junction with Iron Mountain Trail #3389 and turn left. The trail switchbacks up an open slope where yet more wildflowers bloom, gaining

600 feet in 0.9 mile. Reach the summit viewing platform and reap the reward for your efforts, which includes Mount Hood, Mount Jefferson, Mount Washington, the Three Sisters, and Diamond Peak. To the west you can see the distinctive humpback of Marys Peak (Hike 2) in the Coast Range. Also visible are several other destinations in this book: Sand Mountain (Hike 11) to the west, Carpenter Mountain (Hike 13) to the south, and Coffin Mountain (Hike 9) to the north. A mountain locator map placed at the center of the platform helps you identify what you are seeing. Interpretive signs around the edge of the platform describe the floral diversity of Iron Mountain and the Indigenous history.

The Civilian Conservation Corps built an L-4 ground cabin on Iron Mountain in 1933, blasting rock off the summit to flatten it before construction began. After the cabin was destroyed in a 1976 windstorm, it was replaced with an R-6 ground cabin that was moved here from Herman Peak (in the Siuslaw National Forest northeast of Florence). The cabin was lowered onto Iron Mountain with a helicopter, where it was staffed until about 2001. Toxic mold was later discovered in the roof insulation, plus the structural supports were rotting, and the building was a target of vandalism, so it was removed in 2007. The Forest Service later built a viewing platform where the lookout stood.

Iron Mountain is part of the Western Cascades (also known as the Old Cascades), a deeply eroded range of volcanoes that erupted millions of years ago. The rock spire you see just east of the summit is a volcanic plug that formed when magma hardened inside a volcanic vent. Millions of years of erosion left the rock exposed, forming the spire you see today.

To finish the loop, hike 0.9 mile back down to the junction and turn left. After 0.1 mile, reach a junction and stay left. (The trailhead for the shorter hike is to the right; see below). Descend through the forest and cross back over US 20. The trail resumes on the other side to the right, at the edge of a small parking pullout. Reach a junction with Santiam Wagon Road Trail #3413 and turn left for the final mile back to your car.

SHORTER OPTION

If you want to skip the loop and just head straight for the summit, you can park at an alternative trailhead: 1.5 miles west of Tombstone Pass, turn north from US 20 onto Forest Road 035, a good gravel road passable in any vehicle, and follow it for 2.6 miles to the trailhead at the road's end. You'll find the beginning of the trail on the east side of the lot. Hike for 0.1 mile, turn left, and continue for another 0.1 mile, where you will turn right and hike up 0.9 mile to the summit. Return the way you came.

11 SAND MOUNTAIN

YEAR CONSTRUCTED	LOOKOUT ACCESS	LOCATION
1989	Staffed; accessible to the public when invited in by staff; locked when not staffed	Willamette National Forest, McKenzie River Ranger District

Roundtrip distance: 3.6 miles
Elevation gain: 760 feet
Lookout elevation: 5460 feet
Map: USGS Santiam Junction
GPS coordinates: 44.39422°, –121.91852°
Permits and fees: None

After an adventurous drive down a historic wagon road, hike up to a cinder cone and a fire lookout restored by volunteers, where you can enjoy sweeping views of the central Cascades.

Sand Mountain Lookout is on the summit of a cinder cone.

GETTING TO THE TRAILHEAD

On US Highway 20, drive east 5.4 miles from Santiam Junction or 20 miles west from Sisters until you reach Santiam Pass. Turn south onto paved Big Lake Road (Forest Road 2690), signed for Hoodoo Ski Area. After 0.9 mile, the road makes a sharp left turn (straight ahead is the ski area).

After 3.1 miles, the paved road curves a bit to the left and you will fork right onto gravel FR 810. This bumpy, rocky, sandy road follows the old route of the Santiam Wagon Road and requires good tires and high clearance. (Ignore the winter sign for Sand Mountain you will see at 2.4 miles on this road.) At 2.9 miles, park next to the wooden Sand Mountain sign on the left, being sure not to block the gate.

ON THE TRAIL

Walk around the gate and start hiking up FR 810. Sand Mountain looms ahead of you, the lookout visible up on the summit. The sandy dirt road is lined with snowbrush ceanothus, which bursts with white blooms in early summer. Also keep an eye out for low-to-the-ground pink pussypaws growing right in the middle of this seldom-driven road.

The road climbs and curves around the north side of Peak 5438. To your right, you will get a preview of the vistas to come. The road curves to the southwest, then to the southeast, ending at a parking area for the lookout staff at 1.6 miles. Sand Mountain Trail to the summit is on the far side of the parking area on the right. The first short section of this trail follows what was once a continuation of the road. After 400 feet, reach a fork where the old blocked-off road heads right; you will bear left to follow the trail 0.2 mile uphill to the lookout.

On a clear day, the landscape in all directions is stunning! You can see Mount Jefferson and Three Fingered Jack to the north, Black Butte to the east, Mount Washington and the Three Sisters to the southeast, and Diamond Peak to the south. A parade of smaller Cascade peaks march along the western horizon, such as Iron Mountain (Hike 10) with its distinctive volcanic plug. Big Lake can be seen below you to the east, surrounded by burned trees from the lightning-caused 2011 Shadow Lake Fire.

A short distance south of the summit, you can see the former staff parking area with its wooden fence that is slowly being reclaimed by the sand. The road used to end there instead of the parking area you walked through earlier, but erosion made it difficult to keep the road open and it was closed. Just to the right of the old parking area, you can look down into the summit crater, now lined with trees. Remember not to disturb the lookout staffer unless you are invited up, and enjoy the scenery from the ground.

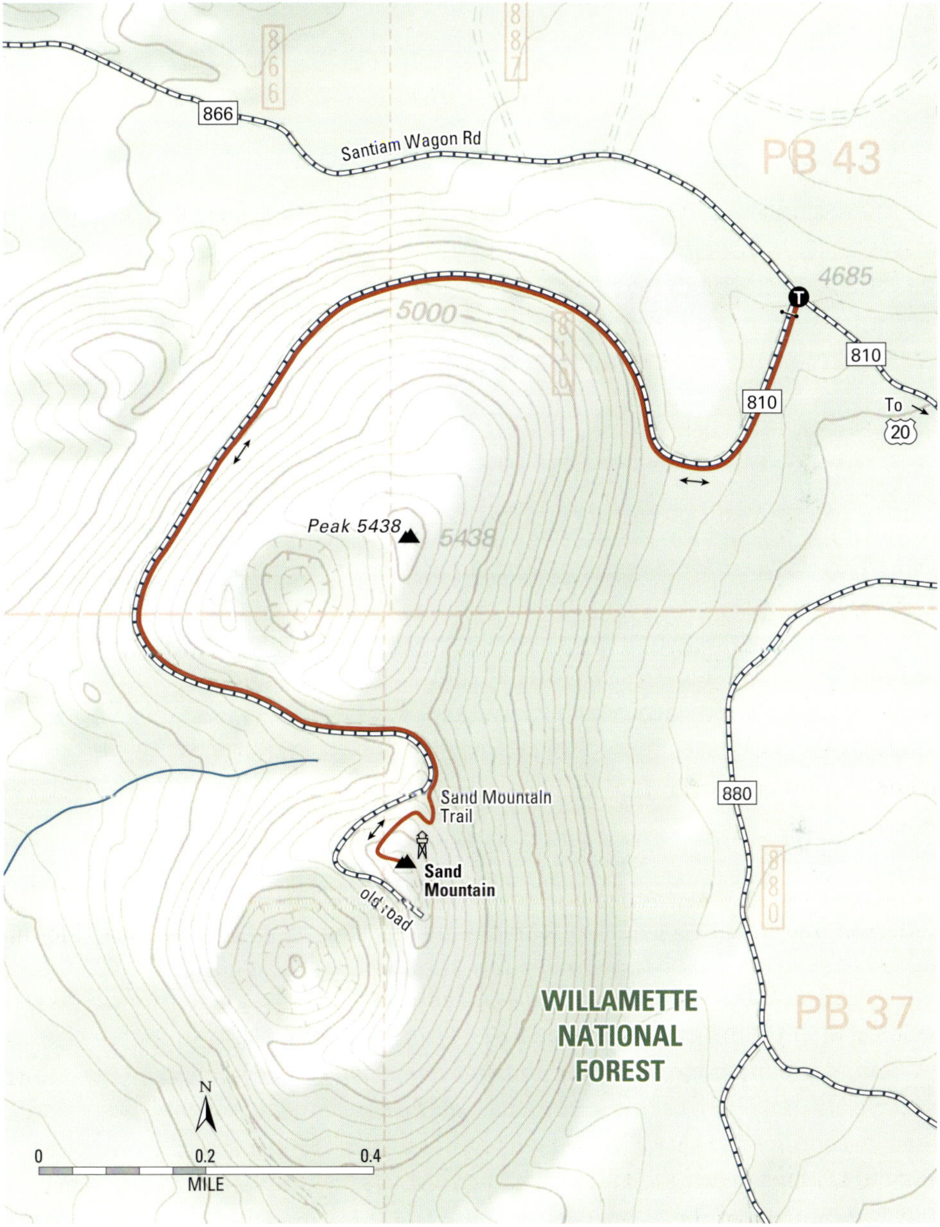

If you can tear your eyes away from the magnificent view and look down at the ground, you might spot the pygmy short-horned lizard, which averages just two inches in length. These little lizards eat ants and hang out in areas with sandy soil.

Distant views of Mount Jefferson and Three Fingered Jack from Sand Mountain

Although lizards are usually associated with hot desert environments, the pygmy short-horned lizard avoids extreme heat. In winter it buries itself a few inches in the sand and freezes solid while it hibernates through the season. It has also adapted to the short high-elevation breeding season by bearing live young instead of laying eggs.

Sand Mountain is part of a chain of cinder cones that erupted three thousand to four thousand years ago, sending lava flows out onto the surrounding landscape. These lava flows affected the McKenzie River channel, creating such familiar features as Sahalie Falls and Koosah Falls (both of which are easily reachable by driving down Oregon Route 126).

The Santiam Wagon Road—part of which you drove to get to the trailhead—was built in the 1860s to connect the Willamette Valley with the eastern side of the Cascades. Wagons traveled this toll road to bring wool west to the mills, returning east with food and supplies, as well as cattle, which were moved to graze in the eastern grasslands. The wagon road was replaced when the construction of US 20 was completed in 1939, but sections remain as roads and trails.

An L-4 ground cabin was built on Sand Mountain in 1931. The cabin somehow survived the 1967 Big Lake Fire, even though the lookout and his family were evacuated by helicopter as heat blistered the cabin's side. The structure survived that wildfire only to burn down the following year while the man staffing the lookout was in town, the cause undetermined.

In 1987, a group of volunteers started working with the Willamette National Forest to reestablish Sand Mountain as a lookout site, with the goals of adding another fire detection point as well as a human presence to keep off-road vehicle drivers from scaling the sides of the peak, causing erosion. In 1989, the Rogue River

National Forest removed the old 1931 L-4 lookout on Whisky Peak in southern Oregon and donated it for use on Sand Mountain. It was the exact same style of gable-roof lookout that had burned on Sand Mountain twenty-one years earlier, the main difference being that the new lookout was raised on a 10-foot tower instead of sitting on the ground.

The project was made possible by 1,800 volunteer hours and $5,000 in donations. The volunteers raced to complete construction in less than three months, finishing up just as the first winter snow started accumulating. The lookout was dedicated in a ceremony the following August. The nonprofit Sand Mountain Society has since gone on to restore other lookouts around the state, Gold Butte (Hike 7) and Pearsoll Peak (Hike 27) among them.

Return the way you came.

12 BLACK BUTTE

YEAR CONSTRUCTED	LOOKOUT ACCESS	LOCATION
1922 (cupola cabin) and 1996 (tower)	Both the unstaffed cupola and the staffed tower are closed to the public	Deschutes National Forest, Sisters Ranger District

Roundtrip distance: 4.2 miles
Elevation gain: 1500 feet
Lookout elevation: 6440 feet
Map: USGS Black Butte
GPS coordinates: 44.39960°, –121.63543°
Permits and fees: Northwest Forest Pass

Black Butte's perfectly symmetrical profile is visible to drivers on US Highway 20 for miles in both directions, but it is best experienced up close on foot. This is one of the most popular hikes in this book, and for good reason. Views from the summit are outstanding, stretching from the Three Sisters all the way up to Mount Hood.

GETTING TO THE TRAILHEAD

From the town of Sisters, drive 5.5 miles west on US 20. Turn north onto paved Forest Road 11, which is signed for Indian Ford Campground. After 3.7 miles, turn left onto gravel FR 1110. After another 4 miles, where the road makes a switchback, the going becomes rough, but it is still passable in low-clearance cars. The road ends at a parking area at 5.1 miles. There is room for about twenty cars here. Toilets are available.

ON THE TRAIL

Head to the signboards at the far end of the parking area where you will see two trails, both of which are Black Butte Trail #4026. You are actually starting your hike at the midway point of the trail; the trail on the right heads downhill to a lower trailhead on FR 1430 (see the note at the end of this entry). You will take the uphill trail on your left.

The trail immediately starts climbing. Towering ponderosa pines provide shade for this first stretch. Chinquapin and snowberry shrubs grow in the understory. The occasional signpost identifies some of the plants growing here with both their common and scientific names.

After 0.6 mile, the trail switchbacks to the right. At the 1-mile mark, it emerges from the forest into a more open area, and soon you will start enjoying views of the mountains to your right, a mere taste of what is to come. At 1.8 miles, reach the edge of a burn scar from the lightning-caused Black Butte II Fire in 2009. Round the corner on the final push to the summit where the staffed lookout tower appears above you, as well as Mount Jefferson and Mount Hood.

The 1922 cupola cabin on Black Butte

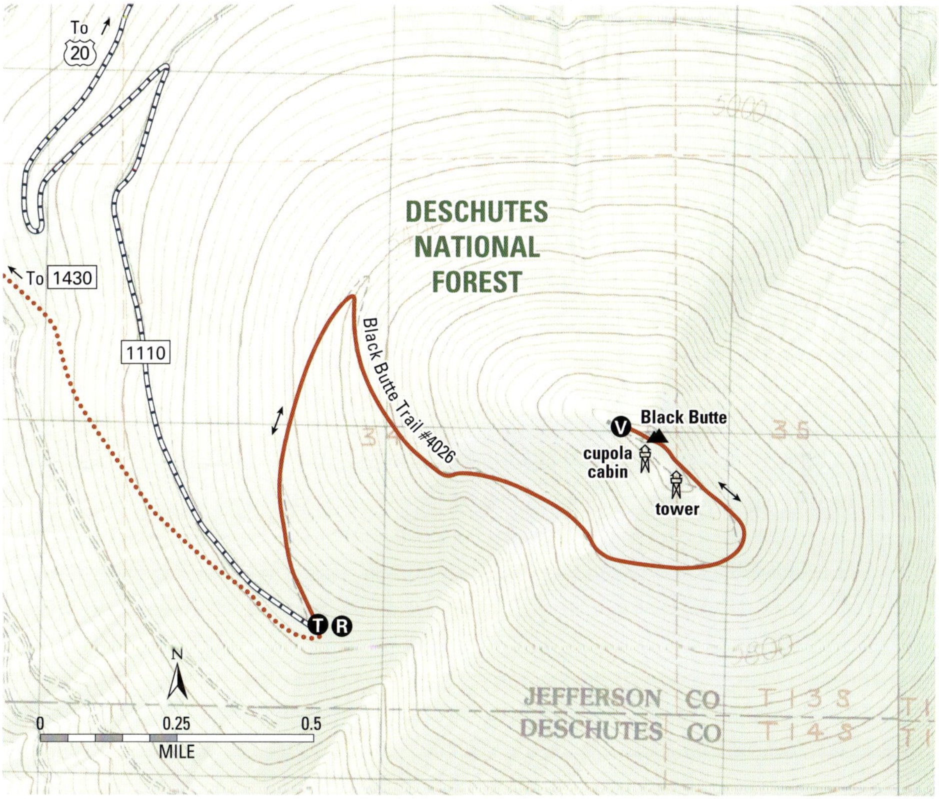

At the summit, the main trail does not take hikers past the staffed lookout, and a sign asks visitors to not disturb the lookout on duty. Instead the trail routes hikers to the historic D-6 cupola lookout where an interpretive sign explains the history of lookouts on this summit. Just beyond is a large viewing platform where signs along the railings help you identify the numerous peaks visible from this spot. On a clear day you can see major volcanic peaks, such as Three Fingered Jack and Mount Jefferson, as well as countless smaller peaks stretching up and down the Cascades.

The summit area is large, and there is plenty of room for the throngs of hikers to spread out. Take a break and soak up your surroundings, keeping an eye out for assertive but adorable golden-mantled ground squirrels, who want to steal your lunch. These rodents hibernate in winter and spend the summer gaining weight. There is a lot of naturally available food for them, such as acorns, insects, and pine nuts, but they are very persistent in begging. Remember that human food is not good for them, and feeding them makes them even bolder in approaching future hikers, so enjoy your lunch and let the squirrels forage for themselves.

Three Fingered Jack is visible on the horizon from the Black Butte Trail.

Black Butte is an extinct stratovolcano that last erupted about 1.4 million years ago. It is older than any of the other High Cascades volcanoes, but it has kept its shapely form due to being in the Cascade's rain shadow and not developing glaciers.

At the foot of Black Butte's north slope 3500 feet below, the Metolius River springs forth from the earth at a rate of fifty thousand gallons per minute and a temperature of 48 degrees. One of the largest spring-fed rivers in the US, it is a popular recreation and fly-fishing spot in the summer. The river, designated a Wild and Scenic River in 1988, flows north 29 miles until it empties into Lake Billy Chinook.

The first lookout on Black Butte was a crow's nest in a tree that went into service in 1910. The cupola lookout was built in 1922. This ground cabin did not provide enough visibility, so the Civilian Conservation Corps constructed an 83-foot tower in 1934. More than a thousand pack loads of construction material were hauled up the trail to construct the tower. In 1979, a cabin was built to serve as living quarters for the lookout. The tower was condemned in 1993 and collapsed in a winter storm in December 2001. (Observe the old timbers from that tower still lying on the summit not far from the concrete footings that once supported the structure.) The old cabin living quarters still remained; however, by 2016, dry rot and a carpenter ant infestation threatened to spread to the cupola cabin, so the Forest Service burned it down. The observation deck was built on the spot where the cabin had stood.

The current 65-foot tower was constructed in 1996 and is still staffed every summer. Volunteers with the Friends of the Metolius worked with the Forest Service in 2019 to restore the cupola lookout, updating it with fresh paint, new floors, and new front steps.

Return the way you came.

OPPOSITE *The Black Butte Lookout tower at sunset*

LONGER OPTION

If you are looking for a longer, harder hike up Black Butte, you can park at the lower trailhead off FR 1430, to follow the original trail up to Black Butte that was used before FR 1110 was constructed. To get to this trailhead, from downtown Sisters, drive west on US 20 for 9.8 miles. Turn right onto paved FR 14, signed for Camp Sherman. After 2.6 miles, fork right to stay on FR 14. Drive 0.1 mile, then turn right onto FR 1430. After a few hundred feet, pull into the unsigned trailhead parking area on your right. The hike to the upper trailhead from this point is 2.3 miles with 1700 feet of elevation gain.

13 CARPENTER MOUNTAIN

YEAR CONSTRUCTED	LOOKOUT ACCESS	LOCATION
1935	Staffed; accessible to the public when invited in by staff; locked when not staffed	Willamette National Forest, McKenzie River Ranger District

Roundtrip distance: 2 miles
Elevation gain: 770 feet
Lookout elevation: 5350 feet
Map: USGS Carpenter Mountain
GPS coordinates: 44.27678°, –122.13610°
Permits and fees: None

This short, quiet trail tucked away in the H. J. Andrews Experimental Forest passes through a shady forest and traverses a wildflower meadow before ending at a summit with barely enough room to accommodate a lookout. It involves a bit of scrambling at the end, but the reward is worth it. Note that much of the forest along the route to the trailhead burned in the 2023 Lookout Fire. Check with the McKenzie River Ranger District for current conditions.

GETTING TO THE TRAILHEAD

From McKenzie Bridge, drive west on Oregon Route 126 for 6.5 miles. Turn right onto Blue River Reservoir Road (Forest Road 15). Drive 3.5 miles, then turn right onto paved Lookout Creek Road (FR 1506), which transitions into a good gravel road

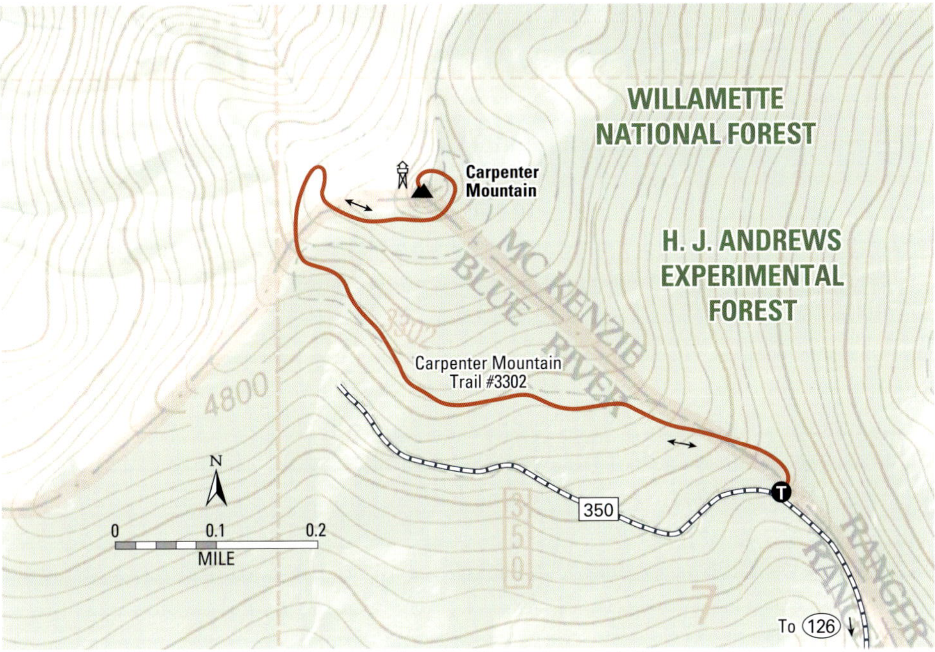

after 2 miles. After 2.4 miles on FR 1506, reach the junction with FR 1507, and keep left to stay on FR 1506. Stay left again at 3.2 miles at the junction with Forest Road 360. After 6.5 miles on FR 1506, fork left onto FR 350. Drive for 5.8 miles to an unsigned parking area on the right.

ON THE TRAIL

After admiring the view of the Three Sisters from the trailhead, walk up the road 100 feet to where Carpenter Mountain Trail #3302 begins on your right, then head uphill through a forest of Douglas-fir, western white pine, hemlock, and Pacific silver fir, which gets its name from the silvery-white undersides of its needles. After half a mile, the trail traverses an open meadow area, a great place to see columbine, delphinium, and tiger lilies if you visit this lookout in July. Here you'll find a nice view to the southwest looking down the drainage of McRae Creek, which feeds into Lookout Creek.

At the 1-mile mark, the trail emerges from the trees beneath the rocky summit. To reach the lookout, you may need to use your hands to navigate the last steep, rocky scramble. Once you reach the top, there isn't much real estate up here—the cabin takes up most of it. The scenery is expansive, stretching for miles, all the way from Mount Hood in the north to Diamond Peak in the south. Iron Mountain (Hike 10) is due north, 8 miles away. If you have a good pair of binoculars, you might be able to make out the lookout on Sand Mountain (Hike 11), 13 miles to the northeast. The rock formation sticking up out of the forest to the north just below Carpenter Mountain is Wolf Rock. Long before the trail network in these parts was converted into a road network, a guard station stood at its east end. The burned trees directly to the south are from the lightning-caused Lookout Fire in 2023 (named for Lookout Mountain where it started, and where a fire lookout briefly stood in the 1930s).

Carpenter Mountain is an ancient volcanic plug made of basalt. It was first used as a lookout around 1915 when an alidade was erected on the summit. Two years later, it was replaced with a firefinder under a roof, although that was destroyed by lightning in 1921. In 1935, an L-4 ground cabin was built, and as no roads came anywhere close to the mountain at that time, building materials were hauled in by pack animals.

Within a 9-mile radius of Carpenter Mountain stood no less than eight other lookouts, all of which are gone now. The lookout on Carpenter Mountain stopped being staffed in the mid-1960s and stood empty for a few decades. It suffered extensive damage in 1986 after being struck by lightning: The door and many windows were blown out, the steps blew off the side of the mountain, and the roof was raised off its frame. The cabin was repaired and returned to service in 1995.

The Blue River Experimental Forest was established by the US Forest Service in 1948. Horace Justin Andrews, the Forest Service Region 6 chief forester, was a supporter of

Carpenter Mountain Lookout is perched on the rocky summit.

Catwalk view from Carpenter Mountain

forest research and involved in selecting the location of the experimental forest on the Lookout Creek watershed in the Willamette National Forest. After he died in a car accident in 1951, the experimental forest was renamed in his honor in 1953.

The H. J. Andrews Experimental Forest is 15,800 acres administered cooperatively by the US Forest Service Pacific Northwest Research Station, Oregon State University, and the Willamette National Forest. The mission of the Andrews Forest Program is to support research on forests, streams, and watersheds and to foster strong collaboration among ecosystem science, education, natural resource management, and the humanities. The forest supports more than 3,000 invertebrate species, 164 bird species, 53 mammal species, 20 reptile and amphibian species, and 9 fish species. The Andrews receives more than eighty inches of rain annually.

Research on the Andrews includes stream ecology, vegetation succession, the effects of climate change, canopy ecology, biological diversity, and more. Logging is also studied here, with the first timber harvest taking place in 1951. Clear-cutting, partial cutting, and a control area that was left in its natural state were studied and compared. In 2023, 10,500 acres of the Andrews burned, so now scientists will have the opportunity to study the effects of wildfire in a forest that has been so thoroughly researched and documented.

The public is welcome to visit the forest; however, fishing and collecting forest products (such as mushrooms and flowers) are prohibited.

Return the way you came.

14 LITTLE COWHORN MOUNTAIN

YEAR CONSTRUCTED	LOOKOUT ACCESS	LOCATION
1960	Open to the public for day use; overnight stays first-come, first-served	Willamette National Forest, Middle Fork Ranger District

Roundtrip distance: 2.2 miles
Elevation gain: 900 feet
Lookout elevation: 4240 feet
Map: USGS Goat Point
GPS coordinates: 44.03733°, −122.51333°
Permits and fees: None

Ready for a quick workout? This steep hike through the forest gains 900 feet in just 1.3 miles, but the views and solitude at this lookout are worth the heart-pumping climb.

GETTING TO THE TRAILHEAD

From Interstate 5 southbound, take exit 188 (or exit 188A if you are driving northbound) and drive east on Oregon Route 58. Drive for 12.8 miles, then turn left onto Jasper-Lowell Road (Pioneer Street), signed for Lowell. Drive 0.7 mile into the little community of Lowell, then follow the road as it makes a sharp left turn. After one block, turn right to stay on Jasper-Lowell Road (S. Moss Street). Drive 1.7 miles, then turn right onto Big Fall Creek Road (Forest Road 18), signed for Fall Creek Recreation Area.

Drive 10.7 miles, then fork uphill to the left onto FR 1817 (just past Dolly Varden Campground). Follow this gravel road, keeping left at 5.6 miles to stay on FR 1817. Keep right at all other junctions. After 11.5 miles, reach the unsigned trailhead on the left at the junction with FR 363. There is room for three to four cars to park on the shoulder.

ON THE TRAIL

Of the two roads you see heading northeast from here, FR 363 on the left is a logging road that soon crosses into private timberland. Forest Road 388 on the right is gated and abandoned. You will ignore both roads and instead look for Little Cowhorn Mountain Trail #3458 on the south side of FR 388 (on the right when looking uphill at the gate). Follow the trail as it switchbacks steeply uphill through a lush forest of

Little Cowhorn Lookout is an R-6 cabin built in 1960.

hemlock, Oregon grape, salal, and sword ferns. Towering vine maples create tunnels of green in the summer and yellow in the fall.

The trail intersects FR 388 at 0.6 mile. Follow the road uphill for 0.1 mile until you see the trail continuing into the forest at the road's end. (The rest of the abandoned roadbed beyond this point has been reclaimed by nature.) The trail makes more than a dozen tight switchbacks. Tall rock pinnacles tower over the trail, and wild rhododendrons produce pink blooms in June.

After 1 mile, the trail reaches a faint unmarked junction. The user trail that goes straight here is a short, worthy detour that heads several hundred feet out to an open rocky area where stonecrop grows in great abundance. The views here are similar to those on the summit. Back at the junction, head uphill. The last stretch of trail is a narrow ledge that has been blasted out of the side of the cliff. There are handrails here, but watch your step and your kids, and keep your dogs leashed. After 1.1 miles, the trail ends at the lookout, perched on the rocky summit. The lookout is unlocked, and while it has been available for first-come, first-served stays in the past, the cabin is now in pretty rough shape.

A D-6 cupola cabin was built on Little Cowhorn Mountain in 1923. Access to the mountain was via a long trail that started at the Fall Creek Guard Station located more than 3000 feet below on Fall Creek. A road was built nearly all the way to the

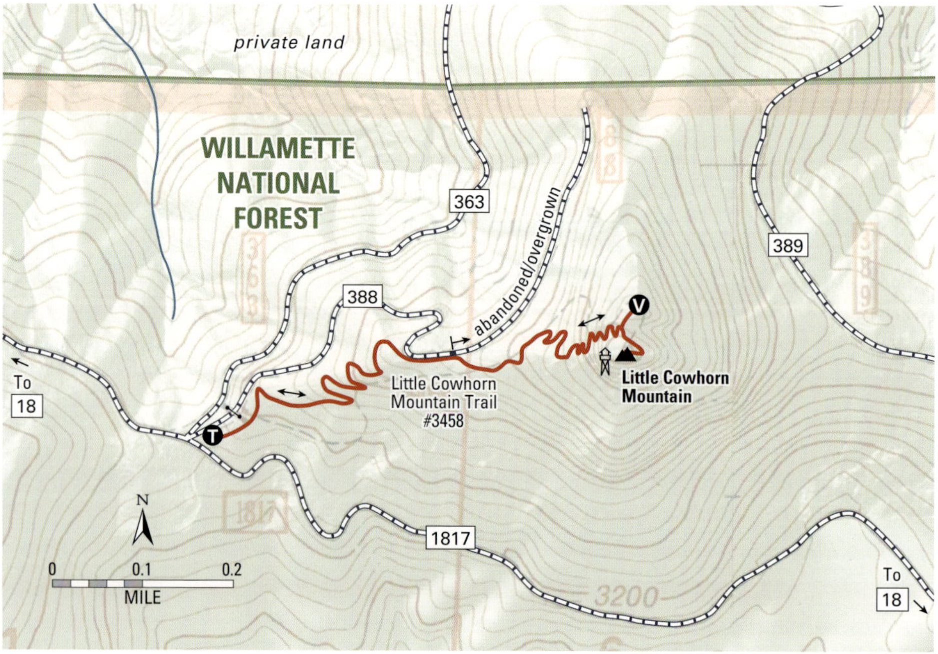

summit in the early 1950s. The R-6 cabin that stands on Little Cowhorn today was built in 1960, but it has not been staffed in decades.

Passport in Time (PIT) is a volunteer program sponsored by the US Forest Service that was established in 1991. Volunteers work with professional staff on public lands to curate artifacts and restore rock art and historic structures. In 1988, PIT volunteers undertook restoration work on this lookout in preparation for it being added to the rental program, but those plans never came to fruition, and the cabin has seen very little maintenance since then. Today, the roof leaks and the floor is rotten; both need replacing. You'll find a lot of mouse and rat poop inside but no toilet for human visitors. The Forest Service is exploring options for restoring this lookout.

On a clear day the numerous Cascade peaks that dot the horizon stretch for miles: From here you can see the top of Mount Hood, Mount Jefferson, Three Fingered Jack, Mount Washington, the Three Sisters, and Diamond Peak. The forest to the south is the Willamette National Forest, and most of the forest to the north between here and the McKenzie River is private Weyerhaeuser land.

This is one of three Cowhorns in Oregon. The 7664-foot peak in the Calapooya Mountains was once known as Little Cowhorn because of a rock pinnacle that resembled a cow's horn. The pinnacle collapsed in 1911, and the peak is now just called

Cowhorn Mountain. The 9182-foot volcano we now know as Mount Thielsen was once known as Big Cowhorn. It was later renamed to honor Hans Thielsen, an early pioneer in the area. Although it is not documented, Little Cowhorn Mountain may have received its name for the same reason the other two did.

The lookout has been threatened by fire several times in the recent past, first by the lightning-caused Jones Fire in 2017, then by the Holiday Farm Fire in 2020 (caused by downed powerlines), then again by the human-caused Bedrock Fire, which started at the Bedrock Campground in July 2023 and burned nearly thirty-two thousand acres. Crews wrapped the cabin in 2023 to protect it in case the fire reached the summit. It was once again threatened in 2024 when a July thunderstorm started numerous small fires, like the one just west of Little Cowhorn, known collectively as the Oakridge Lightning Complex Fire.

You can retrace your steps via the trail, or when you reach FR 388, you can follow this rough, rocky road 0.5 mile back to your car.

15 WALDO MOUNTAIN

YEAR CONSTRUCTED	LOOKOUT ACCESS	LOCATION
1957	Closed to the public; catwalk accessible	Willamette National Forest, Middle Fork Ranger District

Roundtrip distance: 6.2 miles
Elevation gain: 1930 feet
Lookout elevation: 6360 feet
Maps: USGS Blair Lake and USGS Waldo Mountain
GPS coordinates: 43.77642°, –122.14617°
Permits and fees: None

Hike through the Waldo Lake Wilderness to a lookout cabin with 360-degree views. This area contains numerous bodies of water and is infamous for mosquitoes, so bring bug spray if you come in summer, or wait until after Labor Day for a bug-free hike.

At the time of writing, this trailhead was inaccessible due to road closures from the 2022 Cedar Creek Fire, so I have described the hike based on other sources. Also, while the wilderness has reopened to the public, it will take years for all the trails to be cleared. Check with the Middle Fork Ranger Station for road and trail updates.

Approaching Waldo Mountain Lookout

GETTING TO THE TRAILHEAD

From Oregon Route 58 in Oakridge, turn north onto Crestview Street. Drive 0.2 mile, then turn right onto E. First Street, which becomes Salmon Creek Road (Forest Road 24). Drive this paved road for 11 miles to a junction where you will fork left onto FR 2417. Drive 5.5 paved miles, then 0.5 mile on gravel, then fork right onto FR 2424. Drive 3.7 miles to the trailhead on your right, where the road makes a sharp curve to the left.

ON THE TRAIL

The trail heads southeast into the forest. Almost immediately you will reach a junction where you will take the left fork onto Waldo Mountain Trail #3592, where rhododendrons and beargrass bloom in summer. Climb through a forest of Douglas-firs and hemlocks for 2 miles, enter forest burned in 2022, then reach a junction with Waldo Meadows Trail #3591, where you will turn left. Quickly reach another junction, where you will turn right to continue on the Waldo Mountain Trail.

The trail climbs steeply, gaining 700 feet in the next mile. Although almost the entire south slope of Waldo Mountain burned, here on the ridge the fire burned in a mosaic pattern, so you will pass in and out of burned and unburned forest several times before reaching the lookout at the 3.1-mile mark. The cabin sits on the open summit area dominated by manzanita and huckleberry. Burned trees on the south edge of the summit show how close the fire came.

On clear days, the views up here stretch for miles. A string of Cascade peaks can be seen to the north: Mount Hood, Mount Jefferson, Three Fingered Jack, Mount Washington, Middle Sister, South Sister, Broken Top, and Mount Bachelor. Waldo Lake's pristine waters are visible to the east, and on the other side you can see The Twins with its double-humped summit. To the right of The Twins is Maiden Peak. Diamond Peak is visible to the south.

Waldo Mountain has been a lookout site since around 1920, when the lookout on duty had nothing but an alidade at their disposal. Initially there wasn't even a telephone line, so the lookout had to communicate with nearby Huckleberry Mountain using a heliograph (a signaling device using a mirror). The lookout probably slept in a tent until a shake-sided cabin was built in 1926.

A D-6 cupola cabin was built in 1929, its construction material shipped by train to Cascade Summit, transported across Odell Lake by boat, and then by truck to Waldo Lake. From there mules carted it the rest of the way to the summit. An R-6 ground cabin replaced it in 1957. It is kept locked and no longer staffed; however, the catwalk that surrounds the cabin makes for an excellent spot to sit and admire your surroundings.

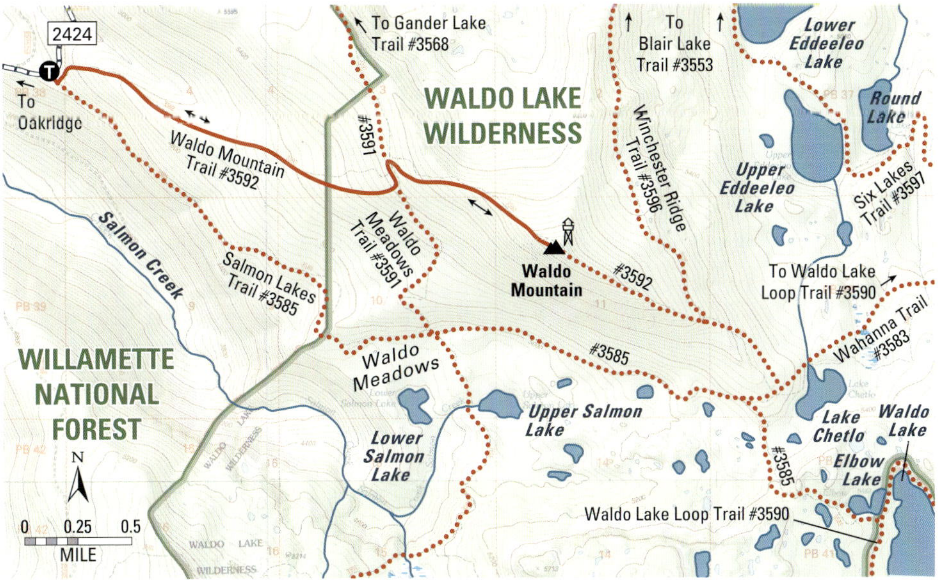

Waldo Mountain looks down on Waldo Lake, named for Judge John B. Waldo, who died in 1907. (Waldo Glacier on Mount Jefferson is also named for the judge.) This lake is Oregon's second deepest, with a maximum depth of 420 feet. (Crater Lake is the deepest lake in both Oregon and the US, at 1943 feet.) Also functioning as the headwaters of the North Fork of the Middle Fork of the Willamette River, it is known for having exceptionally clear water due to the fact that it has no permanent inlet streams; instead, its water comes primarily from snow and rain. Motorized boats and aircraft have been prohibited from using the lake since 2013.

The Waldo Lake Wilderness was established in 1984 and encompasses more than thirty-six thousand acres on the north, west, and south sides of the lake. (Despite the name, no part of the lake is within the wilderness boundary.) More than nine thousand acres burned at the north end of the lake in the lightning-caused 1996 Charlton Fire. That old burn scar burned again in 2022 when lightning started the much larger Cedar Creek Fire, which burned more than half of the Waldo Lake Wilderness as well as forest outside its boundaries. The fire also resulted in the evacuation of the nearby town of Oakridge, and smoke from the fire blew north all the way to Seattle. At 127,000 acres, it was the second-biggest fire in Oregon that year. Fire crews wrapped the lookout to protect it from the flames that would eventually come within a few hundred feet of the cabin.

Return the way you came.

EXTEND YOUR HIKE

For a little more distance, you can also turn this hike into an 8-mile loop. To do so, find the continuation of Waldo Mountain Trail #3592 on the east side of the summit and follow it east as it descends through forest mostly untouched by the fire, passing

Waldo Mountain Lookout offers an expansive vista of the surrounding Waldo Lake Wilderness.

Winchester Ridge Trail #3596 on the left along the way. Shortly after that junction, the trail enters the burn area. At 1.4 miles from the lookout, reach a junction with Wahanna Trail #3583 and turn right. Hike 0.2 mile to the junction with Salmon Lakes Trail #3585 and stay right.

Continue hiking for 1.5 miles to Waldo Meadows, which did not burn in the fire. Wildflowers bloom here in July (and mosquitoes are abundant!). Pass the junction with Waldo Meadows Trail #3591 and continue straight on Salmon Lakes Trail for an additional 2.5 mostly level miles to the trailhead.

16 ROUND MOUNTAIN

YEAR CONSTRUCTED	LOOKOUT ACCESS	LOCATION
1933	Staffed; accessible to the public when invited in by staff; locked when not staffed	Deschutes National Forest, Bend–Fork Rock Ranger District

Roundtrip distance: 2.8 miles
Elevation gain: 700 feet
Lookout elevation: 5900 feet
Map: USGS Round Mountain
GPS coordinates: 43.76211°, –121.71260°
Permits and fees: None

This moderate hike follows a closed road to a staffed lookout with 360-degree views of mountains, lakes, and forest. This is a great destination if you are hiking with kids, since the road is easy to walk and has a steady grade.

GETTING TO THE TRAILHEAD

From Bend, drive south on US Highway 97 for 17 miles to Vandevert Road, signed for Fall River, and turn right. If you are coming from La Pine, drive north on US 97 for 13 miles, then follow signs to double back south briefly, then turn right onto Vandevert Road.

Drive west on Vandevert Road for 1 mile, then turn left onto S. Century Drive. After 1 mile, turn right to stay on S. Century Drive. Follow it for 10.7 miles and turn right onto gravel Forest Road 4250 (almost directly across from the Fall River Guard

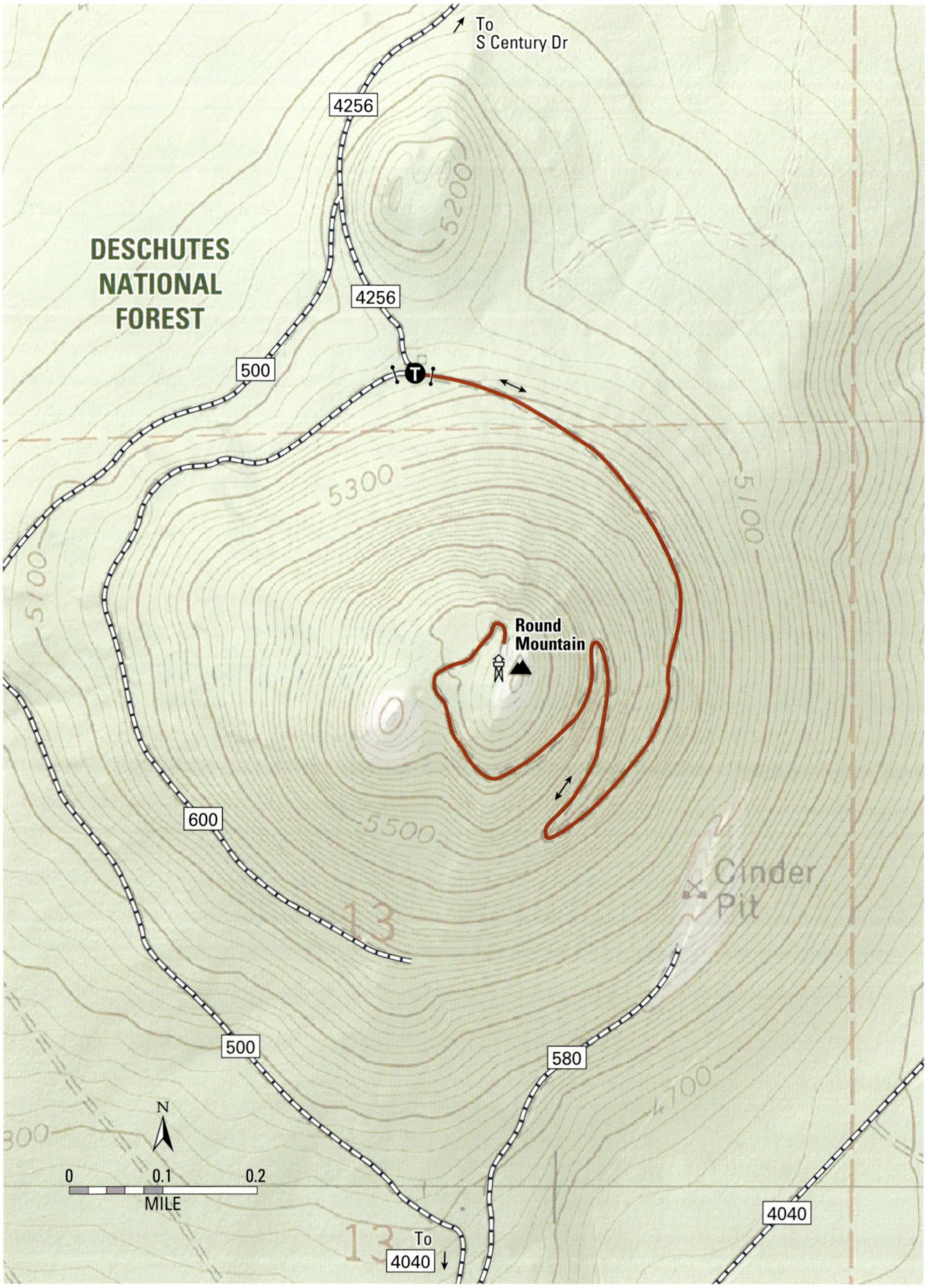
To
S Century Dr
4256
4256
DESCHUTES
NATIONAL
FOREST
500
5200
5300
5100
5100
Round
Mountain
5500
600
Cinder
Pit
13
500
580
4700
N
0
0.1
0.2
MILE
4040
To
4040
13

Station on the left). The road immediately forks; FR 4240 goes right, but you will take the left fork to stay on FR 4250. Drive 3.9 miles, then turn left onto FR 4255.

Drive 0.1 mile, then turn left onto FR 4256. A high-clearance vehicle is recommended, as the drive becomes rough and bumpy in spots at this point. Drive for 0.8 mile and keep left at a fork. Drive 0.2 mile farther, then reach a junction with gated FR 600 on the right. FR 4256, also gated, is just ahead. Park on the shoulder here without blocking any of the gates.

ON THE TRAIL

Hike up FR 4256 beneath towering grand firs and ponderosa pines, where the road is lined with golden chinquapin, sticky currant, and snowbrush. At 0.8 mile, the trail switchbacks uphill to the right. The trail makes another switchback uphill to the left, then passes a sign that says the fire lookout is one-eighth mile away. Do not believe the sign; you still have 0.4 mile to go.

You will be able to see more to the south on this next stretch. At the next switchback, you get a view of The Twins to the west. The road curls around to the right as

Round Mountain Lookout has survived several threatening fires in recent decades.

South Sister and Mount Bachelor are easy to spot from Round Mountain.

it approaches the summit, makes one more switchback, then ends in front of a toilet just below the lookout.

Climb the seventy steps up the slope to the base of the lookout, which is perched atop several massive summit boulders. This 14-by-14-foot L-4 lookout was built in 1933. At that time, a road traveled only as far as the base of the mountain on the north side, at which point a trail went the rest of the way to the summit. Once surrounded by seven other lookouts within a 15-mile radius, now the next closest staffed lookouts are Odell Butte, 21 miles to the south (Hike 18), and Lava Butte, 21 miles to the northeast (Hike 17). Round Mountain is staffed during fire season. You'll also find a remote automatic weather station up here, so you can check the weather at the summit online any time you like at raws.dri.edu.

The Twins and Charlton Butte are visible to the west, along with Cultus Mountain rising up behind Crane Prairie Reservoir. Wickiup Reservoir and Davis Mountain are visible to the south. Paulina Peak (another lookout site) is visible to the east. Lookout Mountain (yes, once the site of a lookout) is visible to the north, with South Sister and Mount Bachelor just beyond.

The Deschutes River starts at Little Lava Lake north of here, flows south, then swings around and starts flowing northeast. Round Mountain is encircled to the west and south by two reservoirs on that river: Crane Prairie Reservoir and Wickiup Reservoir. The 3,400-acre Crane Prairie Reservoir was created in 1922 with the damming of the Deschutes River, which flooded a meadow through which the river flowed that was frequented by cranes. The lake is shallow, reaching a maximum depth of only 20 feet.

Just downstream, the river was dammed again in 1949 to create the ten-thousand-acre Wickiup Reservoir. *Wikiup* is a term used by some Native American tribes to refer to a wigwam or teepee. A riverside spot now flooded by the reservoir was a camping place for Native Americans and known locally as Wikiup. (The spelling was changed to Wickiup in 1939.) Both lakes are popular for fishing and recreation. The name Deschutes comes from the fur-trading era when French trappers called the river Rivière des Chutes, meaning "River of the Falls," referring not to falls on the Deschutes, but on the Columbia. This was probably in reference to Celilo Falls, which has been drowned in the waters of Lake Celilo behind The Dalles Lock and Dam since 1957.

The lookout has been repeatedly threatened by fire in recent decades, including the 1994 Four Corners Fire, the 2001 Crane Complex, and the 2024 Round Mountain Fire.

Return the way you came.

17 LAVA BUTTE

YEAR CONSTRUCTED	LOOKOUT ACCESS	LOCATION
1998	Staffed; closed to the public	Deschutes National Forest, Newberry National Volcanic Monument

Roundtrip distance: 3.3 miles
Elevation gain: 540 feet
Lookout elevation: 5020 feet
Map: USGS Lava Butte
GPS coordinates: 43.90903°, –121.35644°
Permits and fees: Northwest Forest Pass

Lava Butte is popular with the locals, and for good reason: This lookout perched atop a cinder cone volcano provides expansive views, and there is even a place to shelter from the weather. The road is closed to private vehicles, so the only traffic you are likely to encounter is the shuttle bus that ferries visitors to the top.

GETTING TO THE TRAILHEAD

From Bend, drive south on US Highway 97 for 11 miles, taking the exit marked for the Lava Lands Visitor Center. If you are coming from La Pine, drive north on US 97 for 16 miles, then take exit 151 and follow Cottonwood Road north for 2 miles. Park at the Lava Lands Visitor Center.

ON THE TRAIL

The hike starts at the far east end of the parking lot where the road is gated to keep out public vehicles. In 2015, the Forest Service implemented a shuttle bus system for people wanting to visit the top of Lava Butte without walking. This shuttle system replaced the previous timed-entry permit for personal vehicles, which often resulted in long waits. (If you are interested in taking the shuttle bus, head into the Lava Lands Visitor Center for more information.)

Walk around the gate on Lava Butte Road and start hiking along the road, where you will see piles of lava on your left and US 97 on your right. The road makes a sharp left, then begins a long spiral up to the summit beneath the ponderosa pines. In summer, look for purple penstemon and yellow rabbitbrush in bloom. Stay on the road; do not try to take a shortcut straight up the hill, which damages resources and creates hazardous conditions for hikers and the vehicles below.

At 1.5 miles, reach the end of the road and follow the paved trail to the left of the tiny parking lot. In short order you'll reach the two-story lookout, which is staffed during fire season. The upper deck is closed to visitors. The lower level is an enclosed room where you can seek protection from the elements during bad weather. Four panels above the windows identify all the peaks you can see from up here, and on a clear day there are a lot of them. Mount Bachelor and the Three Sisters are 24 miles to the west. Numerous other volcanic peaks can be seen up and down the Cascades, including Three Fingered Jack, Mount Jefferson, and even Mount Hood on a particularly clear day. Paulina Peak (once a lookout site) rises along the rim of the Newberry Caldera to the south. Dozens of cinder cones similar to Lava Butte can be seen in the surrounding area.

Lava Butte is a cinder cone volcano that erupted just once approximately seven thousand years ago. The lava flow from that eruption covers about nine square miles. The cinder cone now rises 500 feet above the surrounding terrain and is part of the Newberry National Volcanic Monument, which was designated in 1990. The Newberry Volcano is a shield-shaped stratovolcano, and its lava flows cover 1,200 square miles. It has more than four hundred vents, the most of any volcano in the Lower 48. Inside the caldera sit two lakes: Paulina Lake and East Lake, both of which are popular recreation destinations in the summer.

The first lookout on Lava Butte was an L-4 ground cabin constructed in 1931. The trail that switchbacked up the east slope was replaced with a road in 1933. A two-story R-6 lookout replaced the first lookout in 1957, the lower level of which was expanded and converted into a small visitor's center in 1960. After forty years, however, the foundation had weakened and the lookout leaked, so the entire structure

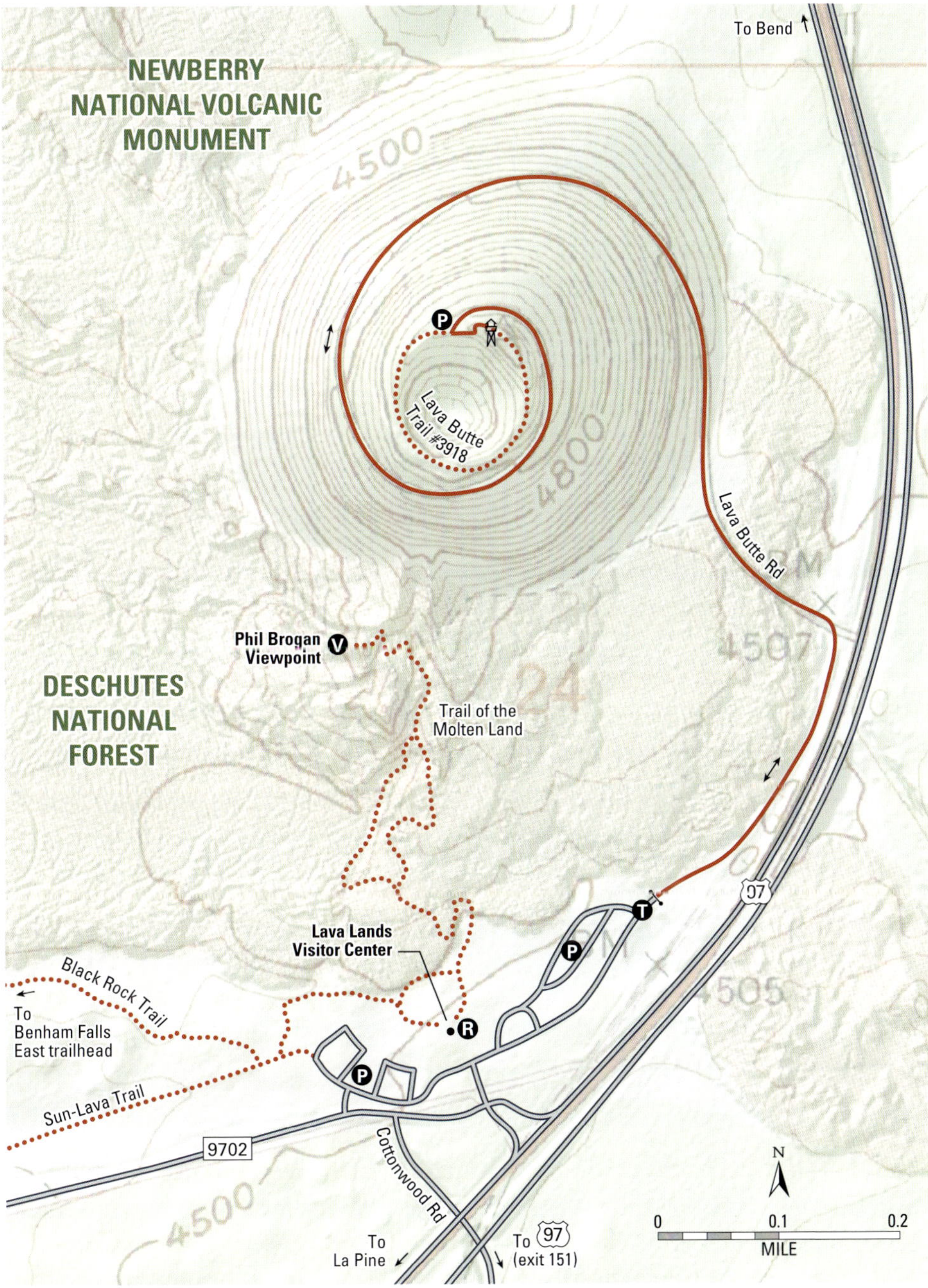

NEWBERRY NATIONAL VOLCANIC MONUMENT
DESCHUTES NATIONAL FOREST
To Bend
4500
4800
Lava Butte Trail #3918
Lava Butte Rd
4507
24
Phil Brogan Viewpoint
Trail of the Molten Land
97
Lava Lands Visitor Center
Black Rock Trail
To Benham Falls East trailhead
Sun-Lava Trail
4505
9702
Cottonwood Rd
To La Pine
To 97 (exit 151)
N
0
0.1
0.2
MILE

Lava Butte Lookout features a viewing room on the ground floor.

was removed in 1997, replaced the following year with the L-4 lookout and lower-level viewing room that stands today.

Return the way you came.

EXTEND YOUR HIKE

You can head back down, or you can continue past the lookout on Lava Butte Trail #3918, a loop that follows the rim of the summit crater. At its deepest point on the north side, the crater is 160 feet deep. Interpretive signs along the way describe the geology of the area. Golden-mantled ground squirrels and yellow-pine chipmunks dart around, hoping for handouts, but please don't give in. Return to the summit parking area, then follow the road back down to the visitor center.

Before you leave, from the Lava Lands Visitor Center you can follow several different trails to explore the lava flow at the base of Lava Butte. The Trail of the Molten Land is a paved accessible loop that travels through the lava at the base of the butte, with interpretive signs describing the area's geologic history; at the far end, at the Phil Brogan Viewpoint, look out over the lava field to the Cascades beyond.

18 ODELL BUTTE

YEAR CONSTRUCTED	LOOKOUT ACCESS	LOCATION
1963	Staffed; accessible to the public when invited in by staff; locked when not staffed	Deschutes National Forest, Crescent Ranger District

Roundtrip distance: 1.6 miles
Elevation gain: 490 feet
Lookout elevation: 7030 feet
Map: USGS Odell Butte
GPS coordinates: 43.47332°, –121.86697°
Permits and fees: None

Like Black Butte to the north, Odell Butte's prominent conical shape is visible for miles around. A short, easy hike leads to the summit, with spectacular views of the Cascades and central Oregon.

GETTING TO THE TRAILHEAD

From the intersection of Crestview Street and Oregon Route 58 in Oakridge, take OR 58 east for 40 miles. Turn left onto gravel Odell Butte Road (Forest Road 5815). If you are coming from Chemult, drive north on US Highway 97 for 8.6 miles, exit onto OR 58, drive for another 9.8 miles, then turn right onto Odell Butte Road.

Drive 2.8 miles on Odell Butte Road, then turn right onto FR 500. Drive 1.6 miles to a switchback, where there is parking on the left and a gate on the right. Do not block the gate.

If you are coming from Bend, drive 47 miles south on US 97 to the community of Crescent and turn right onto Crescent Cutoff Road. Drive 7 miles, then turn left onto Odell Butte Road (FR 5815). Drive 5.2 miles—sticking to the main gravel road at

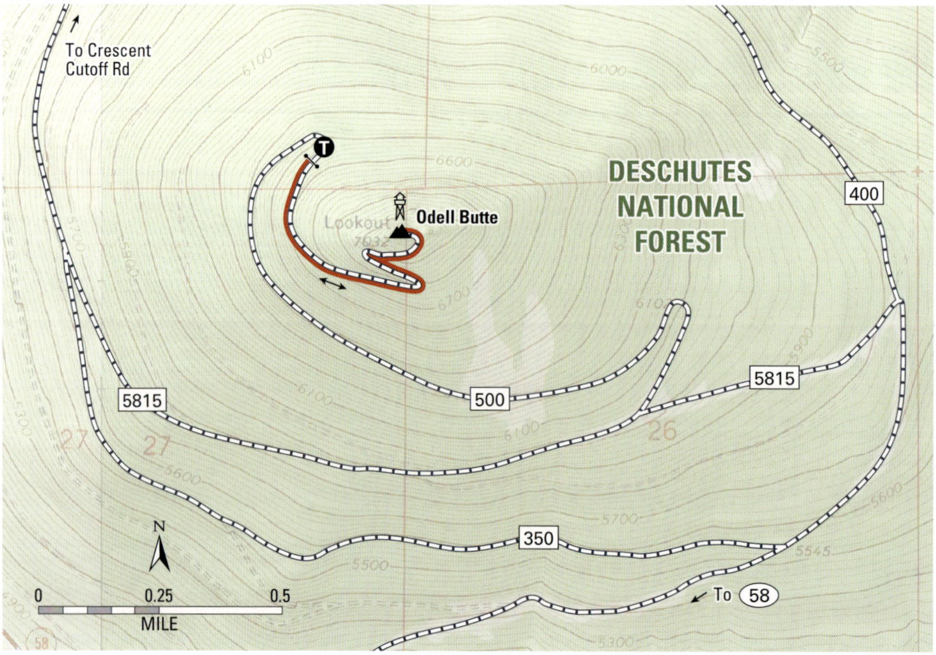

junctions and ignoring logging spurs—and fork left onto FR 500. Drive 1.6 miles to a switchback, where there is parking on the left and a gate on the right. Do not block the gate. All roads are navigable in a low-clearance car.

ON THE TRAIL

Hike around the gate and head up the road through a forest of mountain hemlock and lodgepole pine, where manzanita and snowbrush grow in the understory. You will also see golden chinquapin, which is actually considered a shrubby tree. Soon sagebrush also appears along the road.

As you climb you start to see more through the trees. After 0.8 mile, reach the summit, where you will pass a large cluster of communications equipment on the right. Cross the parking area and take the path to the bottom of the tower stairs. If the lookout is busy and you cannot go up, you can explore the area around the summit to take in the views.

Visible to the north are Maiden Peak, The Twins, the Three Sisters, Broken Top, and Mount Bachelor, along with Davis Lake. The peak to the northeast that is just 6 miles away is Hamner Butte. Walker Mountain is visible to the southeast, where its lookout still stands although it has not been staffed in years, and like Odell Butte the site now bristles with communications equipment. Mount Thielsen's pointy prominence can be seen to the southeast. Cowhorn Mountain's distinct shape is to the west, as is Diamond Peak, rising above Crescent Lake.

A 12-by-12-foot cabin was built atop a log platform on Odell Butte in 1916. This was replaced in 1932 by a 20-foot tower with an L-4 cabin. The building materials for both these lookouts had to be hauled up by pack string, as the summit was only accessible via trail. A 30-foot tower with an R-6 cabin was built in 1963. A road had previously been constructed most of the way up the butte for a logging operation, and it was extended the final 0.9 mile to reach the summit so that construction materials for this cabin could be transported by truck. The resulting lookout is still staffed during fire season.

Odell Butte and Odell Lake are named after William Holman Odell, who was born in Indiana in 1830 and moved to Oregon in 1852. He and Bynon J. Pengra were making a reconnaissance for the Oregon Central Military Wagon Road in 1865 and climbed to the top of a tall butte. (Imagine climbing all the way up here without the benefit of a road or trail!) A lake could be seen to the northwest, which they then visited. Both the lake and the butte now bear Odell's name.

Six-mile-long Odell Lake is sandwiched between the border of the Diamond Lake Wilderness and OR 58. The depression filled by the lake was carved by a glacier, and

Odell Butte Lookout is still staffed during fire season.

Numerous Cascade peaks are visible from Odell Butte.

the moraine left behind impounds the lake at its southeast end. Odell Creek flows out of the lake here, heading northeast to then fill Davis Lake. (Davis Lake was formed not by a glacier, but by a lava flow damming Odell Creek.)

The wagon road that Pengra and Odell were surveying was built between 1865 and 1870. Stretching 420 miles from Eugene, Oregon, to Silver City, Idaho, it was one of five military wagon roads in Oregon that were created to encourage settlement along their routes, as well as increase the ability of the military to move around the state. The wagon road was not built by the military itself, however, but by a private company called the Oregon Central Military Wagon Road Company. They happily accepted 875,000 acres of land in exchange for building the road, yet a wagon road was not what they built. When they declared construction complete, the route was little more than a trail, not built to the required federal standards. The company also deliberately made the road tortuously indirect and circuitous in order to secure the best lands for itself. As a result it was never used for its intended purpose. The section of wagon road from Eugene to central Oregon eventually became OR 58.

Return the way you came.

SOUTHWEST

19 ILLAHEE ROCK

YEAR CONSTRUCTED	LOOKOUT ACCESS	LOCATION
1925 (cupola), 1956 (tower)	Cupola cabin unlocked; tower cabin closed but catwalk may be accessible if unlocked	Umpqua National Forest, North Umpqua Ranger District

Roundtrip distance: 1.4 miles
Elevation gain: 560 feet
Lookout elevation: 5390 feet
Map: USGS Illahee Rock
GPS coordinates: 43.35081°, –122.55410°
Permits and fees: None

This is one of two hikes in this book (the other is Black Butte, Hike 12) where you get two lookouts for the price of one. This short trail delivers hikers to a summit with great views, an old cupola lookout, and a 20-foot-tall lookout tower. *Illahe* is a Chinook word meaning "land," "earth," or "country."

GETTING TO THE TRAILHEAD

From Glide, drive east on Oregon Route 138 for 30 miles. Pass Umpqua's Last Resort, then immediately after crossing Dry Creek, turn left onto gravel Illahee Road (Forest Road 4760). Drive 7.7 miles (continuing straight at an intersection at 1.4 miles), then turn right onto FR 100. Drive for 1.2 potholed miles, then turn left up unsigned FR 104 for 0.2 mile to the Illahee Rock trailhead at the road's end, where there is parking for about five cars. FR 104 can be brushy and overgrown, so if you prefer to walk that stretch, there are places to park alongside FR 100.

ON THE TRAIL

Illahee Lookout Trail #1539 starts at the west end of the parking area. Parts of this trail were burned in the 2017 Happy Dog Fire. A sign at the start warns you of its effects: hazard trees, downed logs, and missing tread. The trail starts out by traversing a slope of blackened snags and thimbleberry bushes, and in summer you can see wildflowers here too: In June you will see arnica, columbine, and rhododendron, and fireweed blooming in abundance in July. This magenta flower loves to grow in open disturbed areas, such as clear-cuts and burned areas.

After 0.2 mile, the trail enters a forest where only some of the trees died in the fire. The trail switchbacks up beneath towering rock cliffs, then traverses a slope forested with Douglas-fir. The trail makes a switchback, then enters another pocket of burned forest on a north-facing slope. Then you'll head over to traverse the south-facing slope where hundreds of blue-eyed Marys bloom in June.

Make another switchback, pass a huge old Douglas-fir that survived the fire on your right, then begin a series of switchbacks up a talus slope. On the final approach to the summit, the trail hugs the cliff, offering dramatic expanses all around. Yellow stonecrop blooms among the rocks. Pass a helipad on your right, then reach the summit, a broad rocky area dotted with trees. The burned trees on the west side of the summit are from a wildfire in 2017, part of the North Umpqua Complex of fires, when the area was hit by hundreds of lightning strikes in early August. More than sixty-four thousand acres were burned by 115 lightning-caused fires that season.

Two unused lookouts stand here. The first lookout is a D-6 cupola cabin built in 1925. Jessie Louetta Wright staffed this lookout during the summer of 1943. The nights were cold at that elevation, even in summer, and she had no heat source until the Forest Service rustled up the old butane cookstove from Mount Bailey and a

Illahee Rock's current tower has stood tall since 1956.

heater from a Roseburg warehouse and hauled them up to the lookout for her. "You can't imagine the luxury of it!" she wrote in her 1982 memoir, *How High the Bounty*.

The cupola was later lowered, probably around 1956 when the 20-foot L-4 tower was built 100 feet to the west. At that time reaching the lookout required a 6-mile journey by trail. Because it took a packtrain of horses and mules a day to make one roundtrip journey to the lookout, the thirteen tons of construction materials that were necessary were transported by helicopter in less than two days.

Now a storage shed, the cupola cabin shows its age, and the tower stopped being staffed sometime around 2016. If the hatch to the catwalk is locked, you can walk around the summit to take in the sights. Bohemia Mountain and Fairview Peak are visible to the north. Neighboring peaks Harding Butte and Spring Mountain can be seen to the northeast, with Diamond Peak visible in the distance. Pointy Mount Thielsen and the rounded hump of Mount Bailey are visible to the south. Twin Lakes Mountain is visible to the southwest. If it is a really clear day, you can even see the top of Mount Jefferson 100 miles away to the northeast.

The view to the southeast looks out over the Boulder Creek Wilderness. This nineteen-thousand-acre wilderness was designated in 1984 and encompasses the watershed of Boulder Creek, a tributary of the North Umpqua River. Most of the wilderness burned in the 1996 Spring Fire and the 2008 Rattle Fire. A portion of

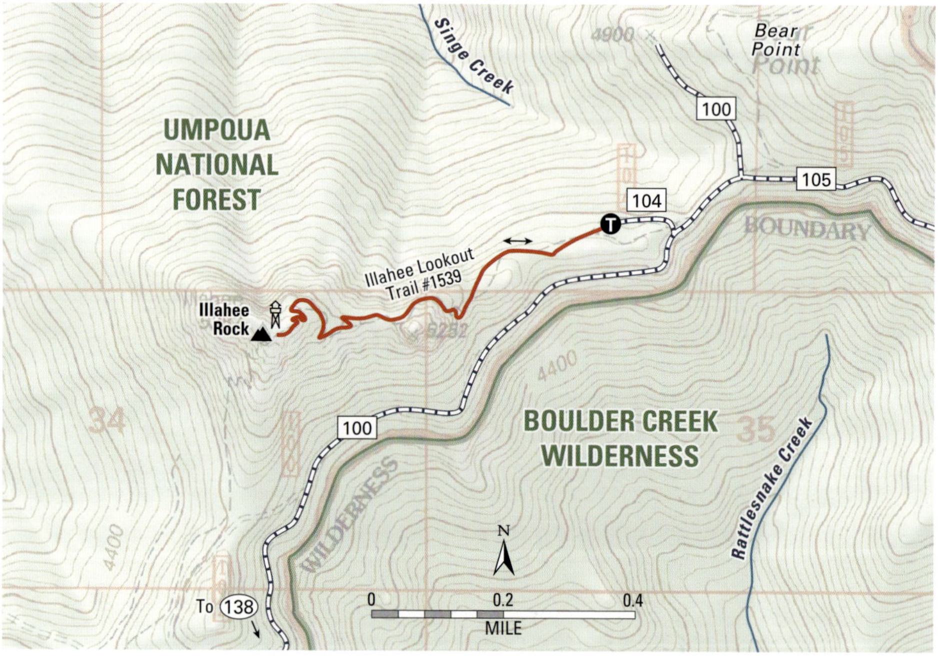

A butterfly lands on arnica on the trail to Illahee Rock.

the Rattle burn scar burned again in the 2024 Pine Bench Fire, part of the Diamond Complex Fire started by lightning. Crews wrapped the tower and removed trees and brush from the summit in case the fire got close, which it did not.

Return the way you came.

20 PIG IRON

YEAR CONSTRUCTED	LOOKOUT ACCESS	LOCATION
1950	Staffed; accessible to the public when invited in by staff; locked when not staffed	Umpqua National Forest, Diamond Lake Ranger District

Roundtrip distance: 6.8 miles
Elevation gain: 1850 feet
Lookout elevation: 4880 feet
Maps: USGS Toketee Falls and USGS Potter Mountain
GPS coordinates: 43.25285°, –122.37353°
Permits and fees: None

If you are looking for a stiff climb and a good workout, hike this lightly used trail to the top of Watson Ridge. The trail receives infrequent maintenance, so check with the Diamond Lake Ranger District for current conditions before heading out.

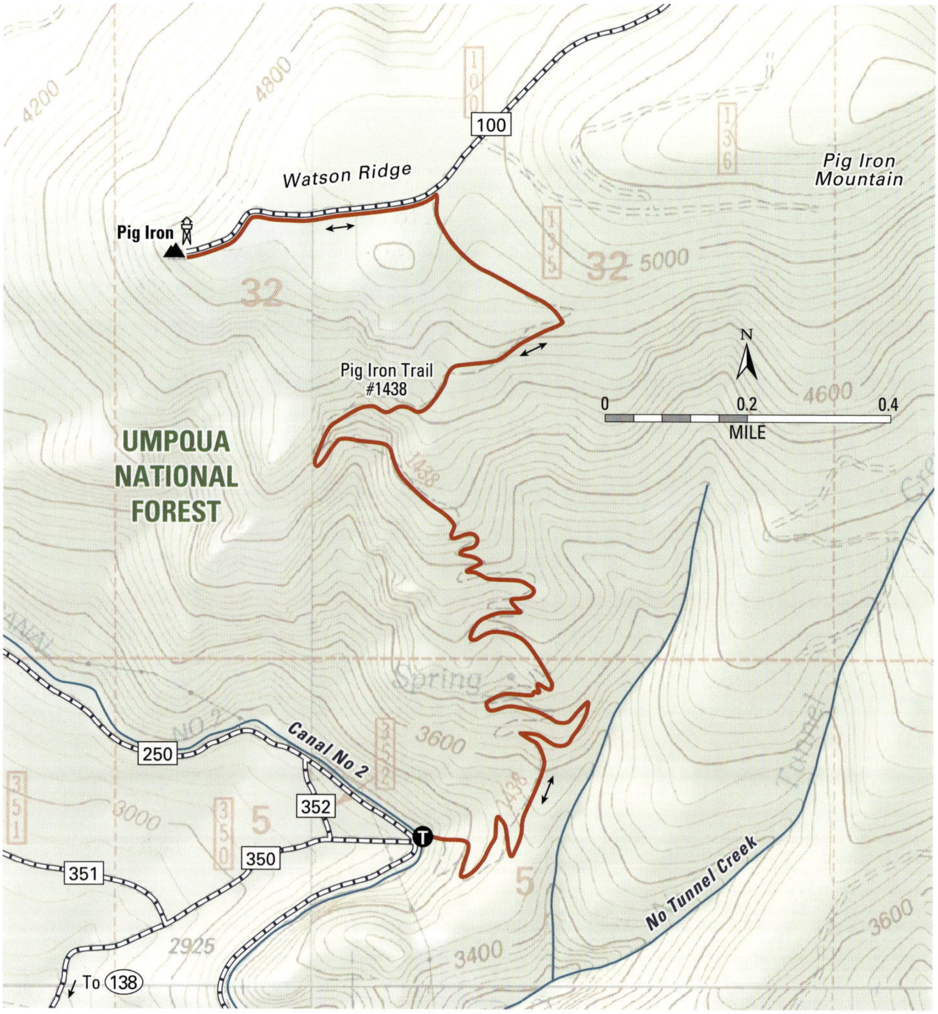

GETTING TO THE TRAILHEAD

From Glide, drive east on Oregon Route 138 for 44.7 miles. Turn left onto Forest Road 4776 at a sign for Toketee Ranger Station. (If you pass a sign for Watson Falls Day Use Area, you have gone too far.) Cross the Clearwater River, then turn right onto FR 300. Quickly reach a junction where FR 200 goes to the left; you should continue straight on FR 300.

From the junction, drive 0.5 mile, then turn left onto FR 350. Follow this road for 0.6 mile until you reach a T junction with FR 250. The trail starts on the opposite (east) side of FR 250, and there is room for two or three vehicles to park alongside the road.

ON THE TRAIL

Pig Iron Trail #1438 starts by crossing the bridge over PacifiCorp's Clearwater Canal No. 2. A sign on the far side warns visitors not to raft, float, or swim in the canal due to the canal's high velocity. The trail wastes no time in gaining elevation and immediately launches up the hillside. You will thank the trees—incense cedar, hemlock, and Douglas-fir—for their welcome shade on warm summer days.

Pig Iron Lookout is staffed in summer.

After 0.3 mile, at an opening in the trees to your right, you can glimpse Twin Lakes Mountain, once a lookout site. Continue climbing up countless switchbacks. At 1.3 miles, the trail traverses a meadow, dotted with wildflowers if you visit in early summer. At 2.3 miles, traverse another meadow with views of Mount Bailey and Garwood Butte.

After 2.9 miles, you will reach FR 100. The road is gated half a mile to your right. However, you will turn left for the final 0.4 mile of easy walking to the lookout.

The lookout sits at the west end of Watson Ridge, which once boasted three lookouts. Elephant Mountain is 8 miles to the east, where a 20-foot pole tower with an L-4 cabin was built in 1933. Six miles to the northeast is Watson Butte, where an L-4 ground cabin was built in 1937. A 10-foot tower with a 14-by-14-foot cabin was built on the other end of the ridge near Pig Iron Mountain in 1950; this is the tower you are looking at now. A trail along Watson Ridge connected all three lookouts to each other. By 1970, a road stretched the length of the ridge.

The tower on Elephant Mountain was destroyed around 1962. After being abandoned for decades, the decrepit structure on Watson Butte finally collapsed during the winter of 2021–2022. Pig Iron remains and is staffed every summer. Despite the name, it is not located on Pig Iron Mountain's summit, but west of it. It is the only staffed lookout with a view of the OR 138 corridor.

Mount Bailey and Garwood Butte (Hike 21) are visible to the southeast. Twin Lakes Mountain can be seen to the southwest. Illahee Rock (Hike 19), Spring Mountain, and Harding Butte are visible to the northwest.

How this mountain got its name is unclear; however, pig iron is a product created by smelting iron ore in blast furnaces and then used in the production of steel. Several landmarks in this area bear the name "Watson," including Watson Falls along OR 138, named after Robert James Watson, a Forest Service ranger who patrolled the forest, fought fires, and maintained trails in this area from 1905 to 1911.

The canal you crossed at the beginning of the hike is part of the North Umpqua Hydroelectric Project, which was constructed between 1947 and 1956. The project consists of eight dams, nine reservoirs and forebays, 21 miles of canals, 9.8 miles of flumes, and 5.8 miles of penstocks and tunnels. Toketee Lake, right at the foot of Pig Iron Mountain, and Lemolo Lake, at the foot of Elephant Mountain on the other end of the ridge, are both popular recreation spots that are part of this complex. As part of its license renewal process, PacifiCorp added fish passage facilities, a project that was completed in 2012.

Return the way you came.

21 GARWOOD BUTTE

YEAR CONSTRUCTED	LOOKOUT ACCESS	LOCATION
1942	Closed to the public; catwalk accessible	Umpqua National Forest, Diamond Lake Ranger District

Roundtrip distance: 3 miles
Elevation gain: 1000 feet
Lookout elevation: 7020 feet
Map: USGS Garwood Butte
GPS coordinates: 43.13018°, –122.27684°
Permits and fees: None

This quiet summit hosts an abandoned lookout cabin and provides fantastic views. With a short hike and a high possibility for solitude, you get a lot of bang for your buck.

Garwood Butte Lookout is boarded up but still a worthwhile destination.

Garwood Butte
6200
1471
Garwood Butte Trail #1471
3704
370
18
UMPQUA NATIONAL FOREST
370
To 230
3703
To 138
N
0
0.1
0.2
MILE
ROGUE RIVER–SISKIYOU NF
1470

GETTING TO THE TRAILHEAD

From the community of Chemult, head south on US Highway 97 for 9.7 miles. Turn right onto Oregon Route 138 and drive for 17.8 miles to the junction with Diamond Lake Highway (OR 230). (From Glide, drive east on OR 138 for 67 miles to this junction.) Turn west onto OR 230 and drive for 3 miles. Turn right onto Forest Road 3703, signed for Three Lakes Sno-Park. Pass the large Sno-Park area on your right and continue straight on the gravel road. Follow FR 3703 for 5.9 miles to the unsigned trailhead, where there is parking for two to three cars on the left shoulder.

Adventurous drivers with high-clearance vehicles may wish to shorten their hike by driving up FR 370 instead. This badly eroded, rock-studded dirt road is rough, rutted, unmaintained, and not suitable for most vehicles. Drive 0.2 mile past the trailhead on FR 3703, then turn right onto FR 370. The trail intersects the road at 0.4 mile and again at 1.2 miles, but neither crossing is signed. There are two pullouts just beyond the second trail crossing.

ON THE TRAIL

Garwood Butte Trail #1471 starts on the north side of FR 3703. Although it is unsigned, look for a wooden signpost just past the start of the trees. Follow the broad dirt path through a forest of mountain hemlock and subalpine fir. After 0.5 mile, reach FR 370, where you will turn right.

Follow the road for 0.2 mile. It briefly levels out and then curves to the right. Just before it starts going up again, look for the unmarked trail on your left. (You can continue the hike along the road, but taking the trail here is more direct.)

The trail heads up through the trees for 0.2 mile before emerging back onto the road, then resuming on the other side just to the left. (If you were brave enough to drive up the road, this is where you will start hiking.) The trail now switchbacks up the south slope of the butte, first through the shady forest, then emerging onto open rocky slopes, where beautiful purple cushions of phlox bloom in July. The lookout cabin appears ahead of you for the last 0.1 mile. After a last steep push to the summit, passing a dilapidated old outhouse on your right, reach the lookout, 0.8 mile from the last road crossing.

In July, watch for hummingbirds visiting the purple penstemon that grows among the rocks up here. Penstemon, sometimes called beardtongue, loves rocky habitat. There are 280 species of penstemon, and it grows only in North America. You may also see columbine and buckwheat in bloom on the summit.

Once called Bear Butte, this peak was renamed in 1946 in honor of Leroy E. Garwood, administrative officer of the Umpqua National Forest. Just two years before his death in 1944, he helped establish the lookout. At the time of the renaming,

The catwalk on the Garwood Butte Lookout offers superb, far-ranging views.

Roseburg's *News-Review* reported that the name change had the added advantage of making one less feature with the name "bear," as the Umpqua National Forest had six Bear Creeks, two Bear Buttes, two Bear Camps, one Bear Bluff, one Bear Bones, one Bear Gulch, one Bear Lake, one Bear Wallows, one Bear Trap Mountain, and two Bear Mountains.

The L-4 cabin on Garwood Butte was built in 1942. It has not been staffed since the 1960s, and although restoration efforts were underway at some point before 2015, those have stalled. The woodstove and most of the furniture have been removed from the lookout, along with the firefinder. Although the cabin is closed up, the catwalk makes a great place to sit and take a break to soak up the scenery.

Look to the north to see Diamond Peak, Middle Sister, and South Sister. To the east Mount Bailey's 8368-foot bulk dominates the view. This shield volcano was the site of a D-6 cupola lookout from 1923 to 1952. Why the lookout on Garwood continued to be used instead of the higher one on Mount Bailey is unclear, but it may have been due to easier access. Even though FR 370 had not yet been constructed, the trail up Garwood Butte was still shorter than the trail up Mount Bailey. (The trail to the summit of that peak still exists and is enjoyed by hikers who do not mind the 10-mile roundtrip hike with 3000 feet of elevation gain.)

To the southeast you can see Mount Scott, Llao Rock, Garfield Peak, and Hillman Butte. To the south are pointy Union Peak and Mount McLoughlin. Between them in the distance on an exceptionally clear day, you might be able to make out the shape of Mount Shasta, even though it is 75 miles away in California. The western landscape is mostly blocked by trees.

Diamond Lake is just 6 miles away to the east but is out of view, obstructed by Mount Bailey. This three-thousand-acre lake is a popular recreation area for camping, swimming, boating, and fishing. In 2006, the Oregon Department of Fish & Wildlife had to kill every single fish in the lake in order to eradicate 90 million invasive tui chub fish, which had taken over the lake and marred its water quality, outcompeting the stocked trout for food. The lake is now closely monitored to prevent a repeat chub invasion.

Return the way you came.

22 HERSHBERGER MOUNTAIN

YEAR CONSTRUCTED	LOOKOUT ACCESS	LOCATION
1925	Open to the public for day use when not staffed; closed to overnight use	Rogue River–Siskiyou National Forest, High Cascades Ranger District

Roundtrip distance: 7.9 miles
Elevation gain: 1400 feet
Lookout elevation: 6200 feet
Map: USGS Fish Mountain
GPS coordinates: 43.03293°, –122.49635°
Permits and fees: None

Hike through a forest of big trees in the Rogue–Umpqua Divide Wilderness to a historic cupola lookout. The trail passes through some areas burned in 2017, so call the High Cascades Ranger District for current conditions.

GETTING TO THE TRAILHEAD

From Tiller, turn northeast onto S. Umpqua Road, which becomes Forest Road 28. Drive for 5.1 miles, then turn right onto FR 29. Drive 14.5 paved miles, then 3 gravel miles to a junction. Turn right onto gravel FR 2947. Drive for 2.3 miles and keep left to stay on FR 2947 at the junction with FR 300. At 1.7 miles past that junction, keep right at a junction with FR 400.

After a total of 8 good gravel miles on FR 2947, reach the Cripple Camp trailhead parking area on your right, at a spot where the road curves left, where there is room for approximately six cars.

The cupola cabin on Hershberger Mountain is listed on the National Register of Historic Places.

ON THE TRAIL

Cripple Camp Trail #1435 starts on the north side of the parking area next to a signboard. A plaque on the left side of the trail commemorates Homer Radford, who built the Cripple Camp shelter with Howard Haskell and Ira Poole in 1937. The trail ascends gradually through the forest for 0.3 mile before descending. After hiking 0.7 mile from the trailhead, reach the junction with Acker Divide Trail #1437 and turn right.

Just 0.1 mile beyond the junction, pass a side trail on the right leading to the Cripple Camp shelter, which faces a lovely meadow. Shelters like these were built for administrative use; at a time when traveling long distances across roadless forest required camping out overnight, Forest Service employees and packers stayed in them. Such shelters, many of which were built by the Civilian Conservation Corps in the 1930s, were often situated near water sources and meadows where livestock could graze. As outdoor recreation increased, the shelters were used by the public as well. Most of the shelters built in the early twentieth century have since collapsed, burned, or been removed, but some like Cripple Camp still stand. Note the enormous Douglas-firs here, and keep an eye out for bog orchids, leopard lilies, and larkspur if you hike here in summer.

Beyond the shelter, the trail travels along the edge of the meadow, becoming faint at times. Enter a section of forest burned in the 2017 Pup Fire, where fireweed blooms in abundance in August.

Leave the burned section behind, cross a creek bed, and continue through unburned forest. Pass a large meadow on your left. This long rectangular meadow stretches east away from the trail, and marshy Toad Lake sits out of sight near the far end.

The trail travels through a forest of hemlock, grand fir, and incense cedar before reaching the junction with Pup Prairie Trail #1434 on the right (mistakenly signed for Rogue–Umpqua Divide), 1.6 miles from the trailhead. Continue straight.

The trail emerges from the trees into Pup Prairie 2.6 miles from the trailhead, where paintbrush, lupine, and columbine bloom in summer. At the far edge of this lush green meadow, the trail crosses Lonewoman Creek and begins climbing uphill through burned trees before reaching a trailhead located at a switchback on FR 530. Rogue–Umpqua Divide Trail #1470 heads north from here; however, you will hike uphill on the road for 0.6 mile, gaining 500 feet. This is a rough, rocky road for vehicles, but it is easily navigated on foot. The road ends at a small parking area next to a toilet and garage-turned-residence for World War II Aircraft Warning Service (AWS) spotters. From the parking area, climb the short trail up to the lookout, which is surrounded by a lovely rock garden full of paintbrush and buckwheat that bloom in July.

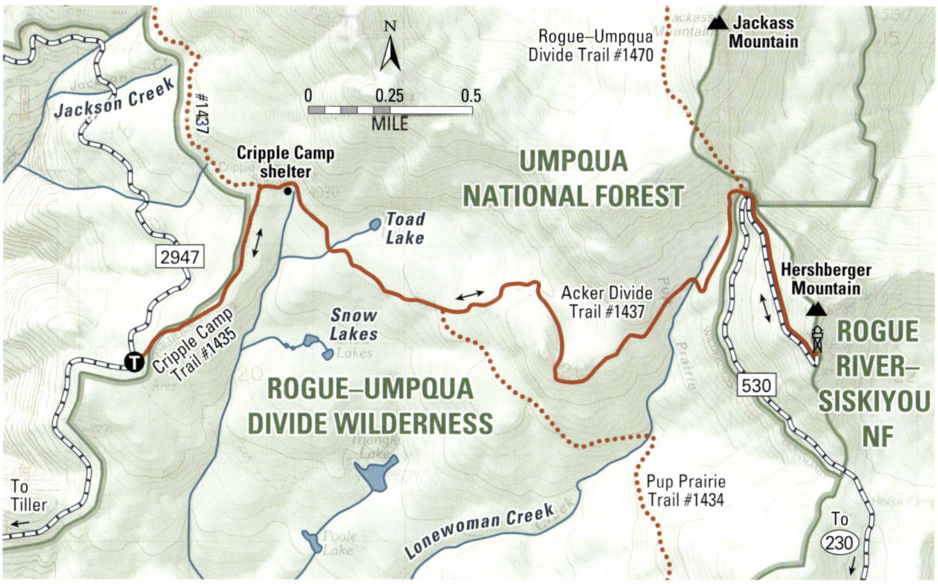

The lookout does not sit on the 6285-foot summit, but rather on a point 85 feet lower and 0.1 mile south of there. The view to the north is blocked by said summit, but Mount Bailey and Mount Thielsen are visible to the east. Mount McLoughlin is visible to the south, along with the distinctive rock formation known as Rabbit Ears. The national forest boundary goes right over the top of Hershberger Mountain, so the land to the east is in the Rogue River–Siskiyou National Forest and the land to the west is in the Umpqua National Forest.

The 12-by-12-foot D-6 cupola ground cabin on Hershberger Mountain was built in 1925, one of only a few such lookouts still standing in Oregon. Clyde Onn served as a lookout on Hershberger Mountain from the late 1920s through World War II. He and his wife also spent the winter of 1942–1943 working as aircraft observers for the AWS. Snowbound at 6200 feet for the winter, the couple received groceries and other supplies via sled dog teams.

The Forest Service worked with volunteers in the 1990s to rehabilitate the lookout, including reshingling the roof. It was listed on the National Register of Historic Places in 2000. In 2012 it received another round of rehabilitation work. There were plans to add the lookout to the rental program, but those never came to fruition. In the summer of 2017, lightning started the Pup Fire along with several other fires, which became known as the High Cascades Complex, ultimately burning 72,000 acres. Crews wrapped the lookout in fire-resistant material to protect it. The fire burned most of the trees on the slopes of the mountain, but the lookout was saved. It is staffed as needed during thunderstorms and emergencies.

Cripple Camp Shelter faces a lovely meadow.

Hershberger Mountain is named after George Hershberger, who trapped and hunted in this area and whose family lived near Central Point. The peak sits just outside the boundary of the thirty-five-thousand-acre Rogue–Umpqua Divide Wilderness, which was designated in 1984. The wilderness gets its name from the fact that the mountains here separate the drainages of the Rogue River to the east and the Umpqua River to the west.

Return the way you came.

23 ACKER ROCK

YEAR CONSTRUCTED	LOOKOUT ACCESS	LOCATION
1964	Closed to the public for day use; open for seasonal overnight rental by reservation	Umpqua National Forest, Tiller Ranger District

Roundtrip distance: 3 miles
Elevation gain: 950 feet
Lookout elevation: 4110 feet
Map: USGS Acker Rock
GPS coordinates: 43.05406°, –122.63119°
Permits and fees: None

This lookout—named for Hiram L. Acker, a Texan who settled nearby in 1913—is perched incongruously atop a giant rock in the middle of the forest. Because there is so little space on the summit around the lookout, consider visiting outside the rental season (before August 1 or after November 15).

GETTING TO THE TRAILHEAD

From Tiller, turn northeast onto S. Umpqua Road, which becomes Forest Road 28. Drive for 18.5 miles, then turn right onto paved FR 29. Drive for 5.7 miles, then turn left onto gravel FR 2838. Drive 1.5 miles to the intersection with gated FR 950, where you can park anywhere along the shoulders of these roads; just do not block the gate. (If you rented this lookout, you will have received a code to unlock the gate and drive through.)

ON THE TRAIL

Walk around the gate and start hiking up FR 950. The road is lined with bracken ferns, sword ferns, and Douglas-fir. You will also see incense cedar, which grows primarily in southwest Oregon and Northern California. The tree is well adapted to the wet, mild winters and hot, dry summers of the region. Its thick, fibrous bark with vertical furrows is used by Native Americans to make baskets, and its leaves for food seasoning.

In June, you will see paintbrush and rhododendrons in bloom along the road. After 0.4 mile, Acker Rock's forested "backside" appears ahead of you, although the lookout itself is not visible from here. You also get a view to the south that includes Abbott Butte and Butler Butte, both of which are former lookout sites. The road continues west, hugging the rock cliffs. At 0.6 mile, pass an unsigned trail on the left. This is the climbers' trail heading to the base of the climbing routes; you will continue on the road.

The road makes a sharp left turn, then at 1.1 miles you will reach a small parking area. The road ends here and Acker Rock Trail #1585 begins. Climb south through a forest carpeted with vanilla leaf and salal. June brings bleeding heart, stonecrop, and small-leaved montia. The trail makes several switchbacks, then emerges from the

A fenced walkway leads to Acker Rock Lookout.

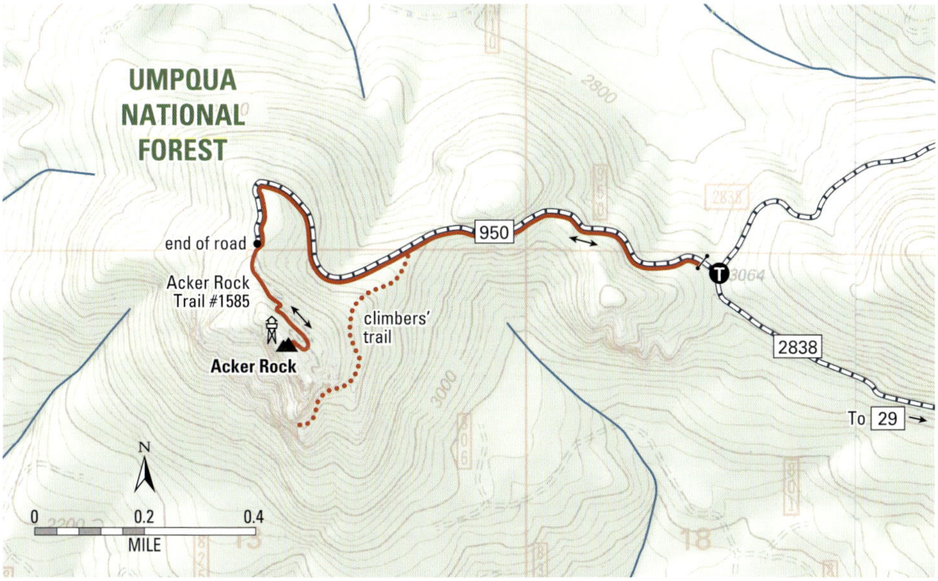

trees onto the open slopes below the lookout. Pass an open-air composting toilet on the left (a loo with a fine view!), then reach the bottom of the wooden stairs up to the lookout. Climb the stairs, then follow the fenced walkway to the lookout. Be mindful of renters if they are present and respect their privacy.

You can see in all directions: To the north are Dumont Butte, Black Butte, Cavitt Mountain, and Quartz Mountain. The pointy peak to the northeast is Black Rock, not to be confused with Little Black Rock, a peak 1600 feet lower just in front of it, both of which are former lookout sites. To the east are the peaks of the Rogue-Umpqua Divide Wilderness, including Rattlesnake Mountain, Highrock Mountain, and Hershberger Mountain (Hike 22). To the south are Abbott Butte and Cougar Butte. To the west are numerous smaller peaks and buttes, such as Deadman Mountain, among others.

It is impossible to get the full scale or scope of Acker Rock while you are on top of it, but it is large enough to support twenty established climbing routes, popular with rock climbers. (Check the satellite images on Google Maps to get a sense of how big Acker Rock is.) Climbers will find the Acker Rock buckwheat that grows here. Only discovered in 2009 and endemic to Acker Rock, it has been found growing on the rock's southwest and southeast vertical faces. This spot is also excellent for bird-watching—especially for bald eagles and peregrine falcons, which often soar past right at eye level. Do not drop anything over the railing or you will never get it back (unless a climber can retrieve it for you, which is rare).

Acker Rock Lookout offers excellent vistas and opportunities to spot soaring birds.

Most lookouts in the Cascades have been built on buttes or peaks, but a few were built on rock formations like Acker Rock. The Forest Service needed a lookout with eyes on this area of the forest, so an L-4 cabin was built here in 1932. All supplies were delivered by pack string from the nearest trailhead down by the South Umpqua River, 2400 feet below, a trip that was 3 miles one-way and required fording the river.

After three decades, the lookout was in bad shape and needed to be removed. In 1963, windows, furnishings, and other items were salvaged from the lookout before it was dismantled and pushed over the north side of Acker Rock to be piled and burned to make way for a new cabin. A helicopter made numerous trips back and forth to transport eight tons of material and tools from a nearby logging landing to the rock's top. The new R-6 lookout was completed the following year. At some point in the late 1970s or early 1980s, the road was built and the old access trail from the river was abandoned.

The lookout was added to the rental program in the 1990s and is available to rent August 1 through November 15. It contains a bed, table and chairs, cookstove, heater, and even a propane fridge!

Return the way you came.

24 THE WATCHMAN

YEAR CONSTRUCTED	LOOKOUT ACCESS	LOCATION
1932	Closed to the public	Crater Lake National Park

Roundtrip distance: 1.8 miles
Elevation gain: 390 feet
Lookout elevation: 8010 feet
Map: USGS Crater Lake West
GPS coordinates: 42.94579°, –122.16926°
Permits and fees: An entrance pass is required, the fee varying by type of vehicle and season. Cash is not accepted, but America the Beautiful Passes are.

This short hike to an old lookout on Crater Lake's west rim provides views of the surrounding peaks and the stunningly blue waters of the lake below. Because it's in a national park, pets are prohibited on this trail.

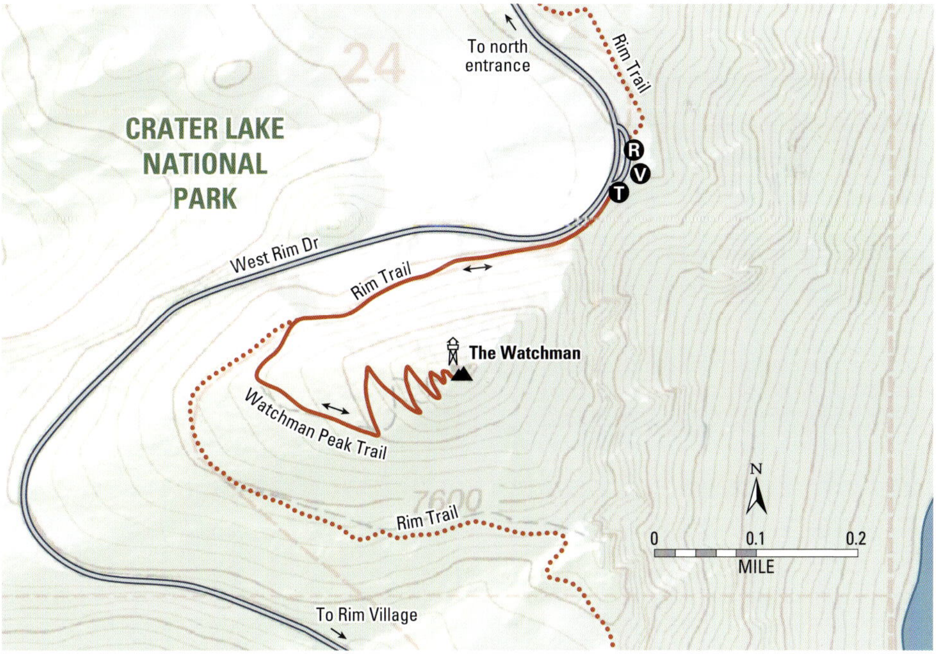

GETTING TO THE TRAILHEAD

From the park's north entrance booth, drive south for 8.3 miles. Pass the junction with East Rim Drive on the left and stay right. Drive 2.2 miles farther to The Watchman Overlook parking area on the left. If the parking lot is full, there is legal parking along both shoulders of the road north of the overlook.

If you are coming from the Annie Spring entrance booth on the south side of the park, drive north on Munson Valley Road toward Rim Village for 6.3 miles, then turn left to follow West Rim Drive another 3.9 miles to The Watchman Overlook parking area on the right. Toilets are available.

ON THE TRAIL

The trailhead is also an overlook with a fantastic view looking out over the lake, and not surprisingly it is a busy spot. It's also popular with photographers, who often congregate at sunrise. To the south you can see The Watchman towering above you.

After checking out the scenery, follow the sidewalk south along the road. The pavement ends and the gravel Rim Trail heads west along the base of the mountain. Watch for western pasqueflower, whose white flowers transform into showy seed heads with feathery strands. You will also see the low-growing, vivid purple blooms of penstemon.

The Watchman Lookout has been overlooking the lake since 1932.

View of Crater Lake from The Watchman

If you are wondering why this path is so wide, this was the route of the old road before the current one was built. A rim road was constructed around the lake from 1913 to 1917, but the narrow, curvy road quickly became obsolete as cars became bigger and heavier. A new road was surveyed in 1931 and 1932, and by 1935, it had been paved. The sections of the old road that had not been incorporated into the new one were torn up; however, this portion at the base of The Watchman was left intact.

A large snowfield can linger on this section of trail into late July, so cross with caution. Just past the snowfield, the Rim Trail continues to the right. You will take the left fork onto Watchman Peak Trail.

The sandy trail climbs through a forest of mountain hemlock. You'll also find whitebark pine, which can grow to be more than a thousand years old. (The oldest known whitebark pine in the park is five hundred years old; the oldest documented whitebark pine anywhere, at 1,270 years old, is in Idaho.) In July, you will also see patches of purple phlox blooming on the hillside next to the trail.

The trail makes several switchbacks as it climbs up the mountain. Reach a short flight of stone stairs that lead up to a stone-lined viewing area in front of the locked lookout—a view that will knock your socks off compared to the one from the overlook by your car. The entire lake is visible from up here, along with Wizard Island directly below. The lake's intense blue color is due to the fact that there is very little else in the lake except 4.6 trillion gallons of pure water. The water absorbs all colors of the light spectrum except for blue, which bounces back and gives the lake its color.

Across the lake is Mount Scott (Hike 25), and to the right are Applegate Peak, Eagle Crags, and Garfield Peak (which has a trail to the summit). To the southwest you can see Mount Shasta, Mount McLoughlin, and the rocky point of Union Peak (a former lookout site that you can still hike to). To the north you can see Mount Bailey in the distance, the jagged edges of Hillman Peak just north of the trailhead, and Llao Rock beyond, farther along the rim.

The Watchman got its name when the US Geological Survey set up a watch point here in 1886, when surveyors sounded the lake's depth with piano wire from a twenty-six-foot-long rowboat called the *Cleetwood*. They recorded a maximum water depth of 1996 feet, pretty close to the current depth of 1943 feet as measured by modern sonar.

The rustic two-story stone and wood structure you see here today is the original lookout that was built in 1932. The 10-by-16-foot lookout has a lower story, in addition to a 14-by-20-foot wing that extends to the south. The lower level was designed to be a museum and observatory for the public, but it has since closed. It was listed on the National Register of Historic Places in 1988. After years of harsh winters, the rundown lookout underwent a $430,000 rehabilitation in 1999 and 2000, when the catwalk, the exterior stairway, the museum roof, and the interiors of the lookout and museum were all restored.

Return the way you came.

25 MOUNT SCOTT

YEAR CONSTRUCTED	LOOKOUT ACCESS	LOCATION
1952	Closed to the public	Crater Lake National Park

Roundtrip distance: 4.4 miles
Elevation gain: 1250 feet
Lookout elevation: 8930 feet
Map: USGS Crater Lake East
GPS coordinates: 42.92919°, –122.02983°
Permits and fees: An entrance pass is required, the fee varying by type of vehicle and season. Cash is not accepted, but America the Beautiful Passes are.

Mount Scott was named after Levi Scott, a pioneer who traveled the Oregon Trail in 1844 and founded the town of Scottsburg in Douglas County along the Umpqua River. His namesake is the highest point in Crater Lake National Park and the tenth-highest peak in Oregon's Cascade Range, plus it boasts the highest-elevation fire lookout in

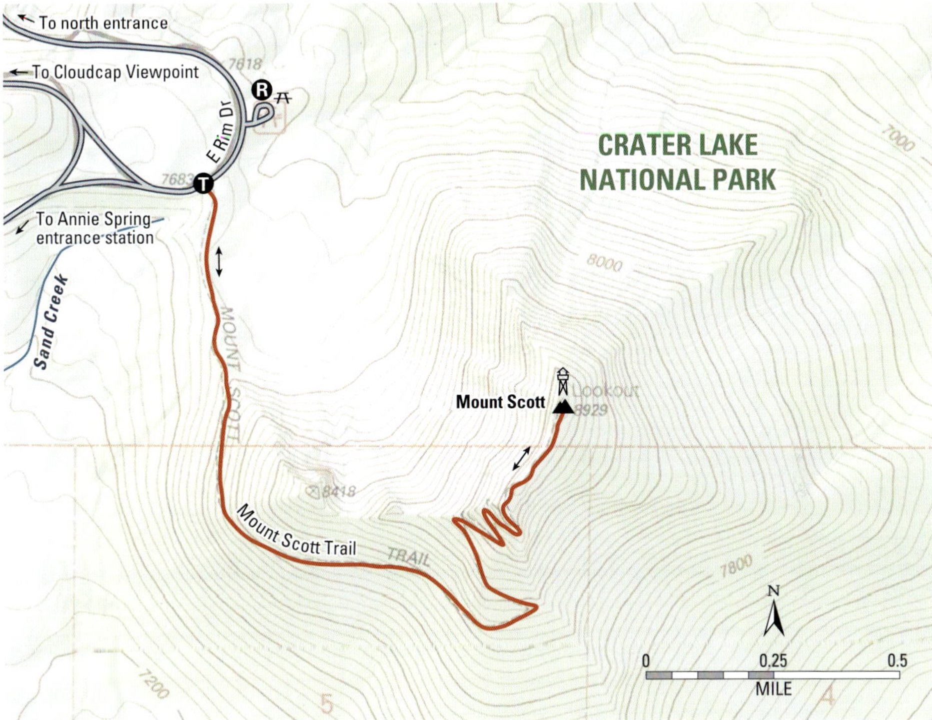

Oregon. But do not let those statistics deter you; thanks to a high-elevation trailhead and a well-graded trail, this hike is not as daunting as it sounds. Because it's in a national park, pets are prohibited.

GETTING TO THE TRAILHEAD

From the park's north entrance booth, drive south for 8.3 miles, then turn left onto East Rim Drive. Drive for 10.9 miles until you reach the trailhead parking area on the left side of the road.

From the Annie Spring entrance booth, drive north on Munson Valley Road for 3.9 miles, then turn right onto East Rim Drive. Drive 12.2 miles to the trailhead parking area on your right.

There is no toilet at the trailhead itself, but just north of the parking area on the east side of the road is a small picnic area with a toilet.

ON THE TRAIL

The trail starts at the southwest end of the parking area, where it immediately begins by heading south, crossing a pumice field dotted with whitebark pine. Mount Scott

and its fire lookout loom above you to the left. Keep in mind that patches of snow can linger here into August.

After 0.3 mile, the trail enters the forest and starts climbing. The higher you climb, the more you will be able to see to the west. In July and August, paintbrush and penstemon bloom here. The trail then curves to the left, traversing the south-facing pumice slope of the peak as it heads east, with views on your right (to the south).

The trail switchbacks uphill to the left, then makes four more switchbacks. (Do not cut the switchbacks here, as it causes erosion and could send rocks tumbling down onto hikers on the trail below.) The trail rounds a corner and the lookout appears ahead of you. Cross a sandy saddle, then make a final push up a rocky slope to the bouldery summit.

The first lookout on Mount Scott was a cupola cabin built in the 1920s. In the 1930s, a wooden tank was erected below the summit with the intention of collecting winter snow to serve as the lookout's summer water supply, but the system didn't work as planned because the tank failed to collect enough snow. By the late 1940s, the cabin had survived more than two decades of harsh winter weather, becoming so unstable that accurate azimuth readings were almost impossible.

In 1952, the cabin was replaced with the current lookout, a two-story 14-by-14-foot design with a lower level for storage. Today, as you look up at the second story, it appears as though the catwalk has been removed, but if you look closer you can see it is actually an unusual fold-up design, with the deteriorating decking folded upright against the sides of the cabin. While the lookout has not been staffed in many years, it now houses seismic monitoring equipment for the US Geological Survey. It is locked up and closed to the public, but you can walk around the summit to enjoy the views.

To the north, pointy Mount Thielsen dominates the horizon, with numerous other peaks visible to its right—Maiden Peak, the Three Sisters, and Mount Bachelor, among others. Yamsay Mountain is visible to the east. Mount Shasta (100 miles away in California) and Mount McLoughlin dominate the southern skyline, with Union Peak to the southwest. Directly across the lake are The Watchman and Hillman Peak.

Crater Lake was formed 7,700 years ago when Mount Mazama erupted, sending an explosion of 12.2 cubic miles of rock, ash, and pumice high into the air. Ash from this powerful eruption ended up as far away as Saskatchewan and Utah. The hollowed-out volcano collapsed in on itself, creating a large caldera that eventually ended up being 5 miles across. Scientists think it took 420 to 740 years for the lake to fill.

OPPOSITE *Crossing the sandy saddle on the final approach to Mount Scott Lookout*

The Klamath people, who have occupied south-central Oregon and north-central California for more than thirteen thousand years, witnessed the eruption of Mount Mazama, which features in their legend that tells of Llao of the Below World and Skell of the Above World battling to a fiery end. They call the lake *giiwas*, which means "a sacred place."

The first white men to lay eyes on the lake were a party of prospectors led by John Wesley Hillman. In July 1853 while looking for gold, they instead came across this huge lake, whose color prompted them to call it Deep Blue Lake (a name that clearly didn't stick). Crater Lake National Park was established in 1902, becoming the fifth-oldest national park in the US and the only national park in Oregon.

Return the way you came.

26 SNOW CAMP MOUNTAIN

YEAR CONSTRUCTED	LOOKOUT ACCESS	LOCATION
2004	Closed to the public for day use; open for seasonal overnight rental by reservation	Rogue River–Siskiyou National Forest, Gold Beach Ranger District

Roundtrip distance: 6.4 miles
Elevation gain: 1420 feet
Lookout elevation: 4220 feet
Map: USGS Collier Butte
GPS coordinates: 42.36455°, –124.17506°
Permits and fees: None

Hike to a rentable lookout that was rebuilt after the original burned in the 2002 Biscuit Fire. Most of the route has burned twice over, but the landscape is awash with vegetation that is regrowing, like the wildflowers you can enjoy in June. It will be several decades before there is shade again, however, so save this one for a cooler day.

GETTING TO THE TRAILHEAD

Drive to the north end of Gold Beach on US Highway 101 and turn east onto Jerry's Flat Road, at the south end of the Isaac Lee Patterson Bridge. Take this winding paved road for 13 miles, then turn right onto Forest Road 3313. Drive 8.2 miles of

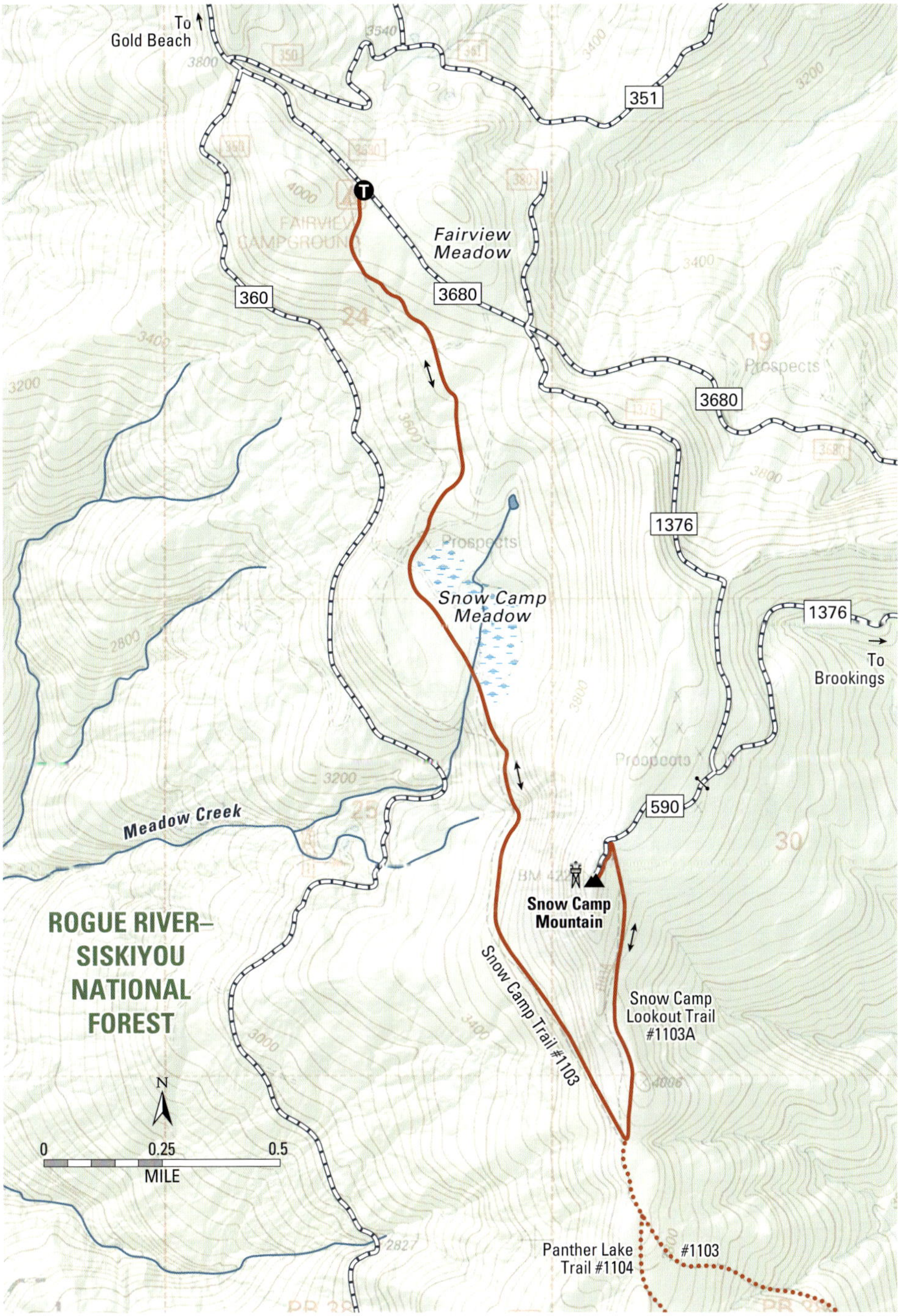
To Gold Beach
351
3680
360
Fairview Meadow
FAIRVIEW CAMPGROUND
24
19
Prospects
1376
Snow Camp Meadow
To Brookings
590
Meadow Creek
25
30
Snow Camp Mountain
ROGUE RIVER–SISKIYOU NATIONAL FOREST
Snow Camp Trail #1103
Snow Camp Lookout Trail #1103A
N
0
0.25
0.5
MILE
Panther Lake Trail #1104
#1103

good gravel road, then reach a junction with FR 3680, where you will turn left. Drive 3.4 miles, always staying on the main gravel road at junctions with side roads and keeping right at the junction where FR 3318 goes left.

Drive another 3.4 miles past that junction, then turn right onto an unsigned short gravel spur and park in a grove of towering hemlocks. On some topo maps, this is labeled Fairview Campground. Although there is a lone picnic table here and flat ground to camp, this is not an established campground and there is no toilet.

ON THE TRAIL

Snow Camp Trail #1103 starts out next to the Snow Camp trailhead signboard. You will first descend, soon entering a short stretch of burned forest where Port Orford cedar and Douglas-fir, among others, are growing back in abundance. Bracken fern grows alongside the trail and rhododendrons display a profusion of pink blooms in June.

Next, enter a section of forest where you will find huge hemlocks; they didn't die, but their lower trunks were singed black. At the 0.9-mile mark, the trail exits the forest and enters an open area of burned snags, Snow Camp Mountain and its lookout appearing on the left. Ponderosa pines are growing back in this burn area, along with chinquapin, manzanita, and snowbrush.

Snow Camp Mountain Lookout bathed in golden sunlight

The trail skirts along the edge of Snow Camp Meadow, ringed by live trees that survived the fire. Yellow irises bloom along the trail in June. At 1.5 miles, cross gurgling Meadow Creek, which originates from within the meadow and flows into the Pistol River west of here. There is no bridge, but rocks and logs will aid in your crossing. On the opposite side, the trail climbs, then levels out, then climbs again as it traverses the west slope of Snow Camp Mountain. Because the trees all burned here (first in 2002 and again in 2017), there are views to the west, but there is also no shade.

Paintbrush and groundsel in bloom along the trail to Snow Camp Mountain

The trail climbs upward until it reaches an unsigned junction at 2.6 miles. Any signage that once existed here has burned up and not been replaced. The Snow Camp Trail continues 3 miles southeast to the Cedar Camp trailhead on FR 1376, and Panther Lake Trail #1104 branches off, heading south 1 mile to an old seldom-used trailhead on FR 369. You will turn left onto Snow Camp Lookout Trail #1103A. The trail climbs, traverses the east slope of Snow Camp Mountain, then meets up with FR 590 at 3.1 miles, where you will come to a large parking area for renters whose vehicles cannot make it up the steep final stretch to the lookout. Turn left and head up the steep gravel road for 0.1 mile to the lookout. Do not disturb the renters if they are present.

The wind often blows fierce and strong on this exposed summit, but the views are worth it. Collier Butte is the close peak to the northwest, just 2.5 miles away. To the west you can see the bulky mountain known as Big Craggies. Bosley Butte is visible to the south. (It hosted a lookout until 2012, when it burned down in a suspected act of vandalism. Since the site already had remotely monitored cameras, the lookout was not rebuilt.) Signal Butte is to the west, along with the Pacific Ocean. If you walk out to the northern end of the summit, you can look down on Snow Camp Meadow, which you passed earlier.

Snow Camp Mountain has been a lookout site for well over a century, first with a tent camp, then a 14-by-14-foot cabin built around 1925. This was torn down in 1958 and replaced with an R-6 ground cabin. However, once the lookout stopped being staffed after 1972, it fell into disrepair. Only after restoration efforts in 1989 was the cabin added to the rental program the following year.

When the lightning-caused Biscuit Fire started in August 2002, crews wrapped the lookout in fire-resistant material and cleared vegetation around it, but the cabin burned anyway, along with the outhouse. In a remarkably short turnaround time, the lookout was rebuilt when a Crescent City contractor and his crew donated thousands of dollars' worth of labor, completing the new cabin two years later. It was not an R-6 cabin like its predecessor, but a replica of similar design.

The cabin was again threatened by the lightning-caused Chetco Bar Fire in 2017, which burned the entire west side of the mountain. Crews wrapped the lookout, and this time, even though the vegetation around it was burned, the cabin remarkably survived. The lookout had to be wrapped again in 2023 when the human-caused Flat Fire started 14 miles to the north near Agness and burned south toward Snow Camp Mountain. Thankfully, this fire was contained before it made it all the way to the lookout.

This lookout—containing a cot, a woodstove, a cabinet, and a table, and two chairs—is rentable from June through September. It is surrounded by a wooden deck on all four sides and has a picnic table out front for renters who are lucky enough to get some wind-free days for eating outside. Because it is so far from the light pollution of any big cities, the stargazing on moonless nights is incredible.

Return the way you came.

27 PEARSOLL PEAK

YEAR CONSTRUCTED	LOOKOUT ACCESS	LOCATION
1954	Closed to the public	Rogue River–Siskiyou National Forest, Wild Rivers Ranger District

Roundtrip distance: 5.4 miles
Elevation gain: 1400 feet
Lookout elevation: 5100 feet
Map: USGS Pearsoll Peak
GPS coordinates: 42.28090°, –123.83067°
Permits and fees: None

The Sand Mountain Society restored Pearsoll Peak Lookout in 1991.

Gaze into the heart of the Kalmiopsis Wilderness from this lofty perch. But avoid this hike on a hot day; wildfires have destroyed all the shady trees along the route. Note that to prevent the spread of Port Orford disease, the last 4.5 miles of road to the trailhead are gated during the wet season.

GETTING TO THE TRAILHEAD

From Grants Pass, drive US Highway 199 south for 20 miles to the community of Selma and turn right onto paved Illinois River Road, which becomes Forest Road 4103. Drive this winding road for 10.9 curvy miles. There are many blind curves, and a lot of traffic on summer weekends, so proceed carefully. Where the road bends

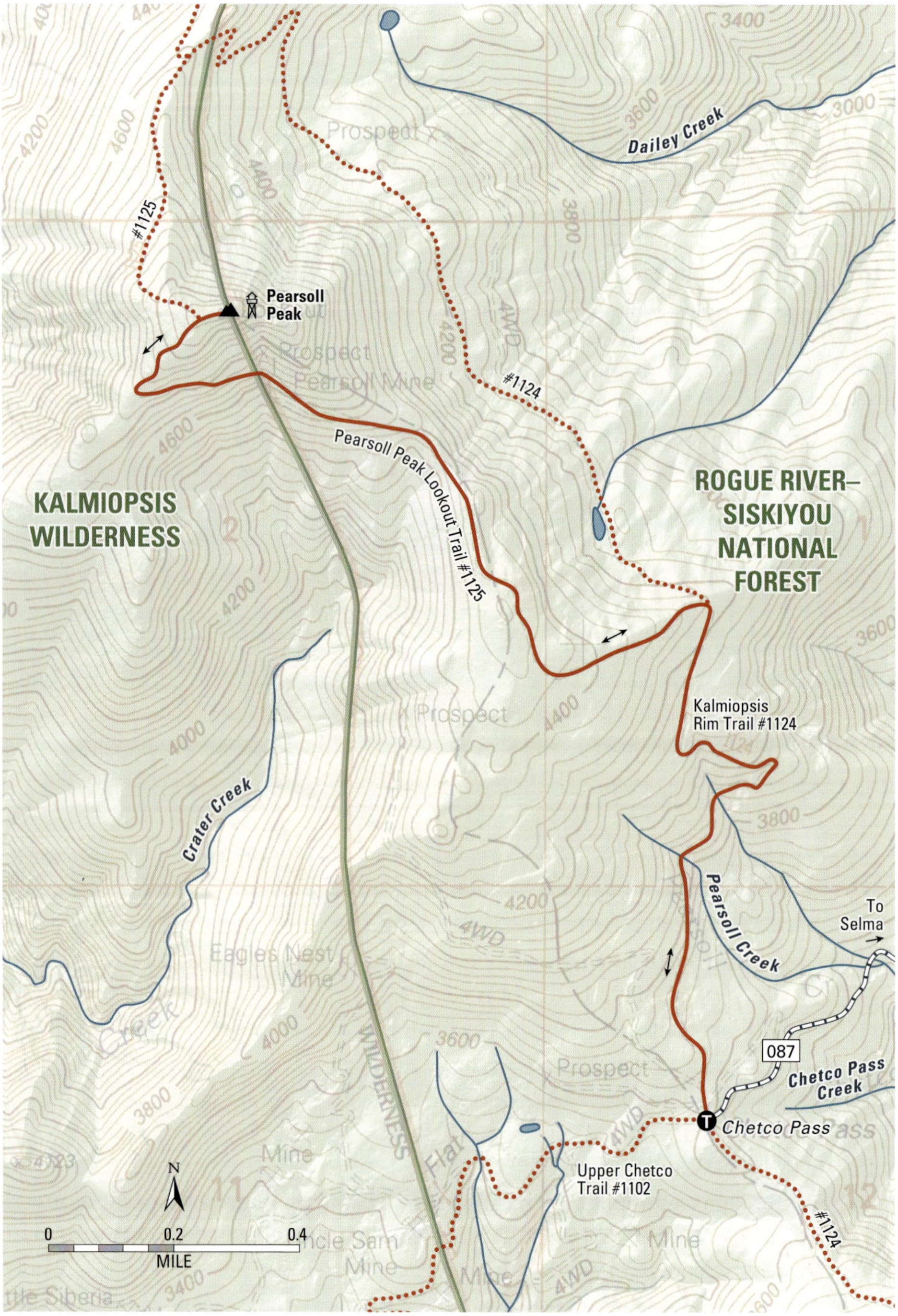
Pearsoll Peak
KALMIOPSIS WILDERNESS
ROGUE RIVER–SISKIYOU NATIONAL FOREST
Pearsoll Peak Lookout Trail #1125
Kalmiopsis Rim Trail #1124
#1125
#1124
Dailey Creek
Crater Creek
Pearsoll Creek
Chetco Pass Creek
Chetco Pass
Upper Chetco Trail #1102
To Selma
087
Prospect
Pearsoll Mine
Eagles Nest Mine
WILDERNESS
4WD
0
0.2
0.4
MILE
N

sharply right, turn left onto gravel FR 087, which descends steeply for half a mile down to the Illinois River. Cross the one-lane bridge, which may be submerged during periods of high water—if this is the case, you should proceed at your own risk and only in a high-clearance vehicle.

Beyond the bridge is a 100-foot stretch of rough road that is not suitable for low-clearance cars. On the left is a parking area with a toilet. McCaleb Ranch Boy Scout Camp is to the right, and the owners allow people to park and recreate in the river at this spot. Straight ahead, follow FR 087 through a gate that is generally open from June 1 to September 30 (before you leave home, call the ranger station to confirm).

If the gate is closed or you are driving a low-clearance car, you will need to park across from the Boy Scout camp and start walking. (I do not recommend visiting when the gate is closed, as it is a long trudge up a shadeless road from here.) Otherwise, drive straight through the open gate and follow the road 4.5 miles to its end at Chetco Pass, where you will park. The road gains 2500 feet from river to trailhead and has several rough and steep sections. It is not suitable for low-clearance cars, and four-wheel drive is recommended.

ON THE TRAIL

On the north side of the trailhead parking area, locate the route of an old mining road, which now serves as a trail, the trailhead itself unsigned. You may have to walk around the end of the wooden fence to reach it. Old mining roads branch out in numerous directions from here, and the fence is a futile attempt to prevent vehicles from driving into the wilderness. Note the rusted body of an old abandoned truck at the trailhead and marvel at how such a vehicle ever made it up here.

Upper Chetco Trail #1102 descends west down to the Chetco River. Kalmiopsis Rim Trail #1124 runs along the eastern boundary of this wilderness; you will follow this trail north. (Heading south from Chetco Pass, the trail goes over Eagle Mountain, along Whetstone Butte, and ends at Onion Camp on FR 141.)

Follow the road uphill, crossing Pearsoll Creek at the 0.5-mile mark. Wildflowers bloom along the route in June, brightening this fire-damaged landscape where burned snags dot the hills. At 1.1 miles, the road reaches a junction with another old road, where you will be able to see Pearsoll Peak and the lookout. The Kalmiopsis Rim Trail continues to the right, but you will follow the road that heads uphill to the left, which is Pearsoll Peak Lookout Trail #1125.

The road begins an uphill traverse along the southeast slope of Pearsoll Peak until it ends at an old mining prospect at the 2.1-mile mark, where it turns into a trail. Cross the wilderness boundary and continue climbing. When you reach a saddle, watch for the trail heading uphill to the right. It is easy to miss. Hike up the rocky

LEFT *Old truck at Chetco Pass* **RIGHT** *View of Pearsoll Peak from the trail*

slope for the final 0.3 mile to the summit, where ghostly snags dot the mountain, staying right at an unmarked fork where trail #1125 continues to the left. The lookout serves as a handy buffer on windy days. A small outhouse sits just downhill from the cabin to the southeast.

On a clear day, you will have 360-degree views. Gold Basin Butte is directly north, its summit just 1 mile away (as the crow flies). Out of sight and far below you to the east is the Illinois River, with the peaks of the Cascades visible in the distance. To the west is the large expanse of the Kalmiopsis Wilderness; along the horizon are Chetco Peak, Red Mountain, and Vulcan Peak. The Chetco River is 4000 feet below you and to the west; its upper 44.5 miles were designated a Wild and Scenic River in 1988. Chetco comes from the name of the Chetco Tribe, who lived along the river; the last of the tribe, a woman named Lucy Dick, died in January 1940.

The first lookout on Pearsoll Peak was a D-6 cupola cabin that was built in 1920. In 1954, it was replaced with the lookout that still stands on the site. The cabin fell into disrepair, but the Sand Mountain Society began restoring it in 1991 and continues doing maintenance on the cabin to this day, no small feat considering the difficult access and remote location. (Read more about the Sand Mountain Society in Hike 11.)

Much of the area visible from Pearsoll Peak has been burned in three different wildfires. In 2002, several lightning-caused fires merged into one massive conflagration known as the Biscuit Fire, which burned 500,000 acres, including most of the Kalmiopsis Wilderness. It was Oregon's largest fire on record until the 2012 Long Draw Fire in southeast Oregon. The 2017 Chetco Bar Fire burned 191,000 acres, then the following year, the Klondike Fire burned 175,000 acres. Both fires were sparked by lightning and both fires reburned areas that had been torched in 2002.

The Kalmiopsis Wilderness was designated in 1964. At 180,000 acres, it is Oregon's third-largest wilderness area, and Pearsoll Peak is the highest point within it (the wilderness boundary goes right over the summit, although the lookout sits just outside the boundary). The wilderness is named for a plant species endemic to the area, *Kalmiopsis leachiana*, which was discovered in 1930 by Lilla Leach in Gold Basin, 2.5 miles due west of Pearsoll Peak. The wilderness is known for its botanical diversity and rugged terrain encompassing deep river canyons and high peaks. A local nonprofit called the Siskiyou Mountain Club has spent thousands of volunteer hours rehabilitating burned trails in the wilderness.

You may be wondering about Port Orford disease. An ornamental grown all over the world, Port Orford cedar is a unique tree with a small native range, stretching just 200 miles across southwest Oregon and northwest California. This limited range is due to the tree's specific growing requirements. Port Orford cedar root disease is caused by the pathogen *Phytophthora lateralis*, which was first discovered on ornamentals near Seattle in 1923 and likely arrived in the US via nursery stock from Asia. In 1952, it was found in southern Oregon within the native population and has since had a devastating effect on the trees. While the fungus is mostly transported in infested water and soil, logging equipment and vehicle tires can easily carry the pathogen across long distances, which is why FR 087 is gated during the wet season to prevent its spread.

Return the way you came.

28 BOLAN MOUNTAIN

YEAR CONSTRUCTED	LOOKOUT ACCESS	LOCATION
2024	Closed to the public for day use; open for seasonal overnight rental by reservation	Rogue River–Siskiyou National Forest, Wild Rivers Ranger District

Roundtrip distance: 3.2 miles
Elevation gain: 780 feet
Lookout elevation: 6270 feet
Map: USGS Oregon Caves
GPS coordinates: 42.02354°, –123.45778°
Permits and fees: None

Both the trail and the lookout burned in a 2020 wildfire, but the trail is once again open to hikers, and the lookout was rebuilt in 2024. Enjoy views, wildflowers, and a rare bonus opportunity to swim immediately after your hike.

GETTING TO THE TRAILHEAD

From the junction with Oregon Route 46 in Cave Junction, head south on US Highway 199 for 0.6 mile, then turn left onto Rockydale Road. Drive 6.5 miles, then turn left onto Waldo Road, which becomes Forest Road 48. Drive 13.3 paved miles, then turn left onto FR 4812. Drive for 4 good gravel miles (taking the left fork at 1.4 miles), then fork left onto FR 040. After 1 mile, follow the road as it makes a sharp right turn at an intersection with FR 530 on the left and FR 535 on the right. (If you're renting the lookout, you will turn right onto FR 535, which heads uphill for 1.5 miles toward Bolan Mountain. There is a locked gate 0.3 mile up for which you will have received the code.)

You will arrive at the Bolan Lake Campground 0.6 mile farther down the road, where the trail starts in the second campground loop. There is limited roadside parking in this loop, especially for larger vehicles. If you are unable to find a spot, you can park on the road shoulder just outside the campground entrance. Also note that the

Bolan Mountain Lookout was rebuilt in 2024 a few years after a wildfire destroyed the original structure.

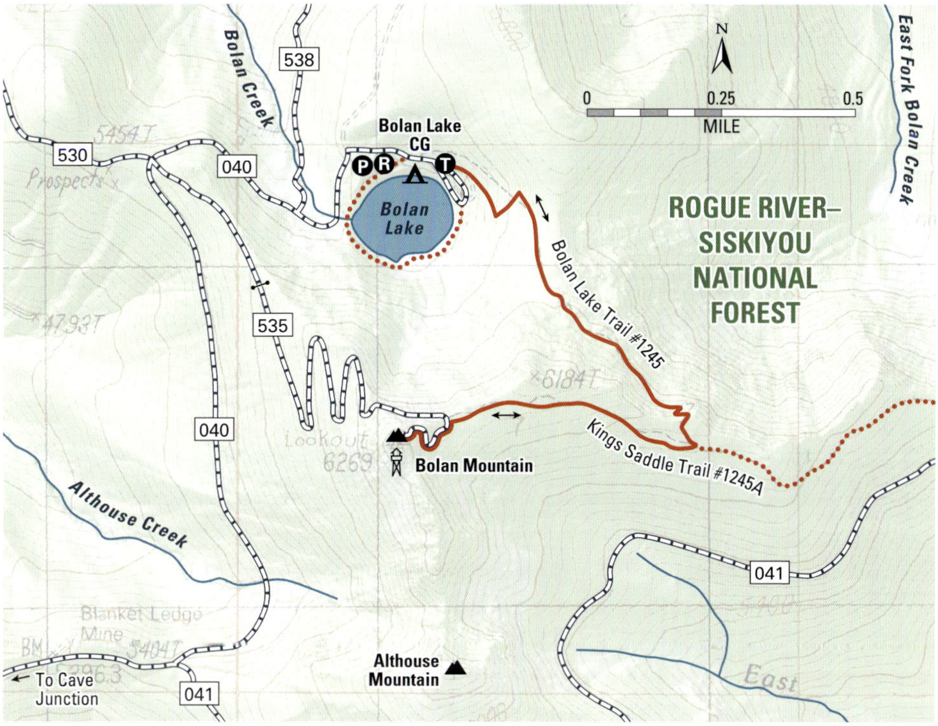

road in the second campground loop is rutted and eroded in one spot and may be tricky in a low-clearance car.

If you plan to camp here, the campground has twelve first-come, first-served sites and two toilets but no water or garbage service. The narrow campground road, tight turns, and small sites are not suitable for large RVs.

ON THE TRAIL

If you parked at the entrance, walk into the campground, staying left at junctions. Pass a toilet on the left, then enter the second loop of the campground, again staying left. Just beyond the fork, look for Bolan Lake Trail #1245 heading uphill on your left. (If you want to check out the lake first, take the right fork when you reach the second loop to find a tiny day-use area and boat ramp on your right. Above the lake you can see FR 535 cutting across the slope just below the summit of Bolan Mountain.)

The trail climbs uphill, heading east. Bracken fern dominates the understory of this burned forest, and you can enjoy beautiful yellow arnica flowers in early July. The trail makes several switchbacks, after which you get a peek of Swan Mountain and other peaks to the east through the burned trees.

Evergreens reflected in the calm waters of Bolan Lake

The trail makes a level southeast traverse at the base of a rocky cliff, threading through a sea of penstemon, knotweed, and wild lovage in late June and early July. You'll then cross several small talus slopes and traverse a slope carpeted in fireweed, then make a switchback uphill to the right. Make another switchback, then climb up a steep rocky section of trail. After yet another switchback, reach the top of the ridge and make a short descent, angling slightly left to meet up with the Kings Saddle Trail #1245A at 0.9 mile. The trail to the left dead-ends 1 mile to the east at Kings Saddle on FR 041; however, you will turn right.

Head west through sprawling meadows of lupine and fireweed. Althouse Mountain and Bolan Mountain are visible through the trees ahead. Half a mile from the junction, reach FR 535 and turn left. Follow the road to its end at the repeater station just downhill from the lookout, then follow the short, steep trail up the rocky slope to the summit and its lookout. (Renters receive a code to unlock the gate at the bottom of this road.)

In 1917, a 12-by-12-foot lookout cabin was built atop a 6-foot-high log base on Bolan Mountain; a cupola was added to the top of the cabin two years later. A road was built to the summit in 1951, which included a rocky cliff traverse with a steep drop-off that to this day makes stomachs flutter. Two years later, the lookout was replaced with a 14-by-14-foot L-4 ground cabin. The lookout stopped being staffed sometime in the 1970s or 1980s and was eventually converted into a rental. In September 2020, the Slater Fire started in Northern California when strong winds brought down powerlines. (It was one of many that season that grew rapidly due to strong east winds.) Spreading north into Oregon, the fire ultimately burned more than 155,000 acres and destroyed seven hundred structures, including the lookout.

In 2024, the nonprofit Siskiyou Mountain Club announced that they were partnering with the Rogue River–Siskiyou National Forest to rebuild the lookout. Over the course of that summer, the cabin and deck were completely reconstructed, largely with volunteer labor. It is now available to rent.

As you enjoy the sights from up here, do not disturb the renters if they are present. Most of the forest that you can see burned in 2020. Bolan Lake and its tiny swimmers and paddlers can be seen 900 feet below to the north; you'll notice that most of the trees on the north side of the lake at the campground survived the fire. Mount Shasta is visible to the southeast, poking up behind the peaks of the Red Buttes Wilderness, which spans the Oregon-California border. Althouse Mountain is the rocky mountain immediately next door to the south, and Preston Peak in California's Siskiyou Wilderness is visible to the southwest.

Return the way you came.

A glorious sunset at Bolan Mountain Lookout

EXTEND YOUR HIKE

This is the only lookout in this book where you can go for a swim immediately after your hike without having to drive to another location. The twelve-acre lake, too small for motorboats, is a popular recreation spot for rafters and paddleboarders. A brushy path starts at the far east end of the campground and loops around the lake.

29 ACORN WOMAN PEAK

YEAR CONSTRUCTED	LOOKOUT ACCESS	LOCATION
1943	Closed to the public for day use; open for seasonal overnight rental by reservation	Rogue River–Siskiyou National Forest, Siskiyou Mountains Ranger District

Roundtrip distance: 11.2 miles
Elevation gain: 1940 feet
Lookout elevation: 4980 feet
Map: USGS Mule Mountain
GPS coordinates: 42.04956°, –123.06361°
Permits and fees: None

This is an excellent spring training hike not only because it is accessible early in the season when other lookouts are still snowed under, but also because these hills are dotted with wildflowers in April and May. Wear long pants, as there is poison oak along the first mile.

GETTING TO THE TRAILHEAD

Set your trip meter at the start of the exit 55 ramp on Interstate 5 in Grants Pass, and follow US Highway 199 west for 2.7 miles. Turn left onto Oregon Route 238 (signed for Murphy and Jacksonville) and drive for 24 miles. Turn right onto Hamilton Road, signed for Cantrall Buckley Park. Drive for 2 miles, then turn right onto Upper Applegate Road. Drive for 13 miles, then turn left onto Forest Road 1075 (labeled French Gulch Road on some maps). Cross the Applegate Dam and drive 1.3 miles. Turn left onto gravel French Gulch Road (FR 490). This road is rutted in several places

OPPOSITE *Acorn Woman Peak Lookout*

and is best for high-clearance vehicles. Drive for 2.1 miles to a saddle where FR 490 heads up and to the right and a sign for the Little Grayback Trail is on the left. There is parking alongside the road here for three or four cars.

Renters and hikers seeking a shorter hike will drive to Hanley Gap. Follow the directions above to Upper Applegate Road. Drive for 7.4 miles and turn left onto paved Beaver Creek Road (FR 20). Drive for 3.7 miles, then turn right onto gravel FR 2010. Drive 5 miles to Hanley Gap. Hikers will park along the road shoulder to hike up FR 350; renters will turn left onto FR 350 and drive 1 mile to the lookout.

ON THE TRAIL

From the road, Little Grayback Trail #921 heads northeast, passing a large metal signboard on your left. The trail climbs through a forest of ponderosa pine, oak, and madrone trees; you will come across two particularly large ones on the right just 0.2 mile up. Madrones, also known as arbutus, have smooth reddish-brown bark that peels off in papery strips. These are not shade-tolerant trees; rather than growing straight up as many trees do, madrones instead grow at angles, twisting every which way to reach the sun. In the fall they produce red berries that birds love to eat.

Watch for poison oak, which is abundant along the first mile of this hike. At 0.7 mile, the trail traverses an open slope with the mountains to your right; you will see them again several times, getting progressively more majestic as you gain elevation. The trail continues to climb at a steady (but not steep) rate, following the contours of Little Grayback Mountain's south side. Continually pass through stands of trees, then traverse meadows with mountain views, then back into the trees.

The interior of Acorn Woman Peak Lookout is bright and welcoming.

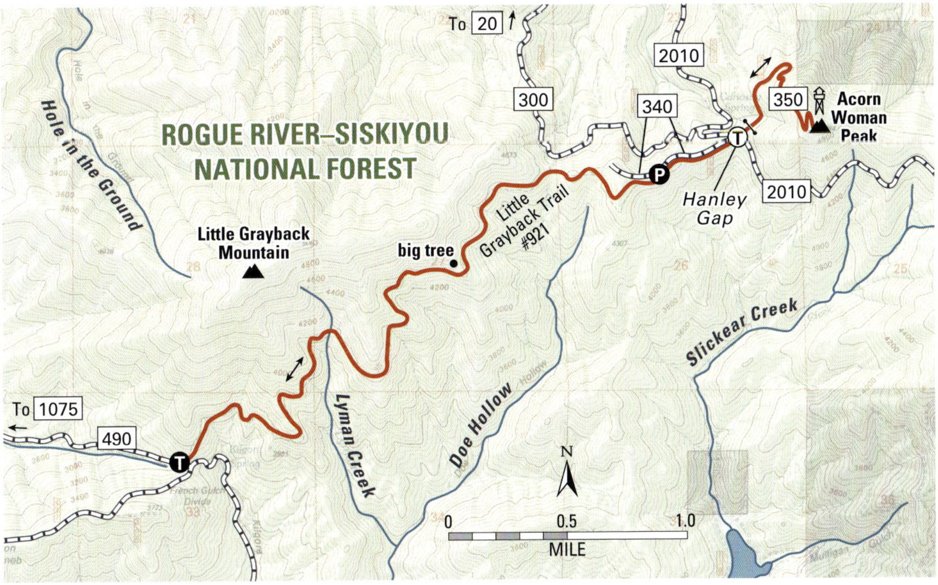

If you happen to visit in spring, watch for lupine, larkspur, ookow, monkeyflower, wild strawberry, and miner's lettuce. You will also notice little white popcornflowers growing by the thousands in many of the meadow areas.

At 2.7 miles, pass a huge old tree, a Douglas-fir, on your left, which provides welcome shade on a hot day. A stunning profile of the mountains from this spot makes this a good place to take a break if you need one.

The trail now levels out for the next mile, and it is an easy stroll through shady forest, followed by another meadow. Then start climbing again, traverse another meadow, and at 4.2 miles reach the upper trailhead on FR 340. Turn right and walk down this quiet road for 0.4 mile to a four-way intersection at Hanley Gap, an alternative starting point, but one that skips the best scenery. Angle right to cross FR 2010 and head up FR 350, hiking around the gate. (Renters will have received the combination to this gate so they can drive through.)

Hike up the road through a pleasant forest of Douglas-firs and ponderosa pines. One mile from the gate, the road ends on the summit of Acorn Woman Peak. The lookout up here is available to rent May through September, so be sure not to disturb the renters if they are present.

Look in all directions: Mount McLoughlin's conical shape is visible to the northeast, and Dutchman Peak (Hike 30) looms in the east. The California border is just 4.5 miles due south, so most of the peaks you see in that direction are across the state line. Scraggy Mountain rises up above Acorn Woman Lakes, and numerous peaks

Sunset vista from the catwalk on Acorn Woman Peak Lookout

can be seen to the southwest, like White Mountain, Black Mountain, and Red Butte. Little Grayback Mountain is in the foreground to the west, and to the northwest you can see the bald south face of Baldy Peak.

The L-4 lookout on Acorn Woman Peak was built in 1943. At that time no roads existed up here; instead, the lookout could be accessed by a route from the north up Hanley Gulch (later superseded by FR 2010), from the west up Mule Creek (now abandoned), from the southwest along Little Grayback Mountain (the way you came today), or from the south from Acorn Woman Lakes (now abandoned).

The lookout stopped being staffed in the 1960s and sat empty for decades, used occasionally on an emergency basis. Volunteers from the Sand Mountain Society worked with the Forest Service to restore the cabin, and in 2019, it was added to the rental program. It is the most sparsely furnished lookout rental in Oregon, containing just a cabinet, a desk, and the firefinder stand. What it lacks in amenities it more than makes up for with 360-degree views and a very dark night sky unblemished by light pollution.

The contraption directly east of the cabin is a remote automatic weather station, one of 2,200 such stations around the US. This solar-powered unit measures air temperature, precipitation, wind speed and direction, and relative humidity. This data is made available online to be readily accessible in firefighting situations, as well as a variety of others.

This peak used to be known as Squaw Peak. The word *squaw* is thought to have originated with the East Coast Algonquin tribes to mean "woman"; however, white settlers used it derogatorily and it is now considered offensive. In 2001, the Oregon legislature passed a bill calling for the removal of the word from public place names and prohibiting its use in naming public property from that point forward. At that time, more than one hundred places in Oregon used the word in their names, and while many names changed after that, by 2021, there were still a few left when the Department of the Interior established a process to review and replace derogatory place names. The US Board on Geographic Names was tasked with removing the term from federal usage. In 2022, this mountain was renamed Acorn Woman Peak.

Return the way you came.

30 DUTCHMAN PEAK

YEAR CONSTRUCTED	LOOKOUT ACCESS	LOCATION
1927	Staffed; accessible to the public when invited in by staff; locked when not staffed	Rogue River–Siskiyou National Forest, Siskiyou Mountains Ranger District

Roundtrip distance: 1 mile
Elevation gain: 160 feet
Lookout elevation: 7420 feet
Map: USGS Dutchman Peak
GPS coordinates: 42.03926°, –122.88479°
Permits and fees: None

An easy road hike among summer wildflowers brings visitors to the summit of Dutchman Peak (named to commemorate a miner named Hensley who died near here in the 1870s during a snowstorm, and often mistakenly called Dutchman's Peak). From this historic lookout, you can take in lovely panoramic views of the surrounding mountains.

GETTING TO THE TRAILHEAD

Due to road conditions, the recommended driving route is from the west. Set your trip meter at the start of the exit 55 ramp on Interstate 5 in Grants Pass, and follow

The D-6 cupola cabin on Dutchman Peak was built in 1927.

US Highway 199 west for 2.7 miles. Turn left onto Oregon Route 238 (signed for Murphy and Jacksonville) and drive for 24 miles. Turn right onto Hamilton Road, signed for Cantrall Buckley Park. Drive for 2 miles, then turn right onto Upper Applegate Road. Drive for 7.4 miles, then turn left onto Beaver Creek Road (Forest Road 20). Drive for 5.8 paved miles and then 4.9 gravel miles. At 10.7 miles, reach a junction with FR 2015 and take the left fork to stay on FR 20.

In another 3.4 miles, reach a confusing junction at Silver Fork Gap and turn left to stay on FR 20, heading east (ignore the left onto FR 819, which doubles back to the north and dead-ends). In another 1.4 miles, reach a junction with FR 805 and turn left. Follow this road 0.5 mile uphill to the junction with FR 800 and turn left. (FR 805 has a few rutted spots that may be tricky in a low-clearance car. You may wish to park at this junction and walk from there.) Drive 0.2 mile on FR 800 to a gate, where you will find parking for two to three cars.

It is possible to approach from the east if you are driving a high-clearance vehicle. From exit 6 on Interstate 5, follow Old Highway 99 S south for 0.6 mile, then turn right onto Mount Ashland Road and set your trip meter. Drive 9.2 miles of pavement, then the road becomes FR 20 and switches to gravel. At 10.3 miles, take the fork left to stay on FR 20. At 11.1 miles, reach a four-way intersection with Forest Road 40S30 called Grouse Gap and go straight to stay on FR 20. Around the 15-mile mark, the road becomes very rough and rocky, and it is slow going the rest of the way. Drive a total of 22.3 miles, then reach an intersection at Jackson Gap and turn right. The road immediately forks. FR 20 continues down the left fork, but you will take the right fork, which is FR 800. Follow this bumpy, rocky dirt road for 0.8 mile to a gate, where you will find parking on the left for two to three cars just before the gate.

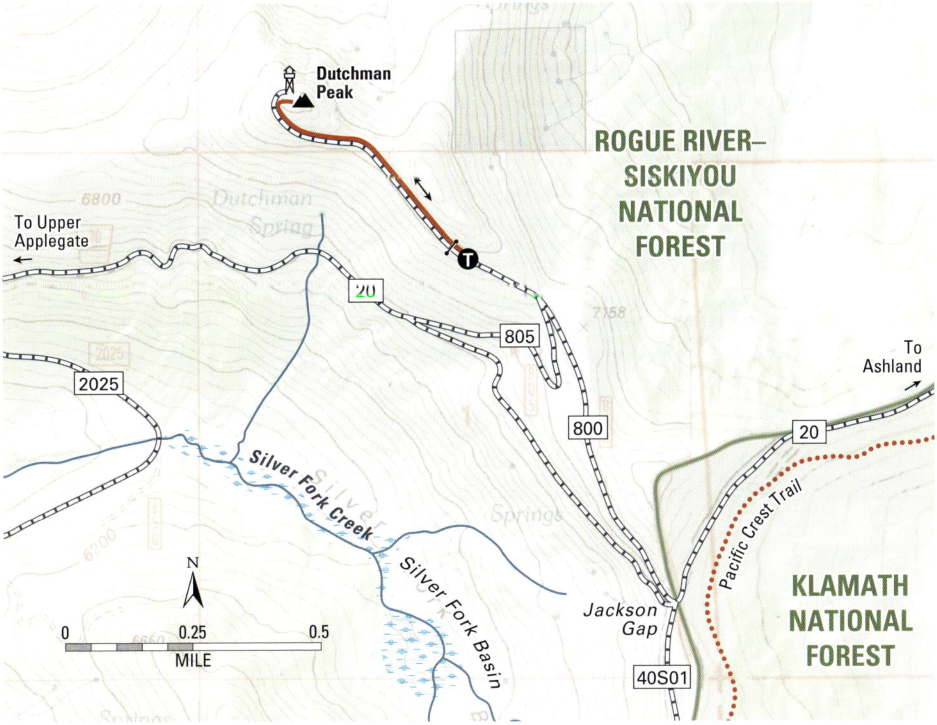

Balsamroot in bloom along the road to Dutchman Peak

ON THE TRAIL

Walk around the gate and start hiking up the road, the lookout visible ahead of you on the summit. The road is lined with sagebrush and manzanita, and if you come in early July, you can walk among balsamroot, paintbrush, penstemon, buckwheat, owl's-clover, and lupine.

Because you are above the tree line, the views begin right away. To your left, you can see Observation Peak immediately to the south and Silver Basin just below it. You may notice ridges on the slopes of Silver Basin. These terraces were built in the late 1950s to slow the erosion caused by livestock grazing.

The road traverses the south slope of the peak, then curls around to the right. Half a mile from the gate, the road ends at a turnaround. From there, follow the short trail uphill to the cabin, which is staffed during fire season. Here, the landscape stretches in all directions: Mount McLoughlin and Mount Ashland can be seen to the northeast and Mount Shasta to the southeast. The funny-looking big white ball on Mount Ashland's summit is a dome that protects a radar dish used by meteorologists to make forecasts and monitor weather conditions. Conditions on Mount Ashland can be rather unforgiving, and the protective dome had to be built to withstand high winds, snow, and ice. Mount Ashland was the site of a fire lookout from 1922 to 1942.

Scraggy Mountain and Preston Peak are visible to the southwest. Grayback Mountain is to the west, and with a good pair of binoculars you might be able to spot the lookout on Acorn Woman Peak (Hike 29) in that direction. Most of the forest you see to the east is in the Klamath National Forest, which is mostly located in California but has a small extension north into Oregon.

A 12-by-12-foot D-6 cupola cabin was built on Dutchman Peak in 1927 and still stands today, one of only a few of this type left in Oregon. The road network in this area did not yet exist then, so pack animals hauled building materials to the summit via a rugged trail. The road was built in 1935, and two years later, the Civilian Conservation Corps built the storage shed, which was then converted into a residence for the Aircraft Warning Service spotters stationed on the summit. The lookout was listed on the National Register of Historic Places in 2000. (Incidentally, there is another standing lookout with a similar name: Dutchman Butte is located in Douglas County and is operated by the Douglas Forest Protective Association. The association no longer staffs its lookouts, having switched to cameras in the early 2000s.)

Dutchman Peak is part of the Siskiyou Crest, an east-west subrange in the Klamath-Siskiyou Mountains of southwest Oregon and northwest California that is known for its rich biodiversity, especially of conifers. Dutchman Peak is also part of the Observation Peak Botanical Area, which contains a diverse array (more than 170 species!) of subalpine flora, some of them endemic.

Return the way you came.

31 SODA MOUNTAIN

YEAR CONSTRUCTED	LOOKOUT ACCESS	LOCATION
1962	Closed to the public	Cascade-Siskiyou National Monument

Roundtrip distance: 4.3 miles
Elevation gain: 840 feet
Lookout elevation: 6090 feet
Map: USGS Soda Mountain
GPS coordinates: 42.08540°, –122.48253°
Permits and fees: None

The summit of Soda Mountain may be overflowing with radio towers and communications equipment, but what you can see when you are up there, more than makes up for it. Visit in summer to see a wide variety of wildflowers.

GETTING TO THE TRAILHEAD

From exit 14 on Interstate 5 in Ashland, follow Oregon Route 66 east for 15 miles. Turn right onto Soda Mountain Road and drive 3.8 miles on good gravel to the Hobart Bluff trailhead, which sits at the edge of a large grassy area beneath powerlines. Most of the parking will be on your right. The trailhead has a single toilet.

ON THE TRAIL

You will begin the hike on a portion of the Pacific Crest National Scenic Trail (usually referred to as the PCT), which starts at the northwest end of the parking area next to a "trail" signpost, immediately turns southeast to run parallel to the road, then turns south to cross under the powerlines. At this point, to your left you can see distant Aspen Butte in the Mountain Lakes Wilderness in the northeast. At 0.2 mile, enter the Soda Mountain Wilderness. Many of the trees around you here are incense

In addition to the lookout, Soda Mountain hosts a lot of communications equipment.

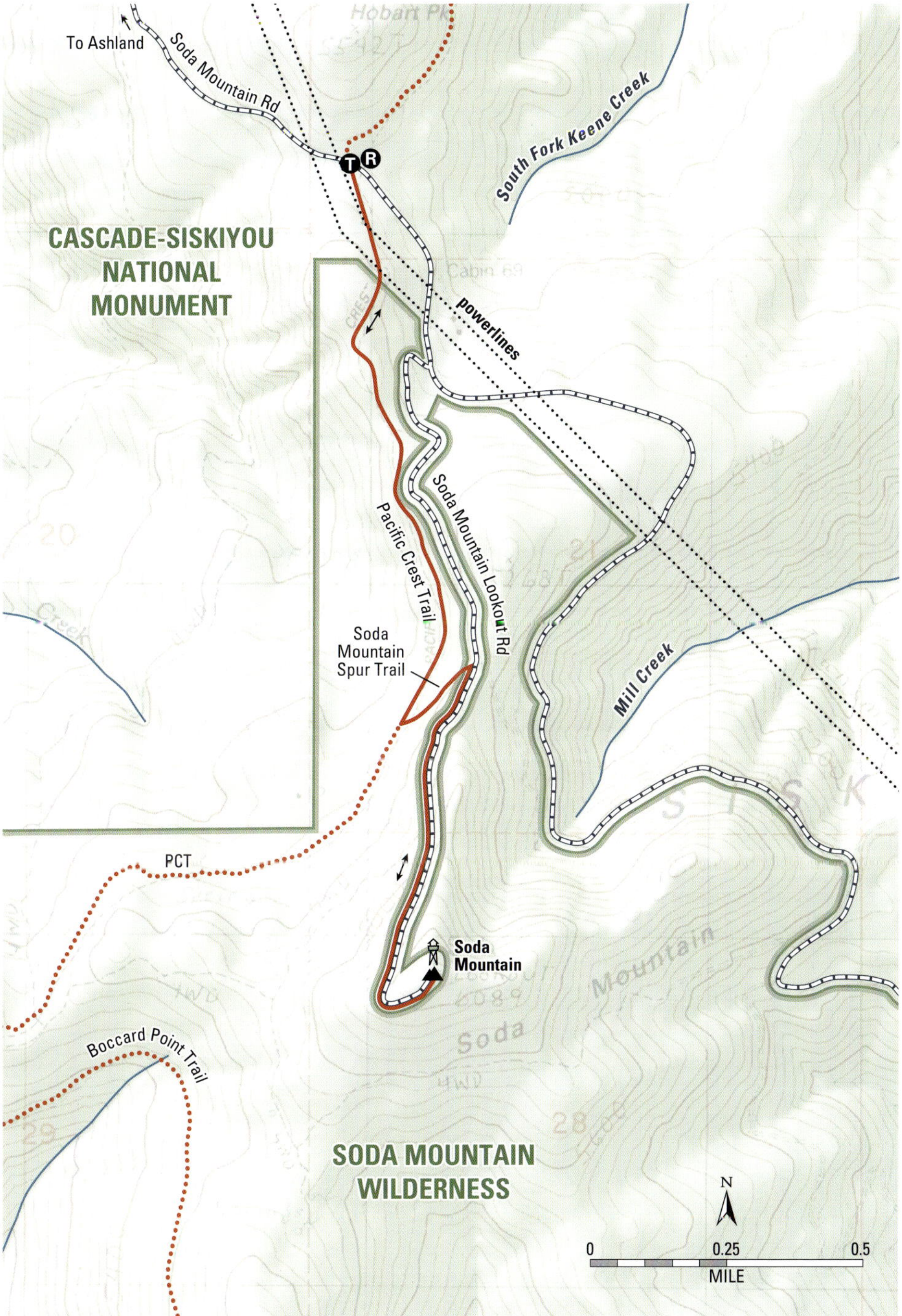
To Ashland
Soda Mountain Rd
South Fork Keene Creek
CASCADE-SISKIYOU NATIONAL MONUMENT
powerlines
Soda Mountain Lookout Rd
Pacific Crest Trail
Soda Mountain Spur Trail
Mill Creek
PCT
Soda Mountain
Boccard Point Trail
SODA MOUNTAIN WILDERNESS
N
0
0.25
0.5
MILE

Phlox on Soda Mountain

cedars, which primarily grow in southwest Oregon and Northern California. Native Americans used incense cedar branches as twirling sticks to start fires, and the foliage was used as flavoring in food.

At the 0.3-mile mark, cross a rock-studded meadow; during a summer hike, look for phlox, daggerpod, delphinium, owl's-clover, Oregon sunshine, and paintbrush. At the far end of the meadow, you can spot Mount Ashland with its white radar-protection dome to the west.

The trail then enters a shady forest of big firs. At 0.7 mile, it emerges from the forest into a sloping, rocky meadow. From here, you will have a view straight ahead to Soda Mountain, where you can see a communications tower poking up above the trees.

After another brief passage through trees, enter another meadow where false hellebore grows. The vivid green leaves of these plants grow in a spiral, which are towered over by their tall white flowers.

At 1.1 miles, watch for an easy-to-miss unsigned junction. Take a sharp left here onto Soda Mountain Spur Trail to head uphill for 0.3 mile until it connects with Soda

Mountain Lookout Road, where you will turn right. This junction is also not marked or signed, so take note of your surroundings so you do not miss it on your way back.

Follow the road uphill through the forest for 0.8 mile to the summit, where phlox and balsamroot can be found in June. On a clear day, you can see Mount Shasta to the south. Mount McLoughlin is visible to the north through a gap in the trees, and to the west is Mount Ashland. Pilot Rock's distinctive shape can be seen to the southwest. This volcanic plug rises 570 feet above the surrounding landscape, a remnant of an ancient volcano that has since eroded away, leaving this basalt pillar from the volcano's interior vent. It has had numerous identities over the years. The Takelma Tribe called it Tan-ts'at-seniphtha ("Stone Standing Up"). Early settlers called it Boundary Mountain. When the US Exploring Expedition saw it in 1841, they renamed it Emmons Peak after Lieutenant George F. Emmons, a member of the group. Later pioneers traveling the Applegate Trail north from California called it Pilot Rock because it was visible from 40 miles away. Today, it is a popular spot for hiking and climbing.

The first lookout on Soda Mountain was built in 1933 by the Civilian Conservation Corps. This was replaced by the current structure in 1962. Although the land is managed by the Bureau of Land Management, the tower is managed by the Oregon Department of Forestry (ODF). Today, the lookout is almost lost among the numerous communication towers; however, notice the cameras mounted on a pole in front of it. ODF stopped staffing this lookout sometime around 2020 but now monitors for fires remotely using these cameras.

The origin of Soda Mountain's name is not documented, but it likely stems from the presence of soda springs (natural springs containing sodium carbonate) in the area. It is surrounded by the Cascade Siskiyou National Monument (one of four monuments in Oregon), designated in 2000, then expanded in 2017 to what is now 113,000 acres. (The 24,700-acre Soda Mountain Wilderness within the monument was designated in 2009.) Known for its biological diversity, including two hundred species of birds, this monument is the only national monument created specifically with the goal of protecting biodiversity. The Cascade Mountains, Siskiyou Mountains, Klamath Mountains, Sierra Nevada Mountains, and Great Basin desert converge here, resulting in five ecoregions: grassland and shrubland, oak woodlands, juniper scablands, mixed conifer and white fir forests, and wet meadows and riparian forests. There are also areas of old-growth forest.

Nineteen miles of the PCT cross the monument. This long-distance trail stretches 2,650 miles from Campo, California, to Manning Park in British Columbia. First proposed by Clinton C. Clarke in 1932, the trail took decades of construction and connecting of existing trails until it was declared finished in 1993. Today, despite the fact that it takes five to six months to complete, hiking the trail from one end to the other—known as a thru hike—has exploded in popularity. In 2013, the Pacific Crest Trail Association issued 1,071 thru-hike permits. In 2022, that number had more than quadrupled, to 4,728. Most people hike it from south to north, but some do it in reverse. Because the PCT connects to hundreds of other trails across California, Oregon, and Washington, countless numbers of hikers, trail runners, equestrians, and mountain bikers use parts of the PCT every year.

Return the way you came.

CENTRAL AND EAST

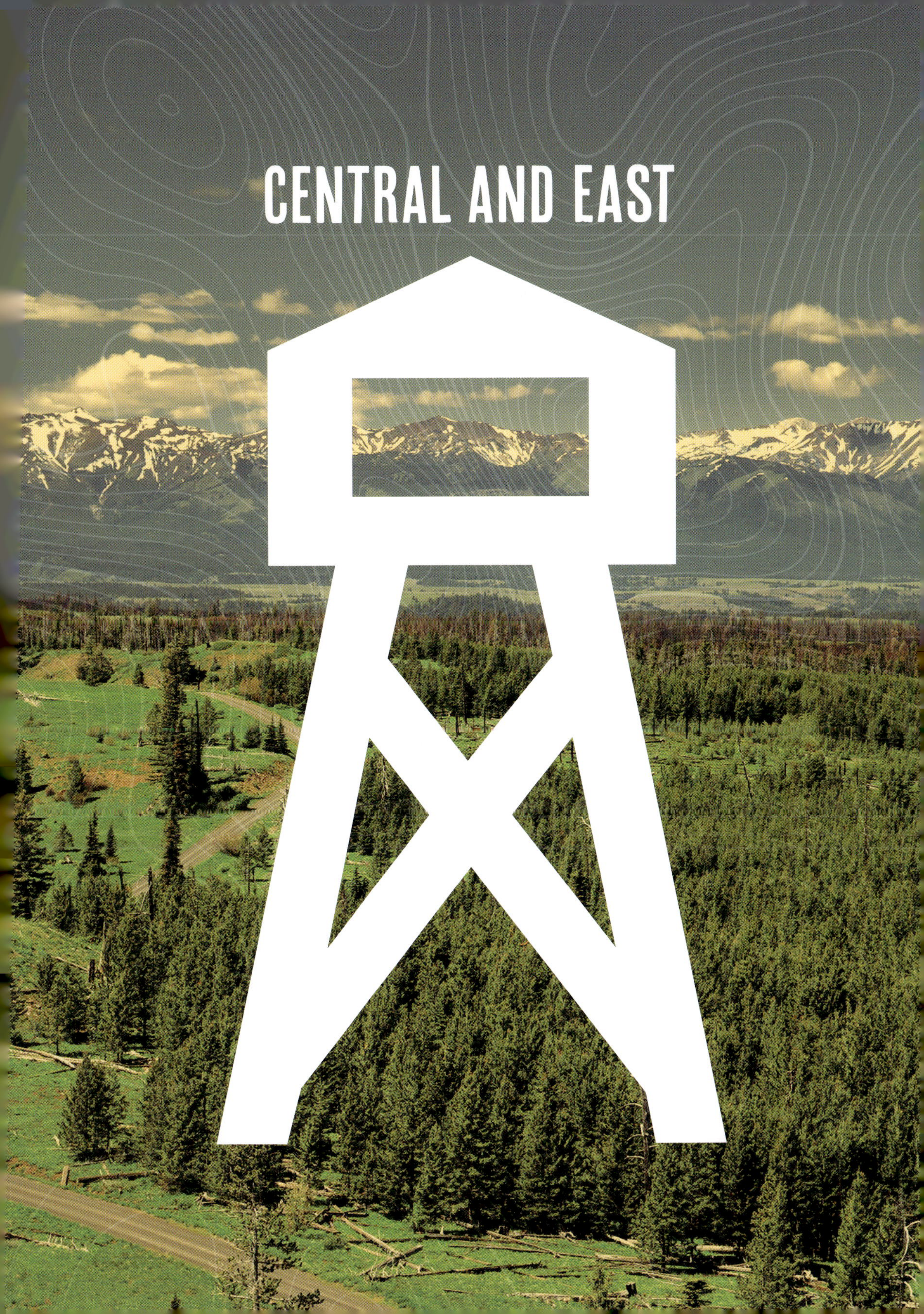

32 GREEN MOUNTAIN

YEAR CONSTRUCTED	LOOKOUT ACCESS	LOCATION
2010	Staffed; closed to the public	Bureau of Land Management, Lakeview District

Roundtrip distance: 0.3 mile
Elevation gain: 50 feet
Lookout elevation: 5190 feet
Map: USGS Jacks Place
GPS coordinates: 43.38603°, –120.72390°
Permits and fees: None

Beautiful this lookout is not, but the views more than make up for it. A perfect hike if you are short on time, traveling with little kids, or cannot walk long distances, this easily accessible hike is also a fantastic spot to watch sunrise or sunset.

GETTING TO THE TRAILHEAD

From Christmas Valley, drive east on County Road 5-14 for 1 mile, then turn left onto gravel Crack in the Ground Road (some maps call this Lava Craters Road), signed for Crack in the Ground and Green Mountain Campground. The road has potholes, but it is passable in most vehicles.

At 7.1 miles, pass the Crack in the Ground trailhead. (You will see parking on the left and the trail on the right. This short 0.2-mile trail takes hikers into a 70-foot-deep, quarter-mile-long rock chasm. It has nothing to do with lookouts but is absolutely worth checking out if you have a half hour or so to spare.) At the 10.3-mile mark, take the left fork to stay on your route. After a total of 12.6 miles, turn right at a Green Mountain Campground sign. Drive 0.2 mile up into the campground and to the far end. Park next to a scenic overlook sign.

If you are coming from the west, from the community of Fort Rock, drive east on CR 5-10 (Fort Rock Road) for 5.7 miles. At a junction where CR 5-10 turns south, continue straight onto CR 5-12. Follow this road as it heads east for 2.2 miles, jogs north for 1 mile, then east for 1 mile, then north again for 3.2 miles (a total of 13.1 miles from Fort Rock). Turn right onto gravel CR 5-12B (Sink Lane). Drive 6.3 miles, then turn right onto gravel Green Mountain Road, signed for Green Mountain and Christmas Valley. Go 3 miles, then turn left into the Green Mountain Campground.

The concrete lookout tower on Green Mountain features an enclosed stairway leading up to an observation area.

Drive 0.2 mile up into the campground and to the far end. Park next to a scenic overlook sign.

ON THE TRAIL

The dirt trail starts at the north end of the parking area and switchbacks up a grassy slope dotted with junipers, the concrete lookout visible above you. Once you have reached the summit, circle around the left side of the lookout along the fence line toward an empty signboard. This lookout is the least charming one in the book: The imposing concrete tower looks like it belongs at a prison, and the chain-link fence topped with barbed wire (meant to keep out vandals) doesn't help.

But the lookout isn't what makes this summit special. To the west, Cougar Mountain rises up out of the desert. Beyond it you can see numerous Cascade peaks, such as Odell Butte (Hike 18), Diamond Peak, Hamner Butte, and Maiden Peak. To the northwest is Hogback Butte just 9 miles away, and beyond that is the rim of Newberry Crater, with its high point of Paulina Peak. Table Rock and Hager Mountain (Hike 33) are visible across the Fort Rock Valley to the southwest.

In 1963, the Bureau of Land Management (BLM) built a two-story lookout on Green Mountain. This lookout, consisting of a concrete base topped with a wood-frame cabin, and its outhouse, were demolished in 2010 and replaced with the 50-foot concrete tower with an enclosed stairway and observation cab that you see today. The lookout is staffed during fire season. In 2024, the BLM, in partnership with the Oregon Hazards Lab at the University of Oregon, installed a wildfire-detection camera on the lookout to help gather information about fire behavior.

The dominant tree you see on Green Mountain is the western juniper. Its bark is thin and fibrous, and sometimes the tree's trunk and branches grow in beautiful

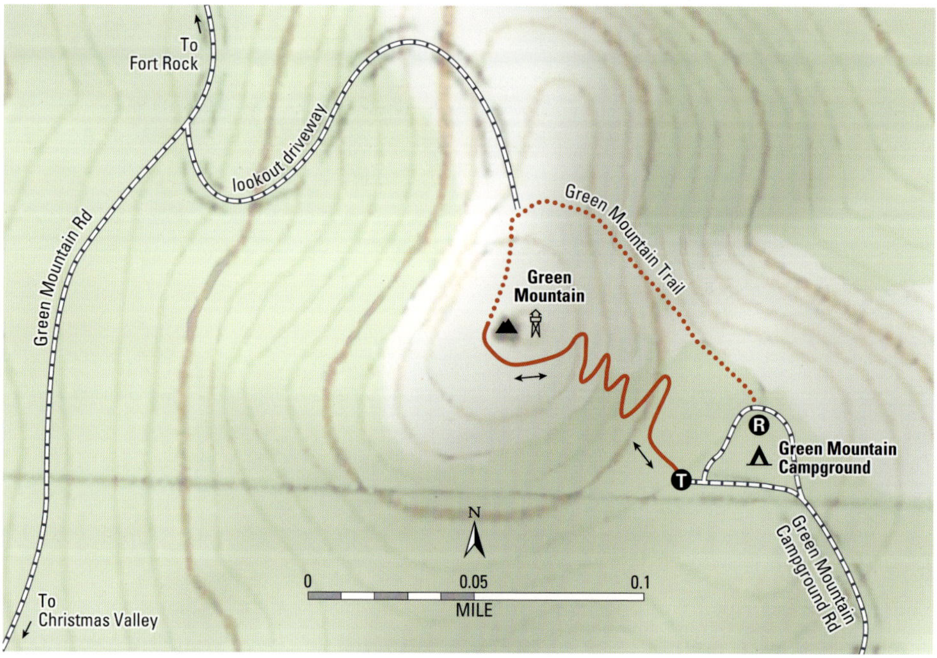

View from Green Mountain

twisted angles. The trees' blue berries, which are actually tiny cones, were used by Native Americans as food and medicine.

Juniper numbers were once controlled by regular naturally occurring, low-intensity burns, but a century of wildfire suppression has caused them to grow like weeds. Left unchecked by the natural processes of the past, these trees, which can live to be 1,600 years old, have taken over large swaths of the desert. In Oregon, juniper occupied 1.5 million acres of land in the 1930s, but it now covers more than 6.5 million acres. When juniper moves in, other desert plants such as sagebrush and grasses die. In an environment where there isn't any water to spare, a single mature juniper tree can draw twenty-five gallons of water from the earth every day in the summer.

Return the way you came.

ALTERNATIVE ROUTE

You can also make a little loop out of this hike. Follow the fence line north until you reach the far end where the lookout driveway ends, then turn right and follow the fence to the northeast corner. From here, a trail descends straight down the hill back to the campground. Once you reach the campground road, turn right and walk a few hundred feet back to your car.

33 HAGER MOUNTAIN

YEAR CONSTRUCTED	LOOKOUT ACCESS	LOCATION
1967	Staffed; accessible by invitation only during fire season; open for overnight rental in winter by reservation	Fremont-Winema National Forest, Silver Lake Ranger District

Roundtrip distance: 5 miles
Elevation gain: 1490 feet
Lookout elevation: 7190 feet
Map: USGS Hager Mountain
GPS coordinates: 43.01190°, –121.04813°
Permits and fees: None

The Klamath people called this mountain Chock-chock-lisk-se, meaning "Bald-Faced Rock," and some early maps call it Bald Mountain. Early settlers called it Hagerhorst Mountain for a pioneer rancher in the Silver Lake Valley. At some point it became shortened to Hager, where today you can hike through a ponderosa pine forest and across wildflower meadows to reach a lookout with 360-degree views of south-central Oregon.

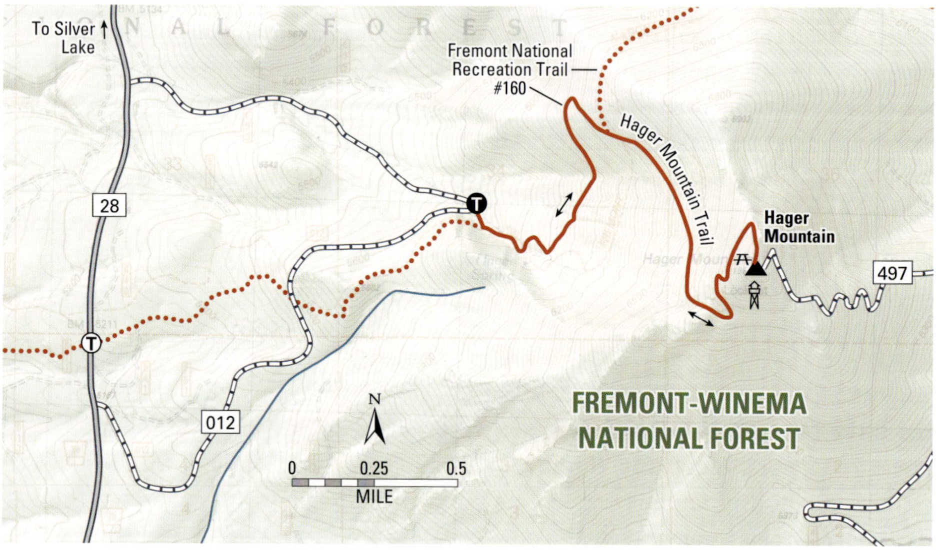

Hager Mountain Lookout stands out on a rocky, sagebrush-covered slope.

GETTING TO THE TRAILHEAD

From Oregon Route 31 in Silver Lake, turn south onto paved E. Bay Road (Forest Road 28). Drive 9 miles, then turn left onto FR 012 and continue for 1.9 miles. This dirt road has a few rough spots and a few brushy spots, but it is passable in most vehicles. Where the road bends sharply left, there is a trailhead parking area on the right with room for three to four cars. There is no toilet or any facilities. (If you are worried about negotiating a brushy gravel road, see the note at the end of this entry for parking at the lower trailhead, which results in a longer hike.)

ON THE TRAIL

The trail begins on the south side of the parking area. Heading into a forest of ponderosa pines, you will quickly reach a junction with Fremont National Recreation Trail #160, where you will turn left. (The lower trailhead on FR 28 is 1.5 miles to the right; see the note for the longer option, below.)

Hike uphill through the trees, where snowbrush and manzanita grow in the understory. Blue diamonds on the trees guide winter renters who ski or snowshoe this trail carrying their gear. The trail swings left. In between the red trunks of the ponderosas you can see the large meadow on the slopes above you, across which you will soon be hiking.

The trail turns right, then left. At 0.8 mile, emerge from the trees and into a more open area at the base of the meadow. In June, the sagebrush slope is covered in the showy yellow blooms of balsamroot, as well as buckwheat, paintbrush, scarlet gilia, and Washington lily. Landmarks to your left start appearing, such as Mount Thielsen to the west.

The trail then makes a switchback uphill to the right. Traverse the lower meadow, passing yet more flowers, the summit and its lookout cabin coming into view ahead of you. Hike through a grove of mountain mahogany, then at 1.1 miles pass a junction where the Fremont National Recreation Trail goes left; you will continue straight on the Hager Mountain Trail. The trail levels out and heads back into the forest, but the reprieve is short-lived and you are soon climbing again.

At the 2-mile mark, the trail switchbacks uphill to the left. You soon enter another open area where the wildflower show continues, making several switchbacks uphill along the sagebrush slope. At the final switchback, enjoy a sweeping panorama to the north that includes the vast area around Silver Lake.

After 2.5 miles of hiking, the trail connects with FR 497 just below the summit next to a picnic table, which makes for a fine place to stop and take a break after that climb. From here, it's a short hike up a trail from the road to the summit. If the lookout is staffed or renters are present, do not go on the deck or enter the cabin without permission. However, it is possible to walk around the summit to see in all directions.

To the north, Paulina Peak at Newberry Crater is visible. Dead Indian Mountain is to the east. From the southwest to the northwest you can see a string of Cascade volcanoes: Mount Shasta, Mount Thielsen, Diamond Peak, the Three Sisters, and maybe even Mount Jefferson on an especially clear day.

Far below to the southwest is the much-diminished Thompson Reservoir. Created for irrigation, the water level is quite low during dry periods, when it looks more like a meadow with a pond in it from this vantage point. Beyond the reservoir is the Sycan Marsh Preserve, a 36-square-mile wetland that is a stopover for migrating birds such as tundra swans and sandhill cranes. The marsh, along with some of the surrounding forest, was purchased by the Nature Conservancy in 1980. The river that flows along the southern edge is the Sycan River, a portion of which was declared a Wild and Scenic River in 1988. The word *sycan* comes from the Klamath people and means "a level, grassy place."

OPPOSITE *Balsamroot, paintbrush, and buckwheat in bloom along the trail to Hager Mountain*

The summit is dominated by sagebrush and bitterbrush. In early summer you may see buckwheat and Oregon sunshine in bloom. If you spot paintbrush that is yellow-green instead of red, it is the green-tinged paintbrush, endemic to the area—95 percent of these flowers grow in the Fremont-Winema National Forest.

Hager Mountain has been a lookout site since 1912, when an unusual octagonal cabin was built. An L-4 ground cabin replaced it in 1936, followed in 1967 by the R-6 ground cabin that still stands today. The winter and summer hikes both follow the same route (starting from the lower trailhead on FR 28), although it is a considerably more difficult trek in winter carrying all your gear through the snow, when the lookout is available to rent. On this exposed mountaintop the icy winter winds can be fierce.

Return the way you came.

LONGER OPTION

If you are worried about driving FR 012, you can start at an alternate trailhead, although it lengthens the hike. The driving directions are the same, except 0.2 mile before the junction with FR 012, you park at the gravel pullout on the left side of FR 28. From there, climb up through the forest for 0.7 mile, cross FR 012, then hike another 0.8 mile to reach the junction near the upper trailhead, described above. The hike from this lower trailhead is 8 miles roundtrip with 2000 feet of elevation gain.

34 LOOKOUT ROCK

YEAR CONSTRUCTED	LOOKOUT ACCESS	LOCATION
1962	Unlocked but unsafe for public access	Fremont-Winema National Forest, Bly Ranger District

Roundtrip distance: 0.6 mile
Elevation gain: 220 feet
Lookout elevation: 6500 feet
Map: USGS Gearhart Mountain
GPS coordinates: 42.46070°, –120.80064°
Permits and fees: None

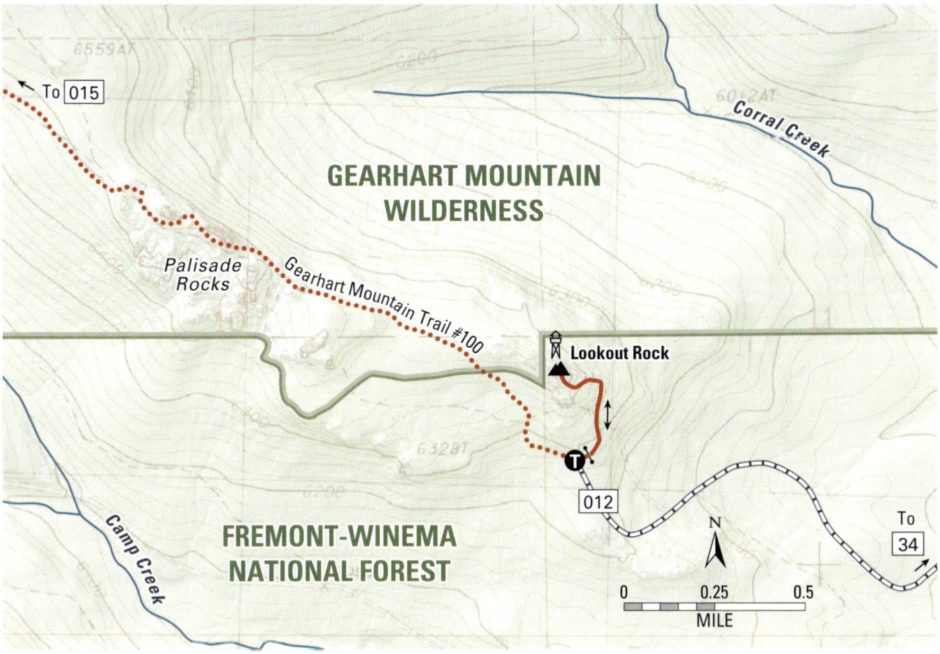

This short hike leads to an abandoned lookout atop a rocky outcrop at the edge of the Gearhart Mountain Wilderness.

GETTING TO THE TRAILHEAD

From the town of Bly, drive east on Oregon Route 140 for 1.4 miles, then turn left onto Campbell Road. Drive 0.5 mile, then turn right onto paved Forest Road 34 (signed for Gearhart Wilderness and Campbell Lake). Drive 14.7 miles, then turn left onto gravel FR 012. Drive 1.4 miles to the Lookout Rock trailhead at the road's end, where there is room for about ten cars.

ON THE TRAIL

At the east side of the trailhead, hike around the gate and follow the old road (what was once a continuation of FR 012) through burned snags. The road swings north and heads up the hill, then curves to the left. As you approach the rock pinnacles, watch for the faint traces of a path on your right. The path angles up toward rocks and the lookout, which now comes into view. Once you are among the rocks, follow the path in the gap as it heads north toward the lookout. Some minor class 2 scrambling is required to reach the base of the tower.

Lookout Rock Lookout is accessed via a brief rock scramble.

A 20-foot tower with an L-4 cab was built on Lookout Rock in 1932. Thirty years later, it was replaced with the current lookout, a 20-foot tower and an R-6 cab. By the 1970s, it was staffed only intermittently for emergencies, and it has not been used in quite a while. The burned trees surrounding this spot are the result of the lightning-caused Bootleg Fire in 2021, the second-largest US wildfire that year, burning more than four hundred thousand acres, including most of the Gearhart Mountain Wilderness. The fire was so big and so hot that it generated its own weather. While 342 vehicles as well as 408 structures were burned, the lookout wasn't one of them. The fire got close enough that several support beams on the tower were scorched, yet amazingly the tower survived. The future of this lookout is uncertain, however, as the damage to the supports has rendered it unsafe, and as of this writing the Forest Service was considering its options.

Through the burned trees you can see Round Mountain and Coleman Point to the east. Fishhole Mountain is visible to the south. Lookout Rock sits just outside the Gearhart Mountain Wilderness, which was designated in 1964. The twenty-two-thousand-acre wilderness is named for the 8370-foot peak at its center, itself named for two pioneer brothers, James P. and William H. Gearhart, who were in the stock business in the 1870s.

Return the way you came.

EXTEND YOUR HIKE

If you would like to get more trail miles before leaving the area, you can return to the trailhead and follow Gearhart Mountain Trail #100 northwest into the Gearhart Mountain Wilderness. (Be sure to check with the Bly Ranger District for conditions.) The rock pinnacles around the lookout are a small preview of what lies ahead. In 0.7 mile from the trailhead, the trail travels among andesite rock formations called Palisade Rocks, or The Palisades, a fun spot to explore and photograph and a good turnaround point, especially if the trail ahead is covered by fallen burned snags.

The trail continues for a total of 13 miles to the North Fork Sprague trailhead on FR 015, passing Gearhart Mountain and Blue Lake along the way, but keep in mind that nearly the entire route burned in 2021—you will have no shade and may encounter many burned, fallen snags across the trail.

35 MORGAN BUTTE

YEAR CONSTRUCTED	LOOKOUT ACCESS	LOCATION
1964	Staffed; accessible to the public when invited in by staff; locked when not staffed	Fremont-Winema National Forest, Paisley Ranger District

Roundtrip distance: 6.7 miles
Elevation gain: 1050 feet
Lookout elevation: 7230 feet
Map: USGS Morgan Butte
GPS coordinates: 42.56985°, –120.55339°
Permits and fees: None

Hike a portion of the Fremont National Recreation Trail to a staffed lookout. Most of this route burned in 2020, which makes for pretty wildflowers in June, but watch out for dead trees that may have blown down across the trail—as well as cows, as this is

MORGAN
BUTTE

open range. There is also a shorter hiking option to reach this lookout (see the end of the trail description and the map for details).

GETTING TO THE TRAILHEAD

From Paisley, drive south on Oregon Route 31 for 5.9 miles, then turn right onto paved Clover Flat Road. Drive 3.4 miles, then turn right onto gravel Forest Road 018, signed for Morgan Butte and Avery Pass. Drive 2.3 miles, then fork right onto FR 020. Continue 1.6 miles to another fork where you have a decision to make: For the longer hike, head right onto FR 019, signed for Avery Pass. Drive 2.2 miles to the trailhead parking area on the left. This road is in generally good condition; however, the last quarter mile is rough and may be muddy after a hard rain.

For the better road and shorter hike, fork left to stay on FR 020 and drive 2.3 miles on a good gravel road to a trailhead on the right just before a locked gate (look for the "trail" sign pointing to the right). There is room on the shoulder for one to two cars. (See the note at the end of this entry for the shorter hike's description.)

ON THE TRAIL

At the Avery Pass trailhead, walk west to the back of the parking area toward a brown metal trail sign. Look for the trail heading left toward Morgan Butte. (The trail to the right heads down to the Chewaucan Crossing trailhead on Forest Road 33.)

This hike follows a portion of the 135-mile Fremont National Recreation Trail and also a part of the Oregon Timber Trail, a 669-mile mountain bike route established in 2015 that follows existing roads and trails from the Oregon-California border south of Lakeview up to Hood River. Follow the trail through a landscape of blackened trees and snowbrush. This area burned in the human-caused Brattain Fire, which spread across more than fifty thousand acres in 2020. The trail levels out and enters a forest of juniper and ponderosa pine that only partially burned. Then reenter the burn area. Wildfire scars like these are often great spots to see wildflowers, and this is no exception: In late June and early July, look for arnica, paintbrush, buckwheat, and balsamroot.

Follow the switchbacks up a sagebrush-covered slope. At 0.7 mile, the trail switchbacks to the right, briefly joining an ancient grassy roadbed. At 1.2 miles, cross an open sagebrush meadow. At the far end of the meadow, a short side trail on the right next to a scenic vista sign heads out to a rocky viewpoint. Gearhart Mountain is visible to the west, and Cougar Peak is visible to the southwest. Both are former lookout sites. Due south is Morgan Butte and its lookout cabin. Far below you the Chewaucan River snakes its way through the valley.

OPPOSITE *The Morgan Butte Lookout survived the 2020 Brattain Fire.*

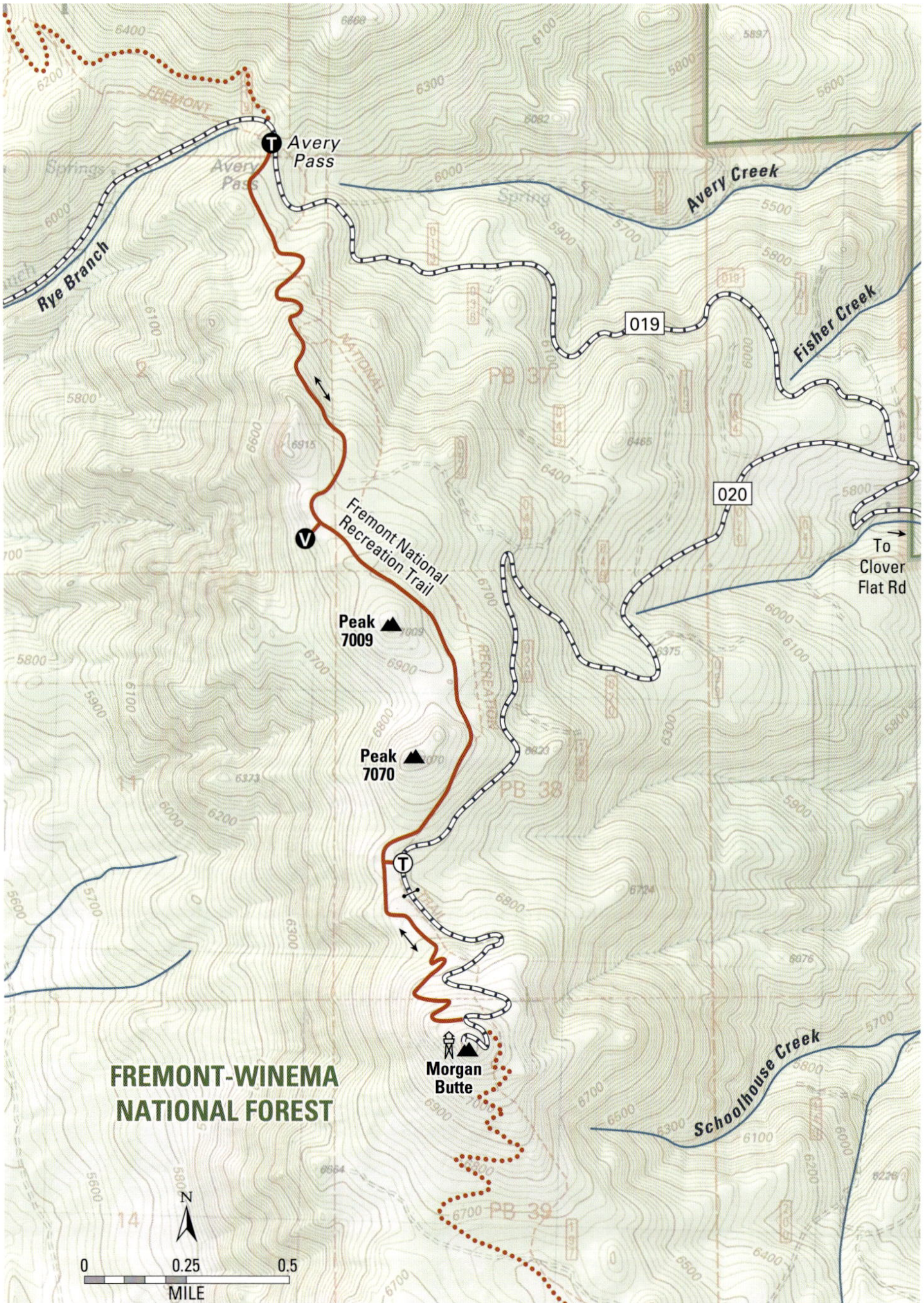
Avery Pass
Avery Creek
Rye Branch
019
Fisher Creek
020
To Clover Flat Rd
Fremont National Recreation Trail
Peak 7009
Peak 7070
Morgan Butte
Schoolhouse Creek
FREMONT-WINEMA NATIONAL FOREST
N
0
0.25
0.5
MILE

A sign indicating the Fremont National Recreation Trail near Morgan Butte

Back on the main trail, continue toward Morgan Butte, where you will pass through a pretty parkland of meadows and mostly live trees. The trail skirts around the northeast side of Peak 7009, then around the rocky prominence of Peak 7070. As you round the end of Peak 7070, you begin descending and the lookout appears ahead of you.

At 2.3 miles, pass the junction with the short connector trail that heads left to FR 020 (see below). Now the trail ascends again, climbing up the sagebrush slope of Morgan Butte. The trail intersects FR 020 and continues on the other side toward Myers Butte and Round Pass. You'll turn right, however, and hike up the road for a final 0.2 mile to the staffed lookout on the summit. Explore the scenery around the summit, but do not enter the cabin without permission.

Gearhart Mountain is to the west, surrounded by acres of burned trees from the 2021 Bootleg Fire. The prominent peak to the south is Round Mountain, where this lookout was relocated from and is now home to communication towers. (That lookout was called Round Pass, even though it was located on Round Mountain.) The farmland south of Paisley is visible to the east, and beyond it is the long ridge known as Abert Rim.

Morgan Butte was a relatively late addition to the list of Oregon lookouts. The 14-by-14-foot lookout (built in 1930) from the aforementioned Round Mountain was trailered north up to Morgan Butte in 1958. An R-6 ground cabin replaced it six years later and still stands today. The Brattain Fire burned much of the surrounding area, but the lookout was spared.

Return the way you came.

SHORTER OPTION

From the trailhead just before the gate on FR 020, head west into the trees and quickly meet up with the Fremont National Recreation Trail. The Avery Pass trailhead is 2.3 miles to the right. You, however, want to turn left for the 1-mile hike up to the lookout, as described above. From this trailhead, it is a 2-mile out-and-back hike with 360 feet of elevation gain. You also have the option of making it a 2.7-mile loop by hiking the road back to your car instead of the trail.

36 MADISON BUTTE

YEAR CONSTRUCTED	LOOKOUT ACCESS	LOCATION
1957	Staffed; accessible to the public when invited in by staff; locked when not staffed	Umatilla National Forest, Heppner Ranger District

Roundtrip distance: 8.2 miles
Elevation gain: 2200 feet
Lookout elevation: 5710 feet
Map: USGS Madison Butte
GPS coordinates: 45.06762°, –119.49472°
Permits and fees: None

Make no mistake, this roller coaster of a trail is a workout, with uphill hiking in both directions. However, it is a pure delight in May and June when the landscape is green and bursting with wildflowers. It is one of the few early-season hikes in this book where snow is usually long gone by Memorial Day. The trail is faint in places, so solid route-finding skills and a GPS device or app are helpful.

GETTING TO THE TRAILHEAD

From downtown Heppner, drive 10.7 miles south on Oregon Route 206/207 to Ruggs. OR 206 continues straight; you will turn left onto OR 207, signed for Hardman and Spray. Drive 14.8 miles, then turn left onto gravel Sunflower Flat Road, signed for Tupper. Drive for 3.7 miles, then turn left onto gravel Tupper Lane (County Road 673). Drive for 3.4 miles, then turn left onto Forest Road 21, signed for Tupper Work Center.

Drive 1.3 miles on good gravel road until you reach the trailhead, a gated dirt spur on your left, signed for Madison Butte Trail. (If you pass the Tupper Work Center on your right, you have gone a few hundred feet too far.) You can drive this short spur to

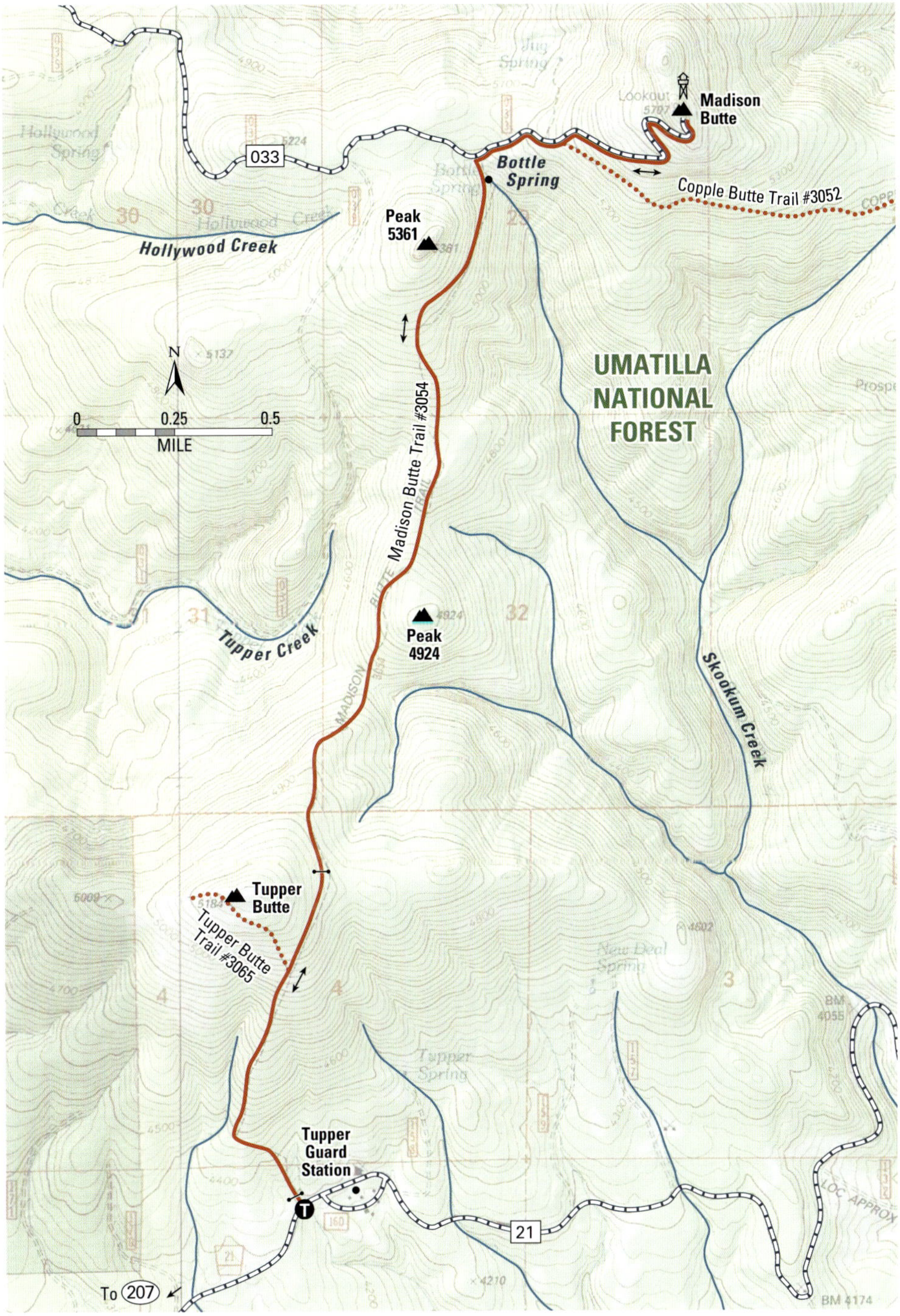
Madison Butte
Lookout
Bottle Spring
Copple Butte Trail #3052
033
Peak 5361
Hollywood Creek
UMATILLA NATIONAL FOREST
Madison Butte Trail #3054
0
0.25
0.5
MILE
Peak 4924
Tupper Creek
Skookum Creek
Tupper Butte
Tupper Butte Trail #3065
Tupper Guard Station
21
To 207

park near the gate, but it is rutted and sometimes muddy. Otherwise, park along the shoulder of FR 21 where there is room for half a dozen cars.

ON THE TRAIL

Madison Butte Trail #3054 starts at the large metal road gate. Open the wire gate to the left, walk through, then close it behind you. The first part of this hike follows an old grassy Jeep track that heads straight uphill through a forest of ponderosa pines, Douglas-firs, and junipers. In May and June, enjoy hiking through a landscape full of barestem desert parsley, arnica, larkspur, groundsel, balsamroot, lupine, and death camas.

At 0.7 mile, pass the unsigned junction with Tupper Butte Trail #3065—another old Jeep track—on the left. This faint grassy path angles northwest across the meadow for 0.3 mile to the summit of Tupper Butte, an interesting detour if you have the time and energy.

Past this junction, the Madison Butte Trail continues climbing, then levels out and enters a dense stand of trees at 0.9 mile, which provides a cool shady respite on hot summer days. You will round the east side of Tupper Butte, then cross a barbed-wire

Approaching Madison Butte Lookout

LEFT *Balsamroot blooming on Madison Butte* **RIGHT** *View from Madison Butte*

fence. This fence may have collapsed enough for you to climb over it, but there is also a gate you can walk through. Scattered among the trees, larches make for a glorious sight in the second half of October when the needles turn bright orange before falling off. The needles grow back in early summer, when it is also a good time to see tiny yellow violets growing low to the ground.

The trail now gradually descends, still in the trees. At 1.4 miles, emerge from the forest with a view of Madison Butte straight ahead. You can see the lookout tower sticking up above the trees, windows glinting in the sun. The trail curves right, still heading downhill, then enters a forest. Reach a saddle and begin climbing again, rounding the west side of Peak 4924.

The trail is faint in some spots, especially when passing through meadows. Pay attention and keep an eye out for the occasional white or silver diamonds on trees that mark the way. Another good indicator of the correct route is previous trail work where a fallen tree across the trail has had several feet cut out of it.

Descend again. (I warned you there was uphill in both directions!) Reach another saddle where the trail briefly flattens out, then begins ascending again. Now it is a steady climb through open forest and meadows. Round the east side of Peak 5361, with Madison Butte's forested southern slope appearing on your right. Pass Bottle Spring, where ice-cold spring water flows from a pipe into a small plastic trough before flowing down the hillside into a murky pond. (Note that even spring water should be filtered before drinking.) Several old, rusted troughs lie scattered about among the false hellebore that grows in the meadow. Beyond the spring, climb up the slope to the junction with Forest Road 033 at 3.2 miles and turn right onto the road.

Your path now climbs steeply, passing through more patches of false hellebore growing on either side of the road. After 0.3 mile on the road, you will pass the unsigned junction with Copple Butte Trail #3052 on the right. (This ridgetop trail heads northeast past Texas Butte and Copple Butte, ending 10 miles away at Forest Road 53.)

Continue up the road, passing beneath towering ponderosa pines and Douglas-fir. Off-highway vehicles are popular in these parts, but this road is gated farther down from May 1 to June 30 and from August 15 to December 1, so if you visit during those times you should see no traffic. After 0.9 mile on the road, reach the summit with its 37-foot lookout tower, which is staffed during fire season.

In 1923, a D-6 cupola cabin was built on Madison Butte. It was replaced by the current 37-foot CL-100 steel tower in 1957. A shed now sits at the base of the tower on the south side where the cupola cabin once stood, but the old concrete cabin foundation makes a perfect spot to sit and admire the landscape to the south, which includes the distant Aldrich Mountains. If you walk to the far west end of the flat parking area on the south side of the tower, you can also see the Strawberry Mountains to the southeast. From the driveway on the east side of the lookout, you also get a view of Black Mountain to the northeast with its telecommunications towers sticking up above the trees. It is the Morrow County high point, at 5932 feet.

Return the way you came.

37 TOWER MOUNTAIN

YEAR CONSTRUCTED	LOOKOUT ACCESS	LOCATION
1935	Staffed; accessible to the public when invited in by staff; locked when not staffed	Umatilla National Forest, North Fork John Day Ranger District

Roundtrip distance: 11.4 miles
Elevation gain: 1800 feet
Lookout elevation: 6850 feet
Map: USGS Tower Mountain
GPS coordinates: 45.01099°, –118.61455°
Permits and fees: None

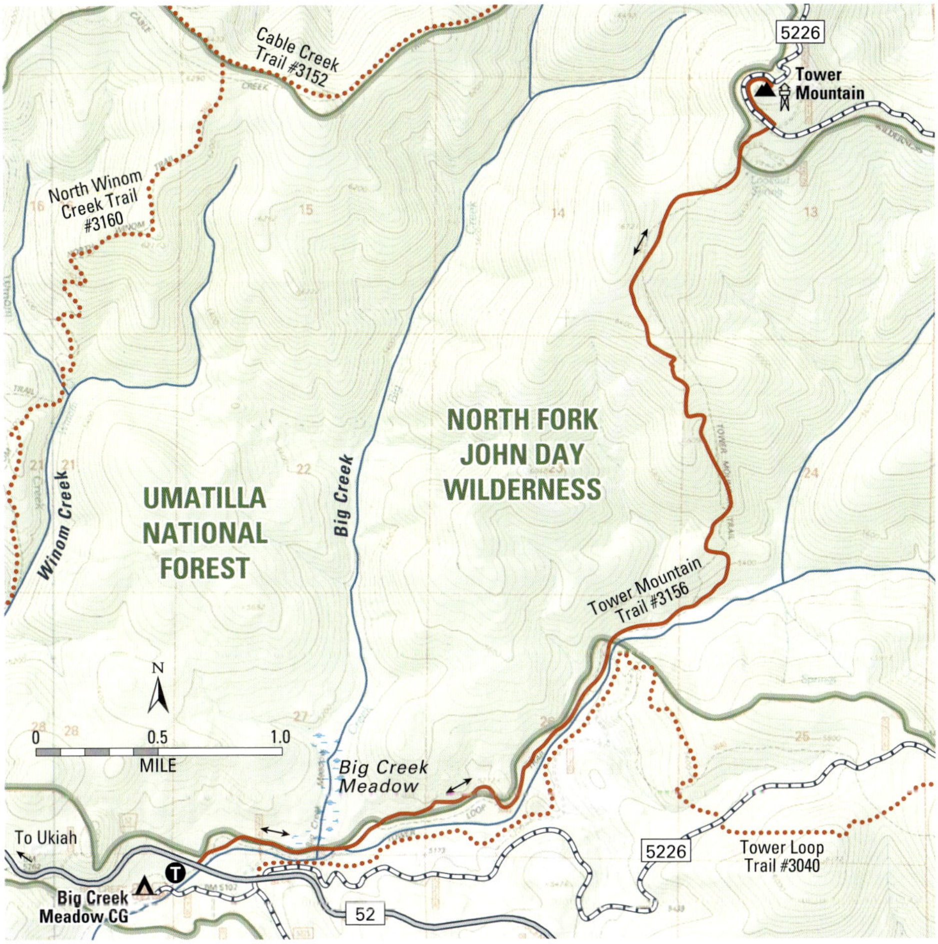

Hike through the North Fork John Day Wilderness to appropriately named Tower Mountain, which hosts the tallest lookout in this book. This hike is long but not steep, and good navigational skills are recommended for the first mile where the trail is faint. You will also encounter several water crossings without bridges, so bring water shoes or some sturdy sandals if you do not want to get your boots wet.

GETTING TO THE TRAILHEAD

From Sumpter, head west on Granite Hill Road (Forest Road 73), also known as the Elkhorn Scenic Byway. Drive 25 miles to a junction where FR 73 goes right, and continue straight on Forest Road 52. Drive for 17 miles, then 0.2 mile past the turnoff

U 16

to Big Creek Campground on the left (FR 5225), look for the unsigned parking area on the left shoulder. The trail starts on the north side of the road.

If you are coming from the north, from exit 209 on Interstate 84 in Pendleton, drive south on US Highway 395 for 47.5 miles, then turn east onto paved Oregon Route 244. Drive 1.2 miles into the town of Ukiah, then turn right onto Camas Street, which becomes FR 52. Drive 23.6 paved miles and watch for a pullout on the right side of the road across from a trail sign on the left, just before the junction with FR 5225 to the campground. There is room for two cars here.

ON THE TRAIL

Trail signs on the north side of FR 52 mark the spot where Tower Mountain Trail #3156 heads into a dense forest of lodgepole pines. The first part of the hike is grassy with faint trail tread in places. Solid route-finding skills are required, as the trail can be hard to follow.

At 0.4 mile, the trail reaches the southwest corner of Big Creek Meadow. Stay to the right at the edge of the meadow, aiming for a break in the trees where the trail continues. After a brief passage through the trees, you will reenter the meadow. A trail to the right heads down to the creek, but you will cross the meadow. The trail angles slightly left but stays to the right of the trees growing in the middle of the meadow.

The trail reenters the trees, then at 0.5 mile crosses Big Creek, your first bridgeless water crossing. Although you can't tell from here, Big Creek Meadow continues north from here for half a mile. You will now skirt a smaller meadow along the tree line and cross another bridgeless creek. Almost immediately the trail crosses the same creek, again without the benefit of a bridge.

Now easier to follow, the trail starts heading northeast, following alongside an unnamed tributary of Big Creek, which comes in and out of view. You will meander in and out of the forest, crossing several meadows where wildflowers bloom in June. Most of the mountainside here burned in 1996 when lightning started the Tower Fire, which spread over more than fifty-one thousand acres.

The trail crosses into the North Fork John Day Wilderness at 2.5 miles, then at around 2.8 miles, it swings north away from the creek, heading gently up the mountain through the forest, where you will start to see western larch. On a clear day, you will get the occasional peek through the trees at the surrounding mountains.

At the 5-mile mark, pass a brown wilderness boundary sign, then 0.3 mile later you will emerge onto FR 5226. (Yes, the public can drive this road to the lookout,

OPPOSITE *The steel Tower Mountain Lookout has been standing tall since 1938.*

although there are several narrow, cliff-hugging sections.) Turn left and hike up the road for another 0.4 mile to the summit with its tower and cabin.

The first structure on Tower Mountain was a 60-foot pole tower topped with a 6-by-6-foot cab that was built in the 1920s. At the time, this spot was known as Lookout Mountain, but to avoid confusion with another Lookout Mountain 66 miles to the northeast, the name was changed to the equally unoriginal Tower Mountain.

That first tower was replaced by a 92-foot Aermotor steel tower in 1935, which still stands today. A cabin was built for living quarters, but it burned down in 1947. Two years later, the Forest Service removed the cabin at Lucky Strike lookout 17 miles to the northwest and relocated it here, where it still stands. The lookout is staffed every year during fire season—one of only a few Aermotor towers in Oregon that still is.

The North Fork John Day Wilderness was designated in 1984. The main unit is 85,000 acres and includes the North Fork John Day drainage. Three satellite units include Greenhorn to the south, Tower to the north, and Baldy Creek to the west in the Wallowa-Whitman National Forest. Tower Mountain is almost at the northernmost point of the entire wilderness complex, save for a small segment of wilderness northwest of here. Together all four units comprise more than 120,000 acres.

Return the way you came.

The living quarters at Tower Mountain Lookout

38 INDIAN ROCK

YEAR CONSTRUCTED	LOOKOUT ACCESS	LOCATION
1957	Staffed; accessible to the public when invited in by staff; locked when not staffed	Umatilla National Forest, North Fork John Day Ranger District, and Malheur National Forest, Blue Mountain Ranger District

Roundtrip distance: 8.2 miles
Elevation gain: 1500 feet
Lookout elevation: 7350 feet
Map: USGS Desolation Butte
GPS coordinates: 44.79625°, –118.69539°
Permits and fees: None

Explore the little-known Vinegar Hill–Indian Rock Scenic Area by hiking to this lookout perched atop a rocky cliff with sweeping vistas of the surrounding Greenhorn Mountains. Come in July for wildflowers or in October for a spectacular fall larch display. Whenever you make the trek, solid route-finding skills and a GPS device or app are strongly recommended.

GETTING TO THE TRAILHEAD

From Sumpter, head west on Granite Hill Road (Forest Road 73), also known as the Elkhorn Scenic Byway. Drive 16 miles to the tiny community of Granite, then turn left onto County Road 24 (Red Boy Road), signed for Olive Lake. After 3.4 miles, fork right onto gravel FR 10. Drive for 18 miles, then turn left onto FR 45 and drive 4.2 good gravel miles to the Indian Rock trailhead. The trail starts on the left, and parking is on the right. There is room for four to five cars.

If you are coming from the north, from exit 209 on Interstate 84 in Pendleton, drive south on US Highway 395 for 75 miles, then turn east onto gravel Texas Bar Road, signed for Olive Lake and Granite. Drive for 0.7 mile and fork right onto FR 10. Drive 21.2 miles, then turn right onto FR 45 and drive 4.2 miles to the trailhead.

ON THE TRAIL

Indian Rock Trail #3039 starts out in a forest of lodgepole pine, subalpine fir, and grand fir. Western larch have returned to this trail since the 1996 Summit Fire,

The R-6 ground cabin on Indian Rock has endured since 1957.

making this an excellent hike in the second half of October when their needles turn a brilliant golden orange.

The trail begins a gradual descent. Pass through a stretch of mature trees that survived the fire. Keep your eyes open: At least three old ceramic phone insulators are attached to the trunks of these trees about ten feet up. These insulators were used back in the pre-radio days when a telephone line was strung along roads and trails for backcountry communication.

At 1.1 miles, reach a meadow where the trail completely vanishes. Angle to the left across the meadow, watching for cut logs and a break in the trees on the far side as signs you are on the correct path (navigating toward 44.78057°, –118.68922°).

Reenter the forest and soon you will cross into the Malheur National Forest, although the boundary is not marked or signed. If you come in July, the understory

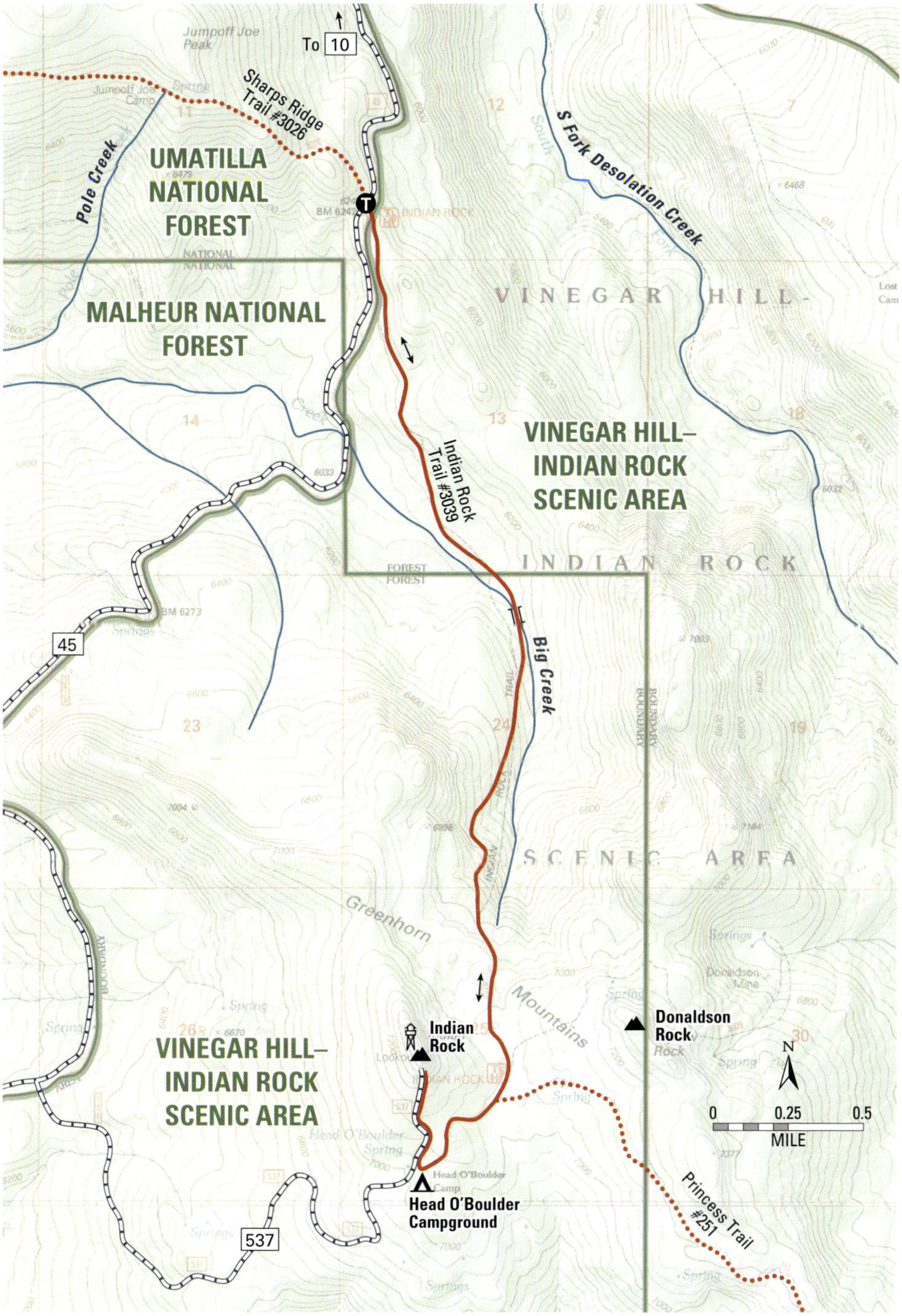
To 10
Jumpoff Joe Peak
Sharps Ridge Trail #3026
UMATILLA NATIONAL FOREST
Pole Creek
MALHEUR NATIONAL FOREST
S Fork Desolation Creek
VINEGAR HILL–INDIAN ROCK SCENIC AREA
Indian Rock Trail #3039
45
Big Creek
Greenhorn Mountains
Indian Rock
Donaldson Rock
VINEGAR HILL–INDIAN ROCK SCENIC AREA
Head O'Boulder Campground
537
Princess Trail #251
N
0
0.25
0.5
MILE

View from Indian Rock

here will be lush with paintbrush, lupine, and fleabane. Big Creek gurgles out of sight to your right, but in short order you will cross it on a large wooden footbridge.

You have only lost elevation up to this point, but that is about to change. Now the trail ascends through a dense post-fire forest. At 2.4 miles, cross a small seasonal creek. There is no bridge, but it is easy to rock hop across. The trail then crosses several dry creek beds. Enter an open meadow area where the Indian Rock lookout is visible ahead on the right; here again look for the cuts in the logs to guide your way. Beyond this is an open sandy area where the trail completely vanishes. Stay to the left along the tree line, then watch for cairns and metal signposts to help you stay on the path. You will then cross another broad open meadow where thousands of western coneflower grow. They grow three to six feet tall, topped by a purple-brown cone made up of disc florets. But don't let those beautiful wildflowers distract you; this stretch requires solid route-finding skills.

At 3.3 miles, reach the tree line on the west side of the meadow, where you will find the signed junction (at 44.75443°, –118.68725°) with Princess Trail #251, which heads east from here. However, you should look for the trail heading west into the trees and follow it. You are now hiking through the burn scar from the 2022 Crockets Knob Fire. In July, paintbrush, Sitka valerian, and lupine bloom here.

Enter unburned forest and descend to FR 537 at 3.6 miles. There is a trailhead here and the tiny Head O'Boulder Campground. Turn right and walk up the road. Hike to its end, then follow the trail up a slope covered in sagebrush and July wildflowers.

There is plenty of room up here to sit down and enjoy the views. To the north you can see the 67-foot lookout tower poking up above the trees on Desolation

Butte. Below you to the northeast is the valley of Big Creek that you hiked up to get here. Also to the east is Donaldson Rock, named for George W. Donaldson, who had a mine nearby (the name was changed from its former pejorative name around 2012). Beyond that in the distance are the peaks of the Elkhorn Mountains, Mount Ireland (Hike 39) among them. Vinegar Hill is visible to the southeast. Dixie Butte and its lookout can be seen to the south. Keep an eye out for the mountain goats that live here.

A D-6 cupola cabin was built on Indian Rock in 1929. It was replaced with an R-6 ground cabin in 1957, which still stands today. The lookout was threatened by the lightning-caused Crockets Knob Fire in 2022. Crews wrapped the lookout to protect it, and the cabin survived. (Crockett Knob is a former lookout site 5 miles southeast of Indian Rock.)

The Greenhorn Mountains are a small range within the Blue Mountains, with a long history of mining. Approximately eighty gold mines have operated in the Greenhorns, and prospecting continues to this day. Indian Rock is within the high-elevation Vinegar Hill–Indian Rock Scenic Area, notable for its open alpine landscapes. It covers approximately twenty-five thousand acres across two national forests, stretching from Sharp Ridge in the northwest corner to Psyche Butte in the southeast corner. The highest point is Vinegar Hill (8100 feet), a former lookout site that is reachable via a rough road suitable for four-wheel-drive vehicles.

Return the way you came.

39 MOUNT IRELAND

YEAR CONSTRUCTED	LOOKOUT ACCESS	LOCATION
1957	Staffed; accessible to the public when invited in by staff; locked when not staffed	Wallowa-Whitman National Forest, Whitman Ranger District

Roundtrip distance: 7 miles
Elevation gain: 2330 feet
Lookout elevation: 8320 feet
Map: USGS Mount Ireland
GPS coordinates: 44.81263°, –118.32837°
Permits and fees: None

This hike to the last remaining fire lookout in the Elkhorn Mountains (and the third-highest standing lookout in Oregon) is a workout, but the scenery is worth it, and you may just spot a mountain goat or two.

GETTING TO THE TRAILHEAD

From Sumpter, head west on Granite Hill Road (Forest Road 73), also known as the Elkhorn Scenic Byway. Drive for 11.6 miles, then turn right onto FR 7370. Drive for 0.5 mile to the junction with FR 180, then keep left to stay on FR 7370. Continue for another 1.7 miles to the junction with FR 150, then fork left to stay on FR 7370. Continue for 0.5 mile, then turn right onto FR 100.

Drive for 0.2 mile, then look for the decommissioned road heading uphill on your left where FR 100 bends to the right. There is room for three cars to park on the shoulder here. A confusing old sign says the trail is half a mile ahead, but in fact the hike starts right here.

ON THE TRAIL

Mount Ireland Lookout Trail #1604 starts out on what used to be FR 130, now closed to vehicles and populated with young trees growing on the old roadbed. At 0.3 mile, you will get a view of Mount Ireland to your left. Just beyond this spot, FR 130 heads right; you will fork left at an unsigned trail. Quickly reach another fork where another closed road goes left; you will stay to the right.

After a stiff climb, the trail levels out as it travels through a forest of Douglas-fir and grand fir. At 1.4 miles from the trailhead, cross FR 142, an old dirt road that heads to the Uncle Sam Mine 2 miles away to the west. Look for the continuation of the trail on the other side of the road.

The trail continues climbing through the forest, sometimes steeply; 1 mile after crossing the road, reach a signed junction in a large meadow and turn left to stay on the Mount Ireland Lookout Trail. (To the right, Downie Lake Trail #1609 descends 1.3 miles to Downie Lake.) The route now follows a narrow boulder-studded two-track that is passable by brave all-terrain vehicle drivers, including the Forest Service workers who work at the lookout. Follow this route as it climbs steadily upward, where the tree cover grows sparser and views to the west start opening up, a preview of the expanse to come and a good excuse to stop and catch your breath.

The two-track turns into a trail as it continues to traverse the southern slope of Mount Ireland. Then it turns east and makes several switchbacks on the last steep haul. The trail ends at the rocky open summit of Mount Ireland, where a few firs grow. Announce yourself to the lookout on duty and keep an eye out for mountain goats.

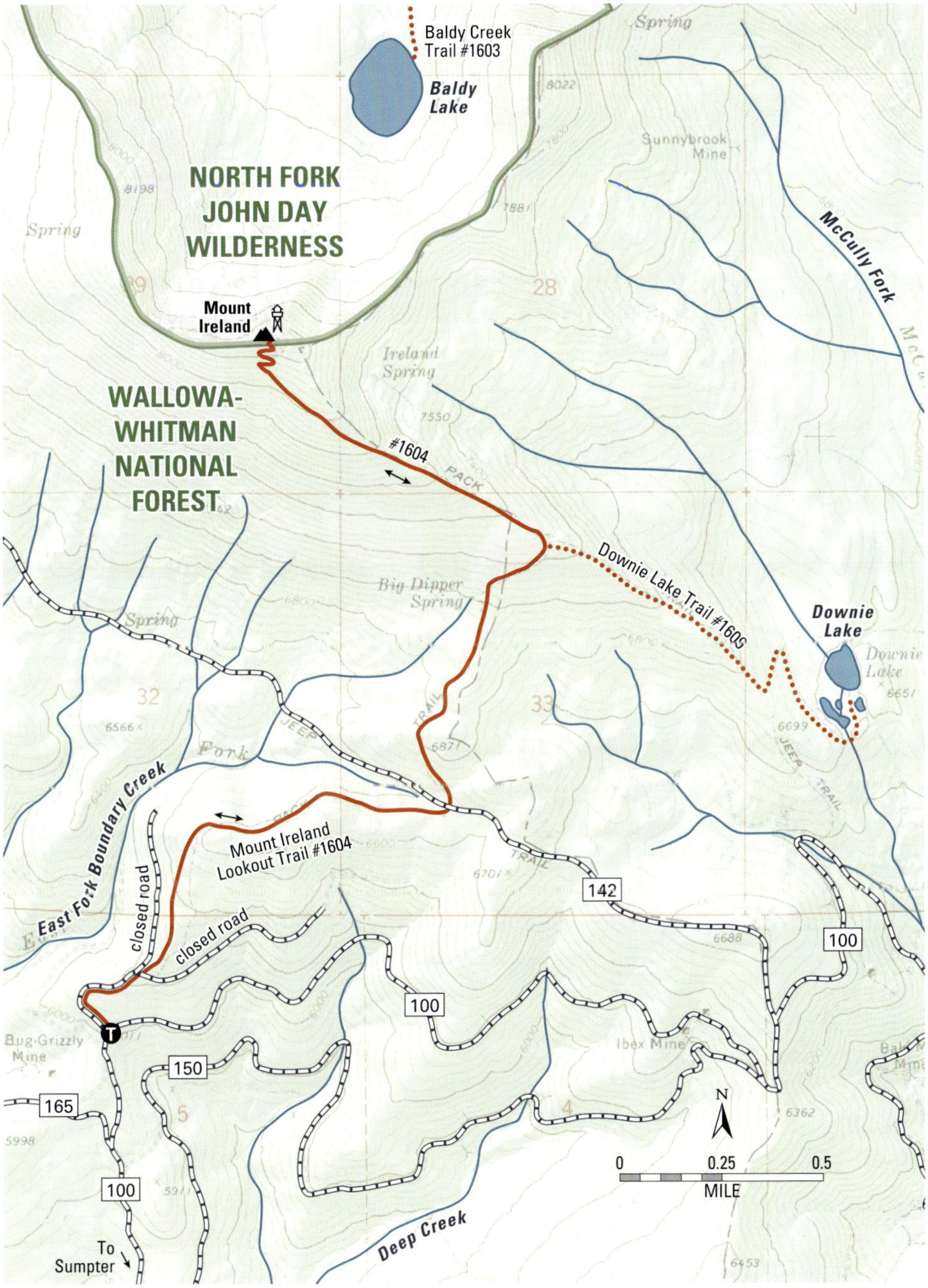
Baldy Creek
Trail #1603
Baldy
Lake
NORTH FORK
JOHN DAY
WILDERNESS
Mount
Ireland
WALLOWA-
WHITMAN
NATIONAL
FOREST
#1604
Downie Lake Trail #1605
Downie
Lake
McCully Fork
East Fork Boundary Creek
Mount Ireland
Lookout Trail #1604
closed road
closed road
142
100
100
150
165
100
To
Sumpter
Deep Creek
N
0
0.25
0.5
MILE

The lake below the summit to the north is Baldy Lake (reached via the 6.3-mile Baldy Creek Trail #1603 from FR 73), and much of the land in this direction is part of the North Fork John Day Wilderness. Lees Peak and Angell Peak are visible in the distance. To the west is Rock Creek Butte (9106 feet), the highest peak in the Elkhorns. Visible to the west is Desolation Butte, the next-nearest staffed lookout 17 air miles away. A bit farther south of that is Indian Rock (Hike 38), which also has a staffed lookout. And farther south still is Vinegar Hill, a former lookout site, and Dixie Butte, with its staffed ground cabin 23 air miles southwest.

In 1916, a cabin was built on Mount Ireland. It had a rooftop observation platform, reached via a ladder, that was replaced by a cupola twelve years later. A new steel lookout was built in 1957 and still stands today, staffed every summer. The Forest Service flies in supplies via helicopter at the beginning of the season; after that, the lookout is responsible for hiking out to get any additional supplies and hauling them back up to the summit.

Once known as Bald Mountain, the name was changed in 1917 to honor Henry Ireland, former supervisor of the Whitman National Forest. It stands at the southern tip of the Baldy Creek Unit of the North Fork John Day Wilderness, which was designated in 1984 to protect the headwater tributaries of the North Fork John

The steel Mount Ireland Lookout is staffed in summer.

Overlooking Baldy Lake from Mount Ireland

Day River. The other three units of the wilderness lie to the west in the Umatilla National Forest.

If you look at a topo map of this area, you will see many mining prospects in these mountains. Gold was discovered west of here on Granite Creek in 1862 and a town sprung to life. Originally called Independence, its name was changed to Granite when the Postal Service pointed out that there was already an Independence in the Willamette Valley. By 1900, Granite had five saloons, three stores, and the three-story Grand Hotel. As the gold petered out and the mines closed, Granite shrank. Its post office closed in 1957.

A town called Fort Sumter was also established in 1862. When it received a post office in 1883, the name was changed to Sumpter. A railway was built between Sumpter and Baker City thirteen years later. By the turn of the century, Sumpter had seventeen saloons and eleven hotels. Mines started closing down in 1906, but dredging started up in 1912. Dredges scooped up the earth, sorted out the gold, and dumped the tailings behind the dredge. Ultimately, three of them would be built and used in the Sumpter Valley. The final one, which was built in 1935 and unearthed an estimated $4 million in gold during its operation, was abandoned in 1954 as operating costs skyrocketed; however, it is now the centerpiece of the Sumpter Valley Dredge State Heritage Area.

Gold mining ceased during World War II so that men, supplies, and equipment could be used for the war effort. The gold mines of the Blue Mountains were largely abandoned due to the high cost of mining and the fixed price of gold, leaving the mining ruins and tunnels still scattered throughout the region to be slowly reclaimed by nature.

Return the way you came.

40 STRAWBERRY MOUNTAIN

YEAR CONSTRUCTED	LOOKOUT ACCESS	LOCATION
1941	Removed	Malheur National Forest, Prairie City Ranger District

Roundtrip distance: 7.4 miles
Elevation gain: 1200 feet
Lookout elevation: 9040 feet
Map: USGS Strawberry Mountain
GPS coordinates: 44.28003°, –118.70331°
Permits and fees: None

This beautiful hike passes mostly through a burn area, but the summer wildflowers and summit views are both amazing. You are also unlikely to see many hikers on the first part of the route, since most people hike up from Strawberry Lake.

GETTING TO THE TRAILHEAD

From John Day, drive south on US Highway 395 for 10.1 miles and turn left onto Canyon Creek Lane (County Road 65), which becomes Forest Road 15. Drive for 13.8 miles, then turn left onto FR 16. Drive for 2.6 miles, then turn left onto gravel FR 1640. Follow FR 1640 for 10 miles until you reach Roads End trailhead (some maps call it the Strawberry Mountain trailhead) on the left where the road bends sharply to the right (although you are not actually at the end of the road). There is room for six to eight cars here. All roads on this route are suitable for a low-clearance car.

ON THE TRAIL

Roads End Trail #201A starts at the north side of the parking area behind the large boulders and follows an abandoned road for the first 1.2 miles. Hiking an old road may sound tedious, but this stretch is truly outstanding in July when thousands of wildflowers bloom alongside—and even on—the old roadbed. Expect to see penstemon, buckwheat, paintbrush, phlox, Sitka valerian, and pussypaws. The old burned snags you see are remnants of the 1996 Wildcat Fire.

At 1.2 miles, the road ends at an unsigned junction where the seldom-used and seldom-maintained Pine Creek Trail #201 drops down to the left. This junction is also a great place to get a good look at pointy Strawberry Mountain ahead of you.

Spring-fed East Fork Indian Creek is down below you in the bowl. The burned snags here are from the more recent 2015 Canyon Creek Complex Fire. From here, you will turn right onto Onion Creek Trail #368, which traverses a slope dotted with yet more summer wildflowers. Although the forest here is gone, the lack of trees allows you to gaze upon Strawberry Mountain ahead during this entire section of the hike.

At 2.6 miles, reach a junction with Strawberry Basin Trail #375. Most hikers who visit the mountain come up that way, via Strawberry Lake. (This is a 12.5-mile roundtrip hike with more than 3500 feet of elevation gain.) You will stay left at the junction, where you will traverse the open rocky east slope of Strawberry Mountain before entering an area of unburned trees. Reach a junction where the Onion Creek Trail heads right. You will turn left for the last push to the summit, where metal cables are the only remaining evidence of the long-gone fire lookout.

There is plenty of room to spread out on the rocky summit and enjoy the scenery, especially Canyon Mountain to the west and the John Day River valley to the north. Dixie Butte can also be seen to the north, but you need a strong pair of binoculars to

On the way up Strawberry Mountain through burned snags

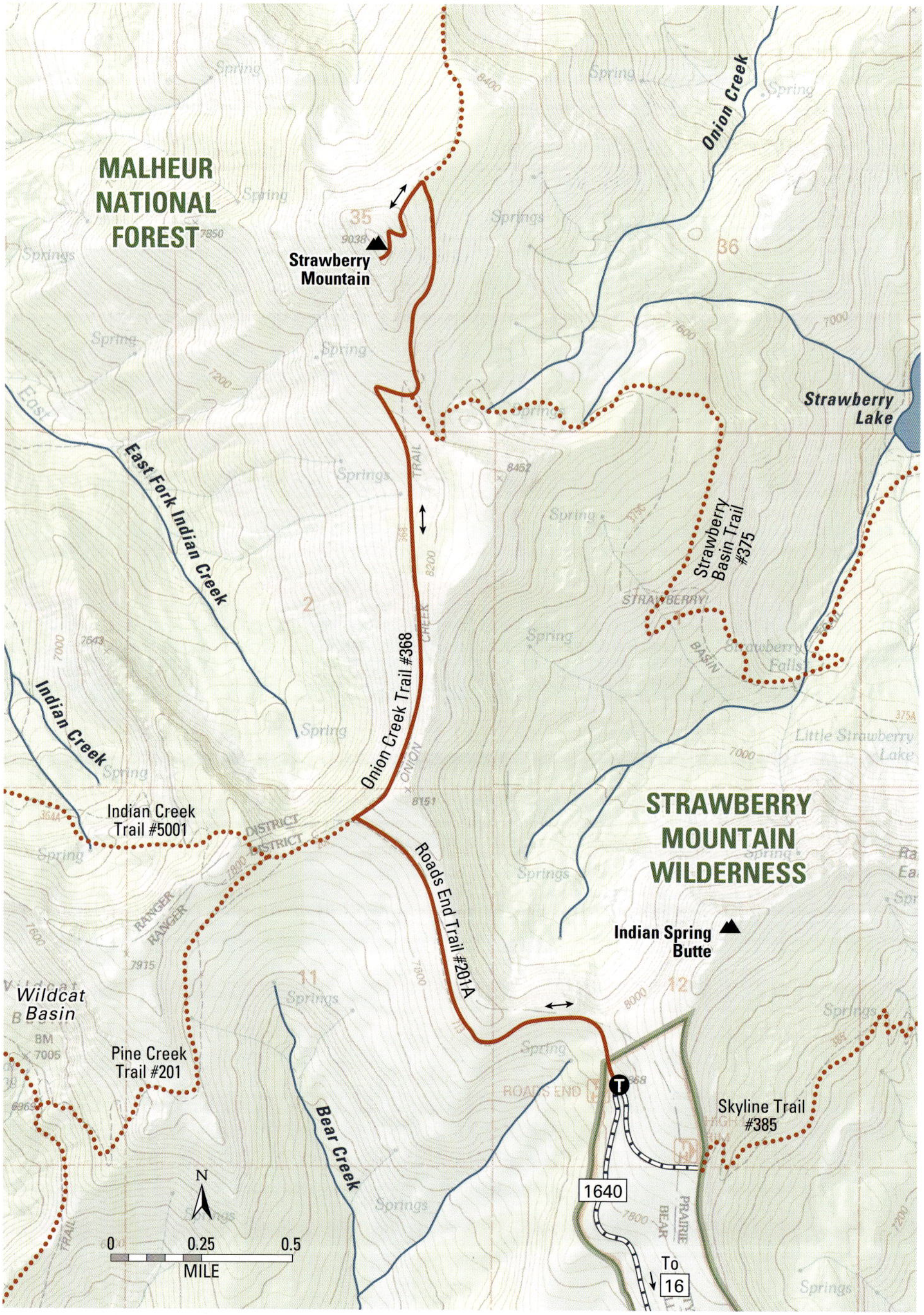
MALHEUR NATIONAL FOREST
Strawberry Mountain
Onion Creek
Strawberry Lake
East Fork Indian Creek
Strawberry Basin Trail #375
Onion Creek Trail #368
Indian Creek
Indian Creek Trail #5001
STRAWBERRY MOUNTAIN WILDERNESS
Roads End Trail #201A
Indian Spring Butte
Wildcat Basin
Pine Creek Trail #201
Bear Creek
Skyline Trail #385
1640
To 16
0
0.25
0.5
MILE
N

Watch for mountain goats while you enjoy the view from Strawberry Mountain.

see its staffed lookout cabin. To the southeast, you will see a pair of distinctive rock formations known as the Rabbit Ears, for obvious reasons. Strawberry Lake is out of sight to the east, 2800 feet below the mountain.

Keep an eye out and you may spot some mountain goats up here. They disappeared from Oregon in the nineteenth century, but the Oregon Department of Fish & Wildlife has been reintroducing them to their habitat, including thirteen that were moved from the Elkhorns to the Strawberry Mountains in 2007. If you are lucky enough to see them, notice their sure-footedness in this steep mountain terrain, for which they are particularly well suited. These herbivores roam the mountains (usually in groups) foraging for moss, lichen, grass, and leaves from shrubs and conifers.

Two tons of steel were transported by pack animal to the top of Strawberry Mountain in 1916 to construct a lookout. It was an especially difficult process. A ranger and the man who would staff the lookout tried hauling a load of supplies to

Wildflowers along the trail to Strawberry Mountain

the summit in late July but encountered snow from the prior winter that was up to fifteen feet deep in places. The ranger's horse fell 70 feet (but was unharmed), and the two had to give up trying to reach the summit. Later in the summer, when the trail was finally clear and construction materials could be transported, another problem was encountered: Some of the steel beams were twelve feet long, too long to be transported horizontally due to the difficulty in navigating corners and switchbacks. Instead, they had to be loaded onto the animals in an awkward vertical position. After all that trouble with construction, the lookout ended up being short-lived, as it was destroyed by wind the following year. In 1921, a D-6 cupola was built, and in 1941 it was replaced with an L-4 cabin, which was ultimately removed in the 1960s.

Strawberry Mountain was called Logan Butte by early settlers. Nathan Willis Fisk established a homestead along a creek north of there and, due to the abundance of wild strawberries, called it Strawberry Creek, a name that spread to other nearby features including Logan Butte, which became known as Strawberry Butte. Over time the word *mountain* supplanted *butte*. The Strawberry Mountain Wilderness was designated in 1964 and expanded in 1984. It stretches 18 miles along the length of the Strawberry Mountains and currently encompasses more than 69,000 acres, much of which burned in 2015, when the lightning-caused Berry Creek and Mason Springs Fires, pushed by high winds, merged to become the Canyon Creek Complex on August 14. The fire ultimately burned a total of 110,000 acres and destroyed forty-three homes. Although the wilderness contains more than 120 miles of trails, the Strawberry Lake and Strawberry Mountain area is by far the most popular with hikers.

Return the way you came.

41 TABLE ROCK

YEAR CONSTRUCTED	LOOKOUT ACCESS	LOCATION
1949	Staffed; accessible to the public when invited in by staff; locked when not staffed	Wallowa-Whitman National Forest, Whitman Ranger District

Roundtrip distance: 5 miles
Elevation gain: 1900 feet
Lookout elevation: 7820 feet
Map: USGS Bullrun Rock
GPS coordinates: 44.35948°, –118.31027°
Permits and fees: None

Ask an Oregonian about Table Rock and they are likely to think of Table Rocks near Medford. This Table Rock sees far fewer visitors, but the views are just as awesome. You will have to work for it, though. This hike gains almost 2000 feet in just 2.5 miles. Due to the steepness and lack of shade, save this one for a cooler day.

Because of a lack of funding and personnel, this trail receives maintenance irregularly. Part of the route was burned in the 2016 Rail Fire, and blowdown may be abundant. Check with the Forest Service for trail conditions before heading out.

Wrapped by fire crews to protect it, Table Rock Lookout survived the 2016 Rail Fire.

GETTING TO THE TRAILHEAD

From the sharp 90-degree turn on US Highway 26 in Unity, turn west onto paved South Fork Burnt River Road, signed for South Fork Campground. Drive for 4 paved miles, then 2.9 gravel miles. Turn left onto Forest Road 6010, signed for Amelia Creek Trail, Table Rock Trail, and Bullrun Trail. Drive for 2 miles, pass a toilet on the left, then fork right. Immediately fork right again onto FR 030, signed for Table Rock trailhead. This road is mostly good gravel, but it does have a few rutted sections in the burn area; drivers in low-clearance cars should proceed with caution. Drive 4.1 miles, then pull into the trailhead parking area on the left.

ON THE TRAIL

Cross the road to where Table Rock Trail #1960 begins next to a signboard. The hike starts out in a forest of Douglas-fir, pine, and larch. Lupine, fleabane, and other wildflowers bloom here in July. Soon you can see Table Rock and its lookout ahead of you—yup, you are climbing all the way up there! The trail passes in and out of open meadow areas and forest. In one such open area you get a view of Bullrun Rock on your left.

At 0.4 mile, cross into the Monument Rock Wilderness. As of 2024, the old wire cattle gate at the wilderness boundary had been destroyed by fallen trees. Now enter an area burned in a 2016 wildfire, where the trail climbs steeply, passing in and out of burned and unburned forest.

After hiking through a forest of young lodgepole pine—regenerating after the 2002 Monument Fire—the trail angles southwest at the 1.6-mile mark, then leaves the live trees behind and enters a large area of burned snags from the 2016 Rail Fire. The trail can be faint and hard to follow, so watch for rock cairns to help guide your way. Life is returning here; baby lodgepole pines dot the hillside, and you can see phlox, fleabane, and other wildflowers in the summer.

The trail swings south, then angles southeast. Table Rock is visible through the burned snags, and the lookout briefly appears again. The trail traverses beneath a rocky cliff on the right, then reaches a fence line, passing through a wire cattle gate (like the earlier one, this one may be broken and lying open on the ground). Cross a cow path that parallels the fence line and head straight across the grassy area toward FR 1370 where the trail ends next to a broken signpost.

Turn left and start hiking up the road. This rough, rock-studded dirt road, used for accessing the lookout, more closely resembles a creek bed in spots. It is not gated, so you may see trucks and off-highway vehicles.

After 0.2 mile on the road, you will reach the lookout. Standing on this broad, flat summit that tilts slightly to the west, you can see how this peak got its name. As you

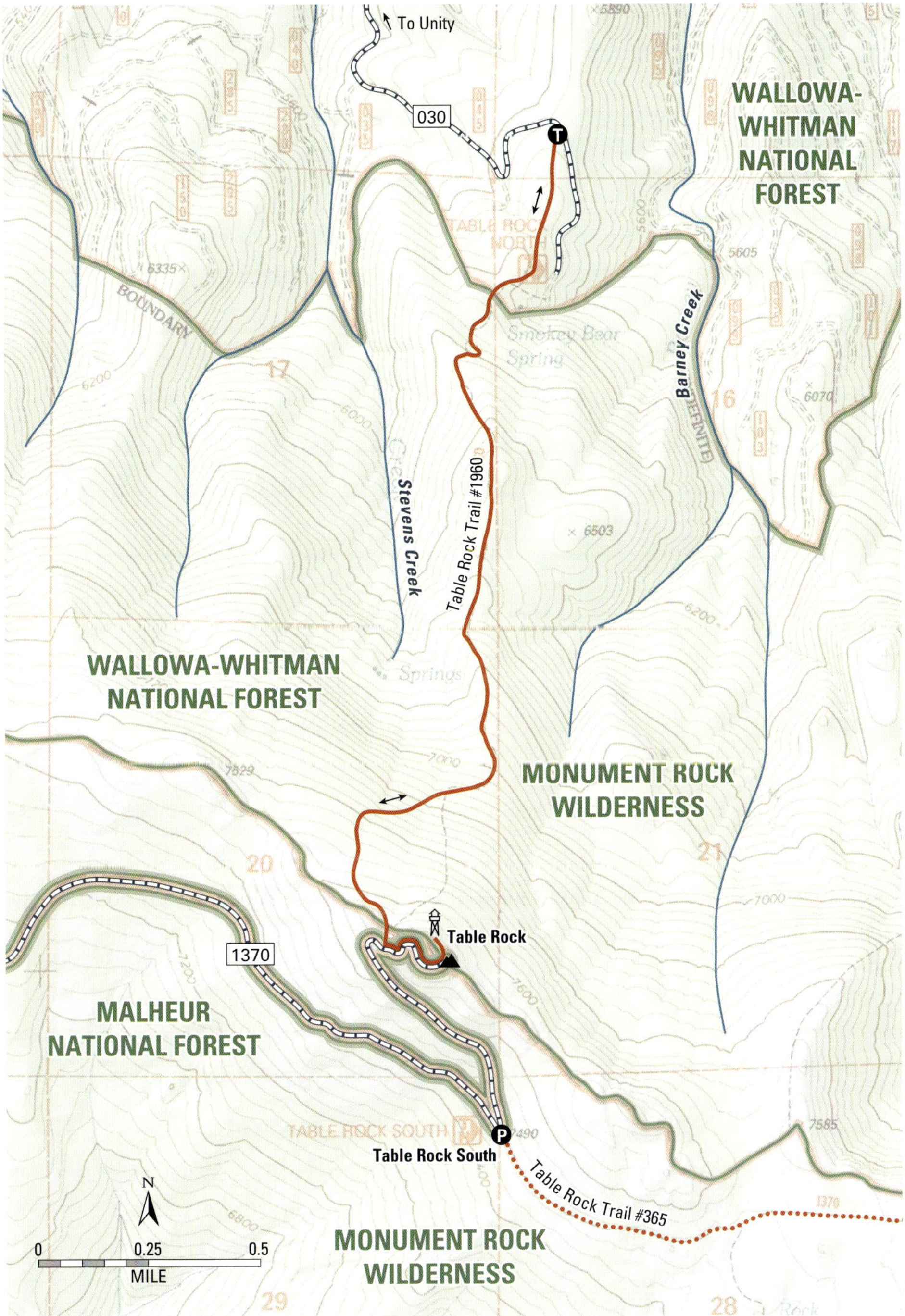
To Unity
030
WALLOWA-
WHITMAN
NATIONAL
FOREST
Smokey Bear
Spring
Barney Creek
Stevens Creek
Table Rock Trail #1960
WALLOWA-WHITMAN
NATIONAL FOREST
Springs
MONUMENT ROCK
WILDERNESS
1370
Table Rock
MALHEUR
NATIONAL FOREST
Table Rock South
Table Rock Trail #365
N
0
0.25
0.5
MILE
MONUMENT ROCK
WILDERNESS

The Table Rock Lookout is surrounded by the Monument Rock Wilderness.

walk around you will get 360-degree views. To the north is Dixie Butte, Vinegar Hill, Mount Ireland, and the Elkhorns. To the southeast are Bullrun Rock and Monument Rock in the foreground, with Ironside Mountain in the distance between them. On an especially clear day you might be able to make out Steens Mountain to the south, 117 miles away. Lookout Mountain and Strawberry Mountain (Hike 40) can be seen to the east.

Table Rock became a lookout site in the 1920s when a D-6 cupola was built here. In 1936, it was replaced by an L-4 ground cabin, which was replaced again in 1949 with another L-4 cabin, which is still staffed every year during fire season. The lookout was threatened by the 2016 Rail Fire, which burned 27,000 acres. Crews wrapped the lookout to protect it and the fire got so close that an old garage and outhouse were consumed by the flames, but the lookout was spared.

The lookout is surrounded by the 20,000-acre Monument Rock Wilderness, which was designated in 1984. (The final 3.3 miles of FR 1370 and the lookout were left out of the wilderness, with the boundary hugging both sides of the road.) The landmark for which this wilderness was named is a rocky prominence crowned by a large cylindrical pile of rocks that may have been constructed by Basque shepherds who grazed their flocks here in the early 1900s. The wilderness has acreage in both the Malheur National Forest and the Wallowa-Whitman National Forest, lying along a watershed divide with the Little Malheur River to the south and the South Fork Burnt River to the north. More than half the wilderness burned in the 2002 Monument Fire, and some of that burned again in the 2016 Rail Fire.

Return the way you came.

42 MULE PEAK

YEAR CONSTRUCTED	LOOKOUT ACCESS	LOCATION
1924	Staffed as needed; accessible to the public when invited in by staff; locked when not staffed	Wallowa-Whitman National Forest, Eagle Cap Ranger District

Roundtrip distance: 10.6 miles
Elevation gain: 3780 feet
Lookout elevation: 8550 feet
Maps: USGS China Cap and USGS Flagstaff Butte
GPS coordinates: 45.10800°, –117.55998°
Permits and fees: None

Oregon's second-highest and most remote lookout is also the hike with the most elevation gain in this book. Sections of the trail are faint and hard to follow, so only undertake this hike if you have reliable route-finding skills.

GETTING TO THE TRAILHEAD

From Main Street in downtown Union, turn onto Beakman Street (Oregon Route 203) headed east, signed for Catherine Creek State Park. Drive for 13.9 miles to Catherine Summit Sno-Park, then turn left onto Forest Road 77, signed for West Eagle Meadows and Boulder Park. Drive for 0.7 mile to an intersection with FR 900, where you will bear right to stay on FR 77. Drive for 9 more miles, then turn left onto FR 600.

Drive 3.6 miles on FR 600, cross South Fork Catherine Creek on a bridge, then immediately turn right onto FR 650 (signed for Pole Creek trailhead). Here you need to open a wire gate, drive through it, and close it behind you to reach the trailhead proper, a small gravel parking area. (If the gate is open, then leave it open. Always leave gates in the state you found them.) If you, like me, struggle to open and close these tight wire gates, you can park here; the trailhead is just 300 feet up the road.

ON THE TRAIL

Sand Pass Trail #1912 begins by crossing bridgeless Pole Creek and continuing straight along the decommissioned continuation of FR 650. South Fork Catherine Creek flows below you out of sight on the right. This road has been closed for so long that trees grow where vehicles once drove, and in places the majority of the roadbed has been swallowed up by the slope to the left. After 0.4 mile, cross Sand Pass Creek, which also has no bridge.

After 1 mile on the old road, the trail forks at an unsigned and easy-to-miss junction. Take the left fork, heading uphill on another decommissioned road. (If you reach another creek crossing, you have missed the junction and gone too far.) At 0.1 mile from the junction, the trail switchbacks to the left, leaving the old road.

Traverse a grassy slope and make several more switchbacks uphill, where you can enjoy wildflowers in July. Catch your breath as the trail levels out, and soon you will hear the sound of Sand Pass Creek out of sight below you on the left. This reprieve is short-lived, however, as the trail once again launches steeply uphill through the pines.

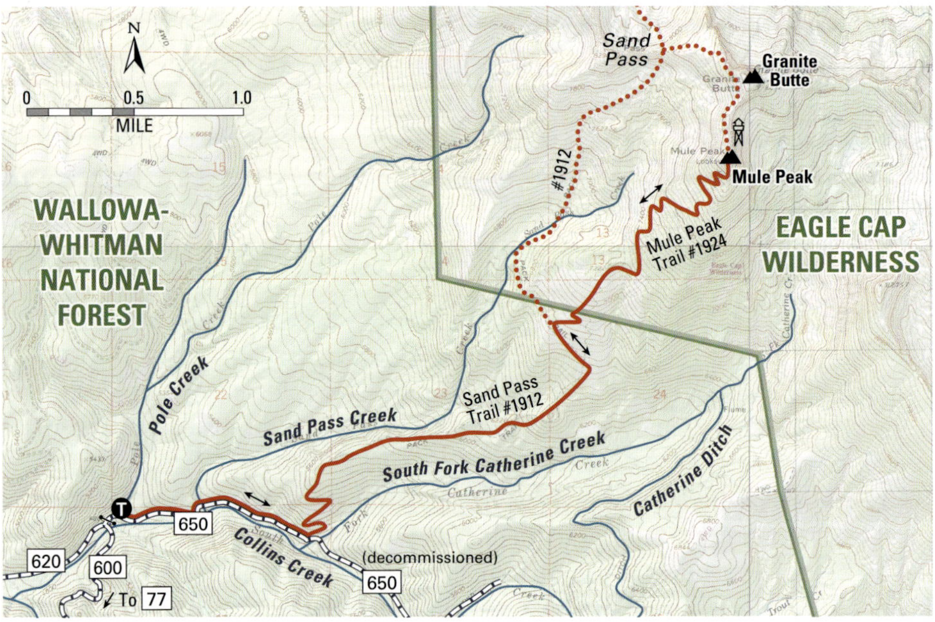

Staffed only in emergencies, Mule Peak Lookout is the only fire lookout in the Eagle Cap Wilderness.

At 3.1 miles from the trailhead, the trail makes a sharp left turn in an open meadow area, and 0.3 mile farther, it reaches a junction with Mule Peak Trail #1924 on the right. Follow this faint trail east. Cross an open area, pass through some trees, then cross an even bigger open area, aiming for a clump of trees. Just beyond them, the trail switchbacks up to the left, then soon makes another switchback to the right, now angling northeast across the open area toward Mule Peak, where you can see the lookout cabin. You will cross the wilderness boundary (which may be unsigned) along this stretch. (If you lose the trail, aim for 45.12378°, –117.51276° on the far side of the meadow.)

At the far end of the meadow, enter an area of snags from the 2005 Mule Peak Fire. Then the trail swings right, where it begins to switchback mercilessly up the mountain for the next 1.5 miles. The climbing feels relentless, especially given the high elevation. The trail is easier to follow up these switchbacks than in the meadow below, but it still gets lost among the boulders at times. If you are running low on water, there is a spring, identified by the lush vegetation that surrounds it, 0.8 mile below the summit at a switchback.

Finally, after 5.3 total miles, reach the summit. Views stretch in all directions. You can see Granite Peak to the north and the numerous peaks of the Eagle Cap Wilderness spread before you. Eagle Cap, the peak for which this wilderness is named, is visible to the east. On a clear day you can see the distant Elkhorns to the southwest. The unnamed green meadow far below has a little creek that becomes South Fork Catherine Creek.

Northeast Oregon was once home to the Nez Perce. Chief Joseph was the leader of the Wallowa Band of the tribe, who made their home in the Wallowa Valley, traveling into the mountains to hunt and gather huckleberries. He resisted the US government's attempts to force him and his people onto reservations, eventually attempting to lead his people to Canada, but he surrendered just 40 miles south of the border.

The D-6 fire lookout on Mule Peak (which is only staffed during emergencies) was built in 1924, the only remaining lookout in the Eagle Cap Wilderness. Designated in 1964 (having previously been designated a Primitive Area in 1930), the wilderness was subsequently expanded in 1972 and again in 1984. The expansion into lower elevations of the mountains was unusual, since these areas were usually excluded from other wilderness designations due to the timber that could potentially be harvested there. At 360,000 acres, it is Oregon's largest wilderness area, containing over 500 miles of trails.

The Wallowa Mountains are full of peaks more than 9000 feet high, so Mule Peak is by no means among the tallest; however, it is one of the few that has an official trail to its summit. The Wilderness Act does not allow for structures to be built, but existing structures were exempted when the Wilderness Act was passed.

Return the way you came.

The far-ranging vista from Mule Peak

EXTEND YOUR HIKE

If you are particularly adventurous, you can keep following the Mule Peak Trail as it curves around the left side of the lookout, passes a toilet, and then continues 0.8 mile along the west slope of Granite Butte to Sand Pass, where you can head north toward Burger Meadows and beyond, or turn south to loop back on Sand Pass Trail toward the junction with the Mule Peak Trail, where you then retrace your steps to return to your car.

43 SUMMIT POINT

YEAR CONSTRUCTED	LOOKOUT ACCESS	LOCATION
1949	Staffed; accessible to the public when invited in by staff; locked when not staffed	Wallowa-Whitman National Forest, Whitman Ranger District

Roundtrip distance: 1.8 miles
Elevation gain: 580 feet
Lookout elevation: 7010 feet
Map: USGS Jimtown
GPS coordinates: 44.97644°, –117.23909°
Permits and fees: None

This short hike leads to a tower on a sagebrush-covered high point at the southern edge of the Wallowa Mountains. From there you can see both the granite peaks and forested slopes of the Eagle Cap Wilderness and the arid lowlands of eastern Oregon.

GETTING TO THE TRAILHEAD

From Halfway, head north on Cornucopia Highway for 5 miles (keeping to the main paved road as it jogs left, then right, at 2.2 miles in Jimtown), then turn left onto Carson Lane, which turns into Forest Road 7710. Drive for 3.4 miles, then turn right onto FR 77. Drive 0.7 mile, then turn right onto FR 7715 across from McBride Campground. Follow this gravel road 4.6 miles to its end at the large Summit Point trailhead parking area. Although it has a few rough spots, it is passable in most vehicles.

If you are coming from Richland, head east on Oregon Route 86 for 6.4 miles. Turn left onto FR 77 and drive for 10.7 miles to the junction with FR 7715, where

Accessed via a short hike, Summit Point Lookout stands tall at the southern edge of the Wallowa Mountains.

you will turn right across from McBride Campground. Follow this road 4.6 miles to the trailhead.

ON THE TRAIL

Cliff Creek Trail #1885 starts out by following the old road (FR 300) at the north end of the parking area. The road is closed to public vehicles—not that you'd want to drive up this rough, rocky track. Hike steadily uphill through scattered trees, sagebrush, and summer wildflowers. Evidence of cows is all around, so watch out for those cow pies.

After 0.6 mile, the Cliff Creek Trail continues straight toward destinations in the Eagle Cap Wilderness, but you will follow the road as it turns right. Soon the lookout comes into view ahead of you. After another 0.3 mile, the road ends at the lookout, which is staffed during fire season.

Even from the ground, you can see in all directions. Cornucopia Mountain (a former lookout site itself) looms to the north. Pine Valley is 4000 feet below you to the southeast. To the south the pointy profile of Little Lookout Mountain is easy to pick out. Looking west you can see the Elkhorns.

A 20-foot tower was built on Summit Point in the 1930s, then replaced with the present 20-foot L-4 tower in 1949. Nearby Cornucopia Peak (8643 feet) has a more commanding view, but the planned road to that summit was never built. Its lookout (and the trail leading to it) was abandoned in the 1940s, possibly because Summit Point was easier to access.

Out of sight below the eastern slope of Cornucopia Peak is the old mining ghost town of Cornucopia. After Lon Simmons discovered gold in 1884, a town quickly sprang

View of Cornucopia Mountain from Summit Point

up as hundreds of miners descended into the area to find their fortune. A post office opened the following year. By 1900, the mines employed more than 170 workers, and the booming, bustling town that accommodated them had grown to include hotels, stores, dance halls, bakeries, livery stables, a barber shop, a blacksmith, and a jail.

A 1922 newspaper article reported that $7 million worth of gold had thus far been extracted from the Cornucopia mines. In the 1940 US census, 352 residents were recorded. However, President Franklin D. Roosevelt shut down gold mining two years later so that the labor and resources could be diverted to mining metals such as lead, copper, and zinc that would help the war effort. Approximately $18 million worth of gold were extracted over a period of fifty-eight years, and 36 miles of tunnels were bored into the mountain. The post office closed and the town was abandoned, never to recover. Today, it is a ghost town with a few buildings and summer homes and a modern lodge that was built in 2008.

Summit Point is just 10 air miles from the town of Halfway in Pine Valley. In the 1880s, when residents submitted a petition for a post office in Pine Valley, they requested the name "Midway," given the location was about halfway between the towns of Cornucopia and Pine. But when the approved petition came back, the name had been changed to "Halfway." The post office was later moved to the site where the town of Halfway would be incorporated in 1908. In January 2000, the town accepted $100,000 in exchange for renaming itself to "Half.com," a publicity stunt that came with a spike in tourists who wanted to see the country's first "dot com city." A year later the name was reverted back.

Return the way you came.

EXTEND YOUR HIKE

If you are not ready to call it a day yet after this short jaunt, hike back down the road to the unsigned junction and turn right to follow the Cliff Creek Trail north. The trail climbs for another mile before topping out at Little Eagle Meadow; you can see Cornucopia Mountain even better from here, as well as more mountains to the north, such as Snowfield Peak. Although the trail is dusty and chewed up from the open-range cattle that graze here, this meadow is carpeted in purple when the lupine bloom in great profusion in July.

Meander as far as you'd like before turning around, keeping in mind that the trail loses elevation as it proceeds north across the meadow and becomes difficult to follow in spots due to the many crisscrossing paths created by the cows. When you are ready to turn back, retrace your steps back to the trailhead.

44 RUSSEL MOUNTAIN

YEAR CONSTRUCTED	LOOKOUT ACCESS	LOCATION
1949	Closed to the public	Wallowa-Whitman National Forest, Whitman Ranger District

Roundtrip distance: 4.2 miles
Elevation gain: 950 feet
Lookout elevation: 7510 feet
Map: USGS Deadman Point
GPS coordinates: 45.07511°, –117.05610°
Permits and fees: None

Hike through meadows and forest in this quiet corner of the Wallowa Mountains. Trails on the south side of these mountains are less traveled than those on the north side, and solitude is easier to find. This trail sees light use and is hard to follow in spots, so a GPS device or app and route-finding skills are helpful.

GETTING TO THE TRAILHEAD

From downtown Halfway, drive north on Cornucopia Highway for 0.4 mile, then turn right onto Fish Lake Road. Drive for 3.3 miles, then turn left onto gravel Clear

Russel Mountain Lookout is no longer staffed and is unsafe to climb.

Creek Road, which becomes Forest Road 66. Drive for 4 miles; then at the junction with FR 6610, make a sharp right turn to stay on FR 66. Drive for 16.2 miles, sticking to the main gravel road at all junctions, then turn left into the parking area for the Sugarloaf trailhead. While there are no facilities at this trailhead, there is a toilet at the Twin Lakes Campground 0.1 mile farther along FR 66.

ON THE TRAIL

Sugarloaf Trail #1887 starts out at the southwest corner of the parking area. The first 1.25 miles of the hike follow an old roadbed, lined with lupine and other July wildflowers. Once the roadbed ends, the trail sets off across a meadow where it can be a bit faint. Watch for sawed-open gaps in the fallen trees from previous trail maintenance to guide your way. The meadow is surrounded by subalpine fir interspersed with old snags that will eventually join the many fallen trees you see all around, evidence of a 1994 wildfire that burned through here.

The trail reenters the forest, then emerges onto another meadow. You are now crossing into the Eagle Cap Wilderness for a short stretch, although it is not signed or marked in any way. After a brief passage through trees, the trail emerges into another large sprawling meadow at 1.5 miles, dotted with a few trees and bleached snags.

Here the trail all but disappears; start across, angling slightly right, heading northwest, aiming for a gap between the trees, and watching for the telltale sawed-out gaps in the logs. (If you are using a GPS device or app, navigate toward 45.0682°, –117.0802°.)

At 1.7 miles, reach the far side of the meadow where the trail becomes more distinct as it climbs up into the forest. Just before reaching FR 450, the trail enters a smaller meadow. Stay along the right side of the meadow, following the tree line, and reach the road at 1.9 miles. Turn around and make a note of this spot so you can

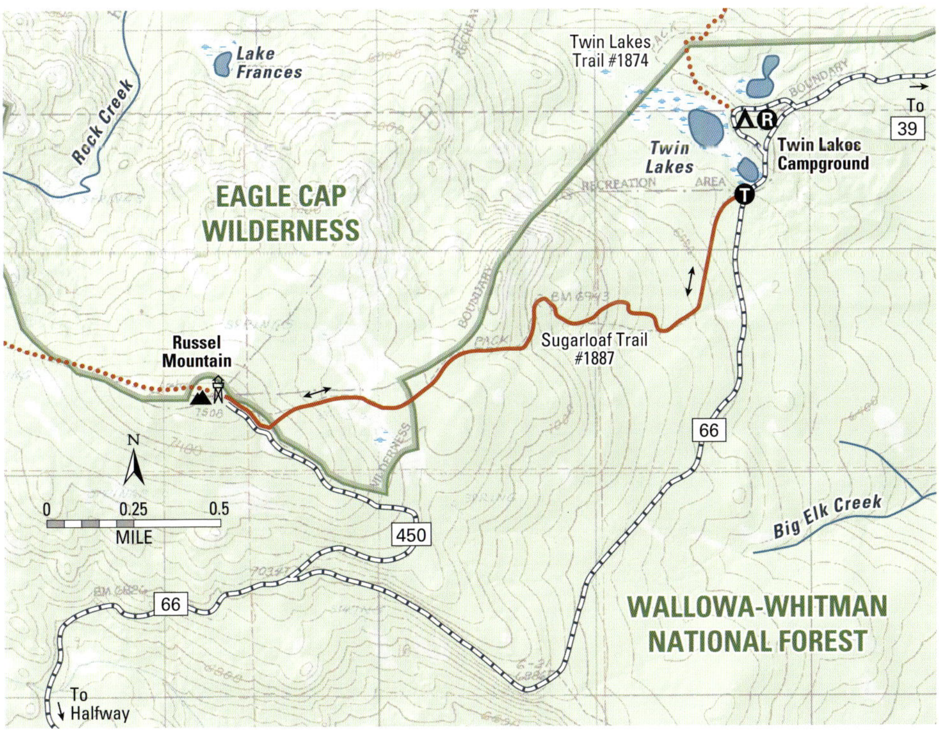

View from Russel Mountain

find it on your way back. Then turn right and start hiking up the road. You may see vehicles, as this road is not gated; however, it is rough and not frequently traveled. The road ends 0.2 mile later at the base of the tower. The Sugarloaf Trail continues beyond the lookout, heading west past an old weathered Russel Mountain Trailhead sign. At 1.5 miles from here, it connects with Deadman Trail near Sugarloaf Lake and Sugarloaf Mountain.

Around 1921, a 50-foot tower was built here, which was replaced in 1949 with the 82-foot tower that still stands today. It has not been staffed since at least the 1980s. The lightning-caused Twin Lakes Fire of 1994 came within 100 yards of the tower after having burned the trees east of here, which were already weakened by drought as well as beetle and budworm infestations. In 2006, several fires merged into the Twin Lakes Complex, which burned 12,000 acres west of Russel Mountain.

The setting is pretty and peaceful, with a nice meadow on the south side of the tower, ringed by firs. The tower is abandoned and structurally unsound and thus closed to the public, but you can still explore from the ground. Walk a hundred feet through the trees to the north and you can see Cusick Mountain, Petes Point, and Aneroid Mountain, among other mountains.

Aneroid Mountain is named after the lake at its base. The lake had been called Sterling Lake, then Anna Royal Lake. In 1897, an expedition by the US Commission on Fish and Fisheries collected specimens from Wallowa Lake. A twenty-five-year-old member of the party, Hoffman Philip, set out on his own into the mountains and came across the lake. Using his aneroid barometer he measured its elevation (7500 feet), naming it after the device. By its sheer proximity, the unnamed 9702-foot mountain to the east also acquired the name.

Out of sight 2400 feet below to the north is the Imnaha River. It originates high in the Wallowa Mountains at an elevation of 8000 feet between Eagle Cap and Cusick Mountain, then flows 77 miles before joining the Snake River at 900 feet, passing through a diverse range of habitats. In 1988, 15 miles of this undammed river were designated wild, and 4 miles designated scenic. (One of several ways to see it is to hike down Twin Lakes Trail #1874, which starts at the Twin Lakes Campground and descends 2.6 miles to the river, losing 1800 feet.)

The Wallowa Mountains are unlike any other mountain ranges in Oregon. All three major rock types—igneous, sedimentary, and metamorphic—can be found here. During the last ice age, glaciers carved the ridges and U-shaped canyons. Remnants of those glaciers are all but gone, including the last one, Benson Glacier on Glacier Peak, 12 miles northwest.

Return the way you came.

45 HAT POINT

YEAR CONSTRUCTED	LOOKOUT ACCESS	LOCATION
1948	Staffed, closed to the public; lower and upper viewing platforms accessible to the public	Wallowa-Whitman National Forest, Hells Canyon National Recreation Area

Roundtrip distance: 0.5 mile
Elevation gain: 50 feet
Lookout elevation: 6980 feet
Map: USGS Hat Point
GPS coordinates: 45.43776°, –116.66176°
Permits and fees: None

Visit this spot high above Hells Canyon, where an accessible trail and two platforms provide visitors with spectacular views for very little effort. Hat Point is named after Hat Creek, where nineteenth-century homesteader Alex Warnock had his hat knocked off while riding an unruly horse—possibly the most amusing name origin story in the book!

GETTING TO THE TRAILHEAD

In the tiny hamlet of Imnaha, reset your trip meter and head south up Hat Point Road (Forest Road 4240), a winding road with spectacular scenery and steep drop-offs. After 21.2 miles, turn right to stay on FR 4240 and drive for 1.5 miles to the day-use parking area.

Much of the forest along this road was burned in the 2022 Double Creek Fire, but there are several spots along the way worth a few minutes of your time: Fivemile Viewpoint (on the right at the 5-mile mark—how did you guess?) by the Imnaha River; Horse Creek Overlook, which is also called the Monument Ridge Viewpoint (on the left at 10.8 miles); and Granny Viewpoint (on the right at 16.5 miles).

ON THE TRAIL

The paved unnamed trail starts by the toilet and heads south past several benches and a sign. Reach an intersection with a gravel service road and switchback up to the left to stay on the paved trail. Your path curls around the north side of the lookout and ends at a wooden ramp that leads up to a viewing platform surrounding the base of the lookout tower.

The surroundings you will see from the lower platform are breathtaking, but if you have the ability and stamina to climb ninety-three steps to the upper platform, they are even better. (The next set of stairs from the upper platform to the cab at the top of the tower are not open to the public, but notice how much steeper they are than the ones you just climbed!) The Seven Devils in Idaho are visible to the east, and the Wallowa Mountains can be seen to the southwest. Way down at the bottom of Hells Canyon, you can spot part of the Snake River. While you are up here, keep an eye out for mountain goats foraging for food along the canyon rim. Back at the base of the tower, walk about 80 feet back down the paved path, then take a right at a gravel path by a bench and head down a rocky slope. Reach a junction by a toilet and turn left. The gravel path loops southeast around the plateau before making its way west back toward the trailhead. If you are here in early summer, look for columbine, penstemon, larkspur, Oregon sunshine, and paintbrush; take a break and enjoy them from one of several benches and picnic tables. (The bleached snags you see here are from the 2007 Battle Creek Fire.) Once you have had your fill, take the path to meet

OPPOSITE *The small cabin at the top of Hat Point Lookout is used only for spotting wildfires, not as sleeping quarters.*

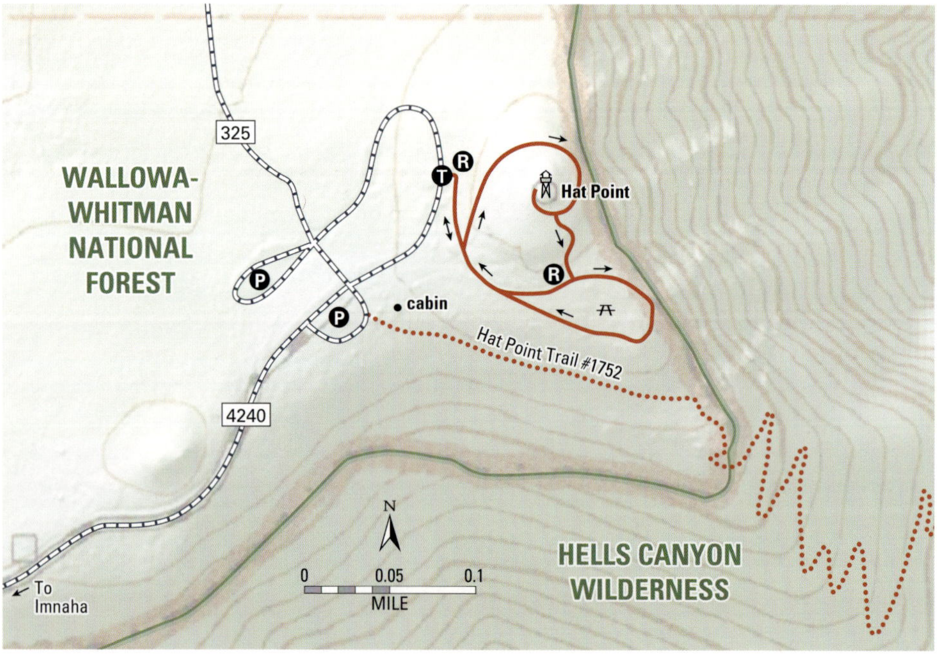

up with the gravel service road, where you will keep left, hike for 100 feet, then keep left to descend the paved path back to your car.

Ten-mile-wide Hells Canyon is the deepest river gorge in North America, measuring 7900 feet from the Snake River to the top of He Devil, the tallest peak in the Seven Devils Mountains of Idaho. (The deepest part of the Grand Canyon is about 6000 feet, but at a width of 18 miles, it has Hells Canyon beat there.) In summer the heat in Hells Canyon can get above 100 degrees, even while snow is still melting high above in the Seven Devils.

The Nez Perce and other tribes fished and hunted in Hells Canyon. In the spring of 1877, Chief Joseph and his band were forced to leave their homeland in the Wallowa Valley. They were given only one month to pack, prepare, and round up their scattered horses and cattle. On May 31, they crossed the Snake River at Dug Bar, 25 miles due north of Hat Point. The water was high and swift so early in the season, and while none of the people died, the same could not be said of their livestock, dozens of which lost their footing in the current and were swept away downstream. Ultimately Chief Joseph was forced to surrender in October after his band had spent the summer trying to flee to Canada.

A party of three men from the Lewis and Clark Expedition ventured into part of the canyon in 1806, but they turned back before they could see much of it. In 1811,

John Jacob Astor hired Wilson Price Hunt to take an expedition out west and find potential locations for fur trading posts. They entered Hells Canyon in December of that year seeking a shortcut to the Columbia, but desperately short of food and impeded by the deep snow, they, too, were forced to turn back. Gold miners arrived in the canyon in the 1860s, many of them Chinese. More than thirty Chinese miners were massacred at Deep Creek in 1887 by a group of six men and boys from Wallowa County, none of whom were ever punished.

The Snake River became a source of hydroelectric power when Idaho Power built three dams: Brownlee Dam in 1958, Oxbow Dam in 1961, and Hells Canyon Dam in 1967. A fourth dam—High Mountain Sheep Dam—was proposed in the 1960s but never built. The 652,488-acre Hells Canyon National Recreation Area was established in 1975 along with the Hells Canyon Wilderness, which currently includes almost 218,000 acres.

A 60-foot tower was built at Hat Point in 1916, then in 1948 it was replaced with the 82-foot tower that still stands today. If the 7-by-7-foot cabin at the top looks tiny, that's because it is. The lookout spends their days up there watching for fires but sleeps and cooks in a cabin near the day-use parking area. In the mid-1990s, the viewing deck surrounding the base of the tower was installed, in addition to the upper viewing platform. The lightning-caused Battle Creek Fire in 2007 burned right up to the base of the tower. The roof of the cabin living quarters was partially burned, as well as some of the boards on the observation platform.

EXTEND YOUR HIKE

Hardy hikers with plenty of water may wish to venture down Hat Point Trail # 1752, which begins near the cabin southwest of the tower. If you decide to explore this trail, keep in mind that it loses a whopping 5500 feet over 7.5 miles as it descends to the Snake River in Hells Canyon—elevation you will need to regain on the hot, grueling hike back up to Hat Point.

ACKNOWLEDGMENTS

This book was a labor of love and would not have been possible without the help of others. Thanks to the incredible team at Mountaineers Books for your support, expertise, and encouragement.

Thanks to all the lookouts who have shared your stories and knowledge with me, including Linn, Rob, Joey, Sunne, Lise, Travis, Evonne, Mike, Karen, Julie, Dwayne, Ryan, Brigg, Brenda, Michelle, and Jim. Thanks to Don Allen for always answering my questions and providing valuable insight, and a huge thanks to all the volunteers with the Sand Mountain Society. Thanks to the many Forest Service employees who answered my questions, and thank you to the lookout community and the hiking community for sharing your photos, reports, and insights, especially Deryl, whose website is a treasure trove of trip reports.

Thanks to Amber Casali for blazing the trail by writing *Hiking Washington's Fire Lookouts*. Your book was an excellent blueprint as I researched and wrote the Oregon version!

Thanks to Rex Kamstra and Ron Kemnow, whose respective websites were invaluable resources. Thanks also to Ray Kresek for showing me around your lookout museum and sharing your stories.

Thanks to Deb and Karl for guiding me across the lake and through the burn in hot weather so I could get photos for the book. I could not have done it without you.

Thanks to my parents for planting the seed. They instilled in me a love of history and a love of hiking and the outdoors (even though it took a long time for that seed to germinate!).

And, of course, a huge thanks to my wonderful husband, Greg, who was always so patient when I dragged him to yet another lookout on our camping trips over the past fifteen years. You held down the fort while I was driving all over the state for this project, and you listened to me think out loud about this book for two whole years. I love you.

OPPOSITE *Mount Washington from Black Butte Lookout (Hike 12) at sunset*

RESOURCES

There are many resources available for people who want to learn more about lookouts and their history. I can't possibly list them all here, but this is a starting point. Contact the managing agency for information on specific lookouts and to check on current trail and road conditions.

MANAGING AGENCIES

See relevant BLM or national forest website for details and links to specific districts.

BUREAU OF LAND MANAGEMENT

Lakeview District
www.blm.gov/office/lakeview-district-office
(541) 947-2177
Medford District (Cascade-Siskiyou National Monument)
www.blm.gov/office/medford-district-office
(541) 618-2200
Northwest Oregon District
www.blm.gov/office/northwest-oregon-district-office
(503) 375-5646

CRATER LAKE NATIONAL PARK

www.nps.gov/crla
(541) 594-3000

DESCHUTES NATIONAL FOREST

www.fs.usda.gov/deschutes
Bend–Fork Rock Ranger District
(541) 383-5300
Crescent Ranger District
(541) 433-3200
Lava Lands Visitor Center, Newberry National Volcanic Monument
(541) 593-2421
Sisters Ranger District
(541) 549-7700

FREMONT-WINEMA NATIONAL FOREST

www.fs.usda.gov/fremont-winema
Bly Ranger District
(541) 353-2427
Paisley Ranger District
(541) 943-3114
Silver Lake Ranger District
(541) 576-2107

OPPOSITE *The historic 1919 cabin on Hawk Mountain (Hike 8)*

MALHEUR NATIONAL FOREST

www.fs.usda.gov/malheur
Blue Mountain Ranger District
(541) 575-3000
Prairie City Ranger District
(541) 820-3800

MOUNT HOOD NATIONAL FOREST

www.fs.usda.gov/mthood
Barlow Ranger District
(541) 467-2291
Clackamas River Ranger District
(503) 668-1700
Zigzag Ranger District
(503) 622-3191

ROGUE RIVER-SISKIYOU NATIONAL FOREST

www.fs.usda.gov/rogue-siskiyou
Gold Beach Ranger District
(541) 247-3600
High Cascades Ranger District
(541) 560-3400
Siskiyou Mountains Ranger District
(541) 899-3800
Wild Rivers Ranger District
(541) 592-4000

SADDLE MOUNTAIN STATE NATURAL AREA

www.stateparks.oregon.gov
(503) 812-0650

SIUSLAW NATIONAL FOREST

www.fs.usda.gov/siuslaw
Central Coast Ranger District, Oregon Dunes National Recreation Area
(541) 563-8400

UMATILLA NATIONAL FOREST

www.fs.usda.gov/umatilla
Heppner Ranger District
(541) 676-9187
North Fork John Day Ranger District
(541) 427-3231

UMPQUA NATIONAL FOREST

www.fs.usda.gov/umpqua
Diamond Lake Ranger District
(541) 498-2531
North Umpqua Ranger District
(541) 496-3532
Tiller Ranger District
(541) 825-3100

WALLOWA-WHITMAN NATIONAL FOREST

www.fs.usda.gov/wallowa-whitman
Wallowa Mountains Office, Eagle Cap Ranger District and Hells Canyon National Recreation Area
(541) 426-5546
Whitman Ranger District
(541) 523-6391

WILLAMETTE NATIONAL FOREST

www.fs.usda.gov/willamette
Detroit Ranger District
(503) 854-3366
McKenzie River Ranger District
(541) 822-3381
Middle Fork Ranger District
(541) 782-2283
Sweet Home Ranger District
(541) 367-5168

BOOKS

Desolation Angels, by Jack Kerouac. Penguin Books, 1995.

Finding Fire: A Personal History of Fire Lookouts in Lane County, Oregon, by Doug Newman. Lane County Historical Society, 2007.

Fire Lookouts of Oregon, by Cheryl Hill. Arcadia Publishing, 2016.

Fire Lookouts of the Northwest (3rd edition), by Ray Kresek. Ye Galleon Press, 1998.

Fire Season: Field Notes from a Wilderness Lookout, by Philip Connors. Ecco, 2012.

Hiking Washington's Fire Lookouts, by Amber Casali. Mountaineers Books, 2018.

How to Rent a Fire Lookout in the Pacific Northwest, by Tom Foley and Tish McFadden. Wilderness Press, 2005.

Lookout: Love, Solitude, and Searching for Wildfire in the Boreal Forest, by Trina Moyles. Random House Canada, 2021.

WEBSITES

REX'S FOREST FIRE LOOKOUT PAGE

Rex Kamstra's website is my go-to online resource when I'm wondering about a particular lookout. The photo archives section has photos and maps for lookouts in Washington, Oregon, Idaho, Montana, Wyoming, and South Dakota. Learn more at www.firelookout.com.

FOREST LOOKOUTS, OREGON

Ron Kemnow has combed through archives, memos, letters, and newspapers to find mentions of lookouts, along with many photos. Check out oregonlookouts.weebly.com for more information.

EVERY LOOKOUT IN OREGON

I have documented my journey toward visiting every publicly accessible standing lookout in Oregon at my website, cherylhill.net/firelookouts.

FACEBOOK GROUPS

Members of these groups post questions, reports of their visits to lookouts, photos, historical items, and experiences staffing a lookout. If you're interested in learning more about lookouts past and present, these groups are a good starting place.

- Fire Lookouts
- Fire Lookouts of Washington
- Fire Lookout Towers of the West Coast
- Forest Fire Lookout Enthusiasts
- Oregon Fire Lookouts
- Staffed Fire Lookouts
- US Forest Service Lookouts
- Wander Fire Lookouts

VOLUNTEER GROUPS

FOREST FIRE LOOKOUT ASSOCIATION

This is the first organization to check out if you want to learn more about getting involved with lookouts. They hold both a western and an eastern conference annually, and every few years the western conference is held in Oregon. It's a great way to connect with fellow lookout enthusiasts. See firelookout.org for more information.

FRIENDS OF BLUE MOUNTAINS LOOKOUTS

Friends of Blue Mountains Lookouts is a local chapter of the Oregon chapter of the Forest Fire Lookout Association. If you're in eastern Oregon and looking to help out with restorations, this is the group for you. Check out their Facebook page at facebook.com/fobmlookouts.

SAND MOUNTAIN SOCIETY

The Sand Mountain Society is an Oregon-based nonprofit dedicated to the preservation and restoration of historic lookouts. For more information, visit sandmountain.org.

INDEX

ABOUT THE AUTHOR

Cheryl Hill is a writer, photographer, and avid hiker. She has worked as a librarian in the Portland area for two decades, after earning a master's in library and information science from the University of British Columbia.

Hill became quite interested in fire lookouts when she took part in a geocaching challenge, the Oregon Forest Fire Lookout Challenge, which inspired her to visit every publicly accessible standing lookout in Oregon. Hill is the author of *Mount Hood National Forest* and *Fire Lookouts of Oregon*, both from Arcadia Publishing.

In her free time when she's not hiking, she enjoys camping, reading, and volunteering. She lives in Milwaukie, Oregon, with her husband and their two cats. Learn more at cherylhill.net.

MOUNTAINEERS BOOKS

SKIPSTONE BRAIDED RIVER

recreation • lifestyle • conservation

MOUNTAINEERS BOOKS, including its two imprints, Skipstone and Braided River, is a leading publisher of quality outdoor recreation, sustainability, and conservation titles. As a 501(c)(3) nonprofit, we are committed to supporting the environmental and educational goals of our organization by providing expert information on human-powered adventure, sustainable practices at home and on the trail, and preservation of wilderness.

Our publications are made possible through the generosity of donors, and through sales of more than 700 titles on outdoor recreation, sustainable lifestyle, and conservation. To donate, purchase books, or learn more, visit us online:

MOUNTAINEERS BOOKS

1001 SW Klickitat Way, Suite 201 • Seattle, WA 98134

800-553-4453 • mbooks@mountaineersbooks.org • www.mountaineersbooks.org

An independent nonprofit publisher since 1960

LEAVE NO TRACE

Mountaineers Books is proud to support the Leave No Trace Center for Outdoor Ethics, whose mission is to use the power of science, education, and stewardship to ensure a sustainable future for the outdoors and the planet. The Leave No Trace program is focused specifically on human-powered (nonmotorized) recreation. For more information, visit www.lnt.org.

YOU MAY ALSO LIKE: